12 MONTHS TO YOUR IDEAL private practice

ALSO BY LYNN GRODZKI

Building Your Ideal Private Practice:
A Guide for Therapists and Other Healing Professionals

The New Private Practice:
Therapist-Coaches Share Stories, Strategies, and Advice (Editor)

A Norton Professional Book

12 MONTHS TO YOUR IDEAL PRIVATE PRACTICE

A Workbook

LYNN GRODZKI

W·W·NORTON

NEW YORK·LONDON

Grateful acknowledgment is made to Susan Jeffers, Ph.D., for permission to adapt (on pages 131–132) the "Pain to Power" concept that appears in *Feel the Fear And Do It Anyway,* © 1987, A Fawcett Columbine Book, Ballentine Books New York, NY.

Composition and book design by Viewtistic, Inc.
Manufacturing by Hamilton Printing
Production Manager: Leeann Graham

Library of Congress Cataloging-in-Publication Data
Grodzki, Lynn.
    Twelve months to your ideal private practice: a workbook/Lynn Grodzki
        p.   cm.
    "A Norton professional book."
    ISBN 0-393-70417-3 (pbk)
    1. Psychotherapy—Practice. 2. Mental health counseling—Practice. 3. Psychotherapists—
Marketing. I. Title.
RC465.5.G763   2003
616.89'14'068—dc21   2003048794

W. W. Norton & Company, Inc., 500 Fifth Avenue, New York, NY 10110
www.wwnorton.com
W. W. Norton & Company, Ltd., Castle House, 75/76 Wells Street, London W1T 3QT

13

contents

Foreword

Wendy Allen, Ph.D.

When I became a psychologist in Santa Barbara, California, 20 years ago, I thought I had the best of all worlds. Santa Barbara is an idyllic, fantastically beautiful small town situated right on the Pacific Ocean, and I loved the idea of building a private practice in my favorite city.

Unfortunately, I didn't realize how many others shared my dream. With four feeder-schools that take students through licensure as psychotherapists, Santa Barbara is packed solid with psychotherapists. I spent long hours as a sole practitioner, building my practice in a fiercely competitive environment. I enjoyed the lush California scenery, but found the world of private practice I inhabited one of considerably harsher surroundings.

In 1986 Lynn Grodzki and I had a long conversation during which she mentioned, with excitement, that she was going to leave her job in management to become a therapist in private practice, too, but in Maryland. I tried to warn her. "Therapy is a calling, kind of like being in a monastery. You will need to practice self-sacrifice."

Lynn laughed. "I want to help people, but I intend to make a good living doing it." She sounded so confident. What did she, with her business background, understand that I didn't? Was there a better way to make a living in this profession? Was she suggesting that I let go of my suffering and sacrifice? I was intrigued.

With this conversation in mind, I began to think a lot about why some therapists did well in private practice and others didn't. Most of us start with the same set of fundamentals: We are caring people who want to help others, we get academic training, we develop a degree of skill in the field, and we try to retain some autonomy over our work lives by working for ourselves.

But beyond these basic ingredients, who makes it in private practice and who doesn't can seem so random. For example, some of the most successful therapists in the profession in my area are very charismatic. Does one have to be an entertainer to have a thriving practice? That hardly seems fair. I wondered what I was not seeing that would explain why some therapists had an edge in the business.

Most therapists are undereducated about business, as I was. Because our graduate schools and professional associations don't offer much in the way of professional development, we therapists are mostly on our own when it comes to figuring out how to make a private practice viable. So we get stuck, often in our lack of awareness.

Lynn's program, workshop, and books about private practice success have made a difference for many therapists, first and foremost in the area of awareness. Lynn highlights that we, as therapists, need more than mere information in order to succeed in business. We need to change ourselves, from the inside out. We must find a way to add some extroverted, entrepreneurial, edgier behaviors to our introspective, gentle, therapeutic selves. We must grow stronger to weather the ups and downs of a small business, show up more vibrantly in the community, and promote ourselves not through selling but by attracting people to our good work.

We don't have to become different people, but we do have to make some deep developmental shifts in our psyche. We have to grow up and evolve as business owners, and we need to do this sooner rather than later. Time is of the essence for those of us struggling to stay current in the ever-changing health-related fields. Speeding up our evolution requires the right fuel.

The right fuel is exactly what this workbook, a companion to Lynn's best-selling book *Building Your Ideal Private Practice*, offers each reader. Month by month, the workbook shows you how to bring your hidden resources as a businessperson into the open. You will develop a new set of muscles as you strengthen your inner entrepreneur. Over time you will shape your environment to help you meet your goals; you will no longer feel as though you are at the mercy of it.

In the publishing world, when a new book comes out and a workbook quickly follows, the workbook is often no more than a brief repetition of the original book. But this workbook, published three years after the original text, contains a large amount of new material developed from Lynn's evolving research, experience, and feedback from the thousands of therapists she has coached in the past few years. It is rich with fresh anecdotes, different case studies, new exercises, and innovative concepts. I regard it as a sequel to *Building Your Ideal Private Practice*.

This workbook, which is written in Lynn's clear, warm, and motivating style, will help you develop into a therapist who provides excellent service *and* enjoys playing the game of business. Everyday obstacles will become another doorway toward creative solutions and paths. As you further develop, you will become more profitable, bring in more clients, and translate your passion in a way that makes people excited about what you have to offer. As a psychotherapist in private practice, I will use this workbook myself. As a business coach who works with therapists, I will use this workbook to help my clients achieve success in an easier, more elegant manner.

And at the end of 12 months of following Lynn's guidance, you will look back and realize that you have stepped up a rung or two on the evolutionary ladder and, even better, you will know what it takes to climb, at your own perfect pace, right to the top.

preface

Building Your Ideal Private Practice:
Making It Easier

In business, I was taught that having a mission—an overriding objective for one's work—was a good idea. A good business owner should review his or her mission from time to time because it could change, sometimes without the owner's awareness. During the past 6 years of working as a business coach, I have kept an eye on my mission, and I see that it is indeed capricious. It develops not unlike a tadpole we had in my second-grade class that I thought was a funny-looking fish, until one day, without my noticing it, it sprouted legs, and then, in another mysteriously timed improvement, became a full-blown frog that croaked.

My business coaching approach has certainly sprouted legs. In 1994 I was a psychotherapist in full-time private practice, living near Washington, DC, a region inundated with psychotherapists. I loved being a therapist, but many of my colleagues were talking about leaving private practice due to managed care or professional burnout. It seemed to me that my profession was reaching a dire crossroads: Too many good, serious therapists, frustrated with their working conditions, were closing down their practices and looking for easier jobs.

I knew a little something about business, having previously been general manager of a mid-sized family business and having taken (and loved) business courses in college. I very much wanted to help my fellow therapists. (I use *therapists*, throughout this book as a form of generic shorthand to mean psychotherapists, psychologists, personal coaches, alternative therapists, body workers, and other helping, healing professionals.)

I thought that if I could compile relevant information about business and put it into a format that appealed to therapists' sensibilities and ethics, then my colleagues could find a way to go beyond managed care, make a decent living, become more profitable, and not leave the profession. The mental health profession could avoid a brain drain, and therapists of all kinds, whose work is so important to society, could have better lives.

So my first mission, as I saw it, was to impart information. I would give therapists all the knowledge, strategies, tips, and ideas I could find to help them succeed in business, adapted into a language they could understand. Over the next 2 years I taught classes, wrote articles for magazines, and talked to any therapist who would listen. Whenever anyone brought up the topic of practice building, my mouth opened and a rush of ideas poured out. I had a million of them. I was the Information Lady.

While some therapists took the information I provided and immediately "got it," using the strategies and ideas to do a lot better in business, the majority of therapists I met during this time stayed stuck or semistuck: They did no better, or made some gains and then fell back to where they were to begin with. I couldn't understand why. These were bright, talented therapists who wanted to be in private practice because it offered them autonomy and independence. A private practice allowed them to deliver the best services possible. What was the problem?

The problem was, as we therapists know so well, that information only goes so far. When I talked at length with any of the therapists who were semi- or solidly stuck, I would find that they had feelings and beliefs that were getting in their way of taking action. Many had negative feelings about money, marketing, organization, profit, and management; old well-learned beliefs or unconscious fight-flight reactions also interfered with their ability to take the information and integrate it. They were frozen in a particular internal struggle.

These therapists suffered from what I began to call a psychic split about their work in private practice: They loved being therapists, but hated being in business. And they had one foot standing squarely on each side.

RELUCTANT ENTREPRENEURS

Most of my colleagues in private practice are reluctant entrepreneurs. I became curious about the cognitive and emotional differences between successful entrepreneurs in business and my reluctant colleagues. As I researched and worked with therapists around their feelings and beliefs, I saw that an entrepreneurial mind-set—the intangible combination of psychology, emotion, and behaviors that defines a successful business owner—could be learned and taught.

I spent more time addressing issues of mind-set, less time developing information and teaching strategies. And I began to see therapists who did not previously consider themselves talented in business blossom into very successful businesspeople. I was integrating my experience as a therapist and doing a form of business therapy: healing the split business owner. Building a successful business begins with building a stronger business owner.

By 1998 I realized that my mission had shifted. I was now working less with information and more with the whole person. The work as a business coach became more satisfying to me, because it allowed me to bring my knowledge and sensibilities as a therapist to my interest in business success. During the next two years I wrote and published *Building Your Ideal Private Practice: A Guide for Therapists and Other Healing Professionals* and began to get a steady stream of letters, e-mails, and phone calls from readers around the country telling me, often in very moving descriptions, how their practices were improving as a result of the book and that in the process they were changing as people.

AN EASIER PATH

I edited a second book, and more coaching opportunities, therapy clients, and speaking engagements came my way. I felt like I was on a fast-moving train and not sure how to slow it down. I liked everything I was doing, but I was overwhelmed. I knew I needed to do less, I just wasn't sure how, since I wasn't ready to let go of anything I had achieved. Not surprisingly, I saw this trend reflected in many of the therapists I met. We all seemed to be working too hard, for lots of reasons.

Managed care made life hard for some. The decision to avoid managed care made life and work hard for others. Family responsibilities weighed heavily on therapists who were raising young children, and those finished with child rearing set big goals and were working hard to grow.

The questions I began to hear in the workshops I conducted reflected problems common to all entrepreneurs: How can I make enough money and maintain a quality personal life? How can I be as successful as I want to be, and feel rested and healthy? What does it take to build a profitable business without expending so much personal effort? Is it possible to be a therapist in private practice and have an easier life?

I didn't know the answers because I was caught in the same struggle. Therapist, heal thyself, I thought. I looked at how I overscheduled myself, at my own balance (or lack of), at my inability to find the easy path. I took 6 months and reevaluated my vision, mission, and purpose statements and began to purposefully change my assumptions about how I ran my practice. I decided to look at everything I did with the idea of promoting more ease and less effort in my life. Then I challenged my coaching clients to do the same.

And, in doing so, my mission evolved yet again.

Like Russian nesting dolls, my current mission incorporates the earlier versions, but moves beyond them. When I was recently asked to explain my work I said, "I help therapists become successful in private practice, because I believe our society greatly needs its therapists. I offer therapists an abundance of information, ideas, and strategies and I also help them heal any negative feelings or beliefs about business that prevent them from being as profitable as they want to be. But these days, I am most interested in helping therapists succeed more easily, with less effort. I love helping my colleagues build ideal lives as well as ideal private practices."

ACKNOWLEDGMENTS

I want to acknowledge the people who helped me in many ways in the process of writing this book:

Deborah Malmud suggested and championed this project from start to completion. Her ideas and thoughtfulness made this workbook more complete and a much better read. She is my ideal editor and publisher. Regina Dahlgren Ardini used her deft hand, as always, to make the text better and smoother. Michael McGandy eased production matters with his eye for details and professional approach.

In Wendy Allen I have both a colleague and a sister; she wrote the perceptive foreword and has been a wonderful associate to have "in the trenches." I benefit greatly from her energy and unconditional support.

Hundreds of clients shared both their challenges and their successes. In the process, they led me to refine my practice-building program and make it more effective. Readers of my earlier books contacted me by way of letters, e-mails, and phone calls. Their willingness to take the time to let me know how the program is working for them was extremely kind and provided me with valuable feedback.

My husband, Tad, provided me with his total support, as well as the space and time to lose myself in a manuscript. To all of the above, I offer my thanks and love.

12 MONTHS TO YOUR IDEAL
PRIVATE PRACTICE

INTRODUCTION

The Business of Therapy

Let's be frank. As therapists we have chosen one of the tougher jobs around. We extend ourselves, hour after hour, to others who are in pain and crisis. We train and hone our services far beyond what most professionals feel required to do, at our own expense. Our work does not stop when the office door closes. We adhere to strict codes of behavior to maintain our licensure and our professional ethics. The complexity and rigorousness of our caseload do not lessen over time, regardless of our years of experience.

When we add to this the stresses and strains of operating a business, it's no wonder many of us feel burned out, defeated, or overwhelmed. To make it even tougher, most of us are unschooled in knowing how to build and operate a successful business. The business side of therapy consistently gets short shrift in the offerings from universities or professional associations.

For example, this year I offered to give a continuing education (CE) course for my alma mater (a major state-run university that offers a master's program in social work) on practice-building strategies and was told, politely, thanks but no thanks. The head of the program informed me that helping social workers develop a private practice was not part of the school's mission of continuing education. Even though I could argue with her that statistics from every major social work association show that 60% of social workers will be in private practice at some point during their career, her bottom line was that the university did not see this type of professional development as important.

So it often falls to therapists who want to succeed in a private practice to figure it out on their own. Although therapists spend considerable time and money refining their clinical skills each year, they give short shrift to the business side of their practices—and then feel like failures if they don't instinctively get a private practice up and running, or keep it running profitably over time. Most therapists spend time in therapy as a way to make sure they practice what they preach, but few bother to take basic business courses or consult with business professionals, such as a business coach.

I have hired coaches at many points in my career, and I know that the experience of working with a coach is quite different from working with a therapist. I once heard the difference between coaching and therapy described in the following way: Imagine you are learning to ride a bicycle for the first time. A therapist would stand off to the side, observe your attempt to stay upright, be understanding and compassionate when you fall, make wise interpretations about why you have fallen, ask some difficult and insightful questions, and perhaps direct you how to get back on and do better, with your new insight. A therapist would want you to develop your own prowess about riding the bike over time, for you to notice how you keep getting your feet crossed, or turn the wheel wrong, and to understand what your history taught you to make you try to ride that way.

A coach would climb on the seat right behind you and ask, "Where do you want to go today?"

As you read this book, you might want to think of me as sitting right behind you where you can lean back into my optimism about you, my pragmatism about business, and my experience about our profession. I know and love the business you are trying to build, having been in the therapy profession myself for more than 15 years, in a fee-for-service practice free of managed care that has provided me with a good income and my clients with a high level of service. I have also been fortunate to meet and coach thousands of your colleagues, and I have a pretty good idea of how a therapist can hold onto his or her integrity while achieving business success. I carry no agenda about where you should go, what you should earn, or what direction your practice should take, other than wanting to help you identify and then manifest your personal and professional vision. I won't indulge you when you give up too easily, short of your stated goals, but I won't leave you stranded either.

Through the pages of this book I will offer ideas, ask leading questions to help you formulate your own answers, and provide a road map to make your journey easier. As I sit behind you, I will elbow you from time to time to look up and enjoy the ride, so that you can find the process of building your business more fun. You will be doing the pedaling and the challenging work; I'll be looking ahead and pointing out the best route I can chart for you. I will also be cheering for you when your efforts pay off, when you gather speed and exclaim with pride; "Look, Lynn! I'm riding! No hands!"

ESSENTIAL ELEMENTS

Two essential elements can make your practice-building efforts much easier:

1. a business model I designed specifically for a professional therapy practice;
2. a set of premises that, if adopted, make it possible to love the business of therapy.

A business model is a road map. Imagine how long it might take to get your bearings in a foreign country where you don't speak the language, don't recognize the landscape, and don't own a map. I know some people hate to use maps and like to figure things out on their own; but we are going for ease and expediency here.

How could you best use a business model? You can envision and plan your business future. It can help you manage your present challenges. You can identify and learn from the mistakes of your past. If you have a user-friendly business model, you can turn to it any time you feel shaky about your situation or just plain lost in the woods. Without a business model, you may not know when to spend versus when to save, when to change gears versus when to hold fast. You may not know what action to take next to expand or grow, how to implement it, what kind of a support system to add as a resource, and how long to stick with your project to see it through. A good business model will help you to see the big picture.

The business model I propose that you use is the core of my practice-building program, which I defined in *Building Your Ideal Private Practice.* It is a flexible, accessible model that has proved useful over time for thousands of therapists. Its based on the metaphor of building a house, because it's a familiar one and the steps of building or renovating a house and building or renovating a small business have many similarities.

The model has three distinct stages, and each stage can contribute to understanding and resolving your business challenges. Here, for your review, is the basic model in a condensed form:

The Private Practice Success™ Business Model

BUILDING A HOUSE	BUILDING A PRIVATE PRACTICE
Preparation Stage	*Preparation Stage*
Survey the site.	Assess your professional and emotional support.
Create a design.	Craft a business vision.
Dig a foundation.	Install an entrepreneurial mind-set.
Building Blocks Stage	*Building Blocks Stage*
Construct the rooms.	Implement strategies and actions.
Finishing Touches Stage	*Finishing Touches Stage*
Add finish and polish.	Position your practice.

Preparation

When a builder wants to build a house, long before he takes up his hammer and nails and begins to put boards together, he has some essential preparation to do. This preparation has three phases:

1. *Surveying the site.* The builder walks the property to see if the ground can hold the weight of the house, looking for hidden faults in the ground that might cause it to sag under the substantial load of the house. Similarly, you as the business owner can sag under the weight of your business. A small business places a tremendous burden on the shoulders, heart, and mind of the owner. To counter this, you will need sufficient support, internally and externally, to help you manage the inevitable stresses and strains from owning your business. No matter where you are in your business development, if you are feeling stressed, burned-out, bored, exhausted, or depressed, your support is the first thing to examine.

For example, do you have excellent professional support in your life? Sometimes therapists are part of a professional or peer support group, but the nature of the group does not offer good support. I want you, as the business owner, to have a support system of other entrepreneurial people, not necessarily therapists, who want you to be as successful as you can, without placing any complicated personal agenda onto you. Your support system needs to function without envy or competition among its members. It needs to be pure, safe, and inspiring—a group where everyone wants for, and celebrates, each other's success. If you don't have the right support, you can create it, and I will show you how in Months 1 and 3 of this workbook.

2. *Create a design.* No builder would ever attempt to begin to build without some kind of plan on paper, even if it's just a simple sketch. It's folly to start construction without a visual blueprint. In the same way, you need a blueprint or guide for the future direction of your practice. This is your business vision, which can be a casual sketch or a finely drafted document. It will define where you are trying to go, a year, two years, or five years from today.

Most business owners say that having a business vision is one of the best and most important tools they possess, but few therapists in private practice have one in place. We will change that to help you make your practice building more efficient. If you have been concerned with a lack of professional direction, if you feel like you don't know what is in store for you or your practice a year from now, if you feel bored with your current practice, you probably suffer from not having a coherent and compelling business vision in place. You will design your vision in Month 4.

3. *Dig the foundation.* The builder thinks ahead to the way a building settles over time, and digs a foundation to strengthen a house, so that it stays straight and strong. Likewise, you need to have some strength and muscle in your makeup, to help you weather the highs and lows, the challenges of running a business, to keep you strong in the face of the pressures and anxieties any business owner faces. Your strength will be your mind-set, and I will help you to install an entrepreneurial mind-set, how other successful entrepreneurs think and behave. If you feel confused about what to do next, can't see a project through to the goal, if you are uncomfortable with the talk of profit and money, if you struggle with how to respond to the ups and downs of business, this step of preparation is one that needs your attention. You will learn how to adopt this mind-set in Month 2.

Building Blocks

After the preparation phase, the builder is ready to start using a hammer and nails and construct the rooms of the house. At this point, most builders have considered lots of options about how and what to actually build, so that the resulting home reflects some personal choices. Similar to this, I want the actions you take to build your practice to reflect your choices, so that your practice is custom-designed for you. I want you to have lots of strategies and techniques in your knowledge base, so that you know many different ideas and tips for marketing, handling and managing your money, making a profit, setting and raising fees, expanding, diversifying, simplifying, setting policies, and managing your practice. Then I want you to choose the strategies that are most natural to you, or most interesting, so that you won't feel pressured to do anything that is too outside your natural inclinations. (We are trying to do this the easy way, remember? The easiest way for you to succeed is to feel that you have chosen strategies for success that are the most appealing to you.)

If you have felt clueless in how to generate sufficient referrals, market your practice well, set a reasonable missed session policy, or use an alternative to a sliding scale, it is time to increase your storehouse of knowledge. The building blocks stage of the business model includes tools and strategies that you can pick and choose from to custom build-your practice. A lot of the middle section of this workbook, Months 5 through 8, is about implementing this phase. If you need to explore additional ideas or strategies to aid implementation, my first book is a companion guide that offers an abundance of information, strategies, and actions.

Finishing Touches

Sometimes the first thing you notice upon entering a house are the fine details—the interior decoration, polish, and all the finely crafted points that make a house distinctive and unique. Similarly, you want your practice to shine, to reflect your uniqueness and creativity. You want your mastery and artistry to show in your practice, as your way to overcome competition. The way to add finish is to know how to position your practice well into the future, how to add services that clients desire, and how to keep your practice evolving and on the cutting edge. If you have been feeling that there is nothing special about your practice, that you are unable to withstand competition, or can't get excited about your work after many years in business, look to Months 9 through 12 for help.

LOVING THE BUSINESS

Therapists in private practice do two jobs at once (clinician and business owner), but usually only love one. You will need to love them both, equally, to be truly successful in private practice.

I have identified three premises that help therapists love business. Premises are not necessarily truths, but rather strong suggestions about reality. I find that therapists who have adopted these premises as though they are truths have more affection for the business they have built.

Premise 1: You Are Not Your Business

You may be a sole proprietor in your business and be doing it all—providing the therapy services, paying the bills, even emptying the trash—but I strongly suggest you see your private practice as a separate entity. A major cause of hating business comes from overidentifying with one's practice.

Differentiate yourself from your business. See your business as distinct from you, even if you built it, even if it only exists as a result of your actions. Think of it as a child you birthed who has a lot of you in it, but is not you. Your business has its own needs, and even its own personality and behavior. As a good parent or good business owner, it's your job to give your business what it needs, but not to confuse its needs with your own.

For example, my business needs between 24 and 27 client hours each week to stay highly profitable. I understand this and try to keep my practice full, to give my business what it needs. But I personally don't need to see that many clients and work at that pace in order to be happy. I could spend my days being very happy by seeing only 2 or 3 clients. I keep a fuller schedule for the sake of my business. It needs this full schedule to thrive, so if I want to keep my business viable, I do what it takes to keep its calendar full.

My business also has its own nature, which does not match my personal nature. For example, my business goes down in the summer. I don't. Summer is often a time of great energy and satisfaction for me personally. I love warm weather and long days of sunlight. Knowing this about the nature of my business helps me not to take the drop-off of clients personally, not to get depressed, and to plan accordingly.

Premise 2: Your Business Reflects Your Strengths and Weaknesses

Even though you are not your business, your business will mirror aspects of you. For example, if you have strong boundaries regarding time, have always been a prompt person and manage your time well, this will probably be reflected in your business. Your sessions probably start and stop on time, your business calendar is clear and exact, and you schedule the weekly administrative tasks and follow through without a problem.

If you are very disorganized and live with clutter and chaos, chances are your business mirrors your disorganization. Your paperwork is hard to find and file, your treatment reports are late.

If you have a good relationship with money, your business reflects that as well. Your finances are up to date, you talk easily to your clients about fees and their financial responsibilities, and you pay your estimated taxes on time without a problem.

Recognizing that your business is a good reflection of you means that when you want to make a change in your business, you may be able to address this change easier by making it in yourself. Now, as therapists some of us are so tired of working on ourselves that we groan at this, because it signals an AFGO (another "frigging" growth opportunity). But others of us see this as a saving grace: "Thank goodness I can work on myself, I know how to do that!"

One of my coaching clients had a goal to find more focus in his practice that was extremely diversified. He had five separate, very small businesses operating under one roof: a publishing company, a therapy practice, a bookstore, a coaching practice, and a clothing store. All of them were doing poorly and he told me that the only solution he could see was to add one more into the mix: a recording studio. I disagreed with this idea and tried to get him to see the bigger picture, but he was stuck on it and we had a nonmeeting of the minds.

Rather than try to work this issue through in the business, I asked him to take a look at what was driving his personal need to diversify this way. The next time, he said, "I realize that my problem in business comes from inside me. I am always going in all directions and can't settle on one. This is the story of my life. I have three different academic degrees, have lived in six different states as an adult, and been in four marriages. I now see that until I work some of this out on a personal level, I won't be able to find a focus for my business." He was wise to see that the easiest path for him was to work first on his own lack of personal cohesiveness, rather than having to try to tame his many-headed business.

Premise 3: All Actions You Take in Business Are Fear-Based or Love-Based

You will need to take a lot of specific actions in order to make your business successful. Feeling frightened when taking action, or taking action because you fear what will happen if you don't, is a good way to foreclose on feelings of love for your business.

For example, you may need to make several marketing cold calls to potential referral sources. Doing this from a basis of fear means that you will make the calls from a basis of survival. You think, "If I don't make this call, my practice won't survive. And it's not just making the call, I have to get results, and soon. If this doesn't go well, I will be out of work for good." Imagine the pressure that kind of thinking places on you as you try to develop professional relationships. Who could love a business that puts one into this kind of a spin?

If you take action from a basis of love, you make the exact same call, but do it from a different perspective. You think, "I am calling this person to let him know how much I love the work I am doing, and out of a sense of not just getting but also giving. I want to give him an awareness of who I am, what I do, and offer a win/win suggestion of how we can support each other. Even if no results come from this call, I love to talk about my work, so I will just call the next person and the next." Same action, different basis, different experience of marketing, different feeling about the actions needed to keep a business operating.

Every time you take action in regard to your practice, see if you can do it from a basis of love—love of self, love of others, love for your business, or love of the profession. This feeling of love makes you feel expansive and open-hearted, a good way to proceed in business.

Adopting these premises will make your relationship to your business easier. When you can give your business what it needs while not taking those needs personally, see your business as a natural reflection of yourself, and take business actions based on positive affect, you will naturally and logically learn to better love the business of therapy.

HOW TO USE THIS WORKBOOK

True to my business mission, this workbook is designed to make your life and work easier. Whereas my first book, *Building Your Ideal Private Practice*, was a comprehensive guide to practice building, this workbook is a month-by-month coaching program, to give you the experience of being coached for a year.

MONTH BY MONTH

As you go through each month, completing a progressive series of assessments, written exercises, and skill sets, you also identify the action steps to take and follow that month with fieldwork suggestions (things to do in the real world once you set the book down). You have a prep form each month on which to record your wins and challenges, and to help you set your monthly goals, just like my coaching clients do. Your prep forms are in two places for your convenience: a brief version on the first page of each monthly chapter, and a full-page version for each month in Appendix A. In the Appendix D you will find a Master Plan. This is an outline of the objective for each month, the fieldwork assignment, and words of advice to help you stay on-track. If you feel lost or overwhelmed at any point while going through the workbook, use the Master Plan to see the big picture of the yearly plan and to understand where you are on your personal business journey.

Throughout the book you will find anecdotal examples, new ideas to consider, and lots of suggestions about actions you can take as I help you develop a more sophisticated understanding of the business of therapy. During our last 4 months, I will introduce you to a fascinating model of business evolution and show you the strategies that can help you position yourself and your practice for the future, so that you can stay on the cutting edge of your profession.

The workbook is a yearlong, progressive practice-building program; each month builds on the one before it. In keeping with the Private Practice Success business model, the first 4 months of the workbook focus on aspects of preparation, the second 4 months highlight building blocks, and the final 4 months craft the finishing touches. If you skip a month, or only pick and choose certain exercises to follow, you may not have the necessary foundation in place for the next, so my first suggestion is to take your time and go month by month through the book the way the program is offered.

The workbook is structured differently than my earlier books, and even if you have read *Building Your Ideal Private Practice* you will find that the practice-building program in the workbook moves you forward in a different way, with new exercises, skill sets, and concepts. The earlier book and this workbook together constitute my most up-to-date practice-building program. For those who are adding coaching to their practices, my edited book about coaching, *The New Private Practice: Therapist-Coaches Share Stories, Strategies, and Advice,* may also be an important addition to your practice-building library.

You can begin to use this workbook in any month of the year, but do continue to work with the program for the following 12 months. You can review and reuse the workbook year after year, as your annual practice-building program. After you read through the book, you can highlight certain strategies and exercises, and use them repeatedly. My hope is that you allow the workbook to support you, that you keep it handy and nearby, so when you need to be motivated, less anxious, or more focused, it's easily available and you can get back on track.

Although I am trying to help you build an ideal private practice in the easiest way possible, the reason it's called a workbook is that there is work for you to do. The 90/10 law applies here: Ninety percent of the value of this program lies outside the time you spend reading this book. I will really be doing my job as your coach when you take the information and strategies and put them to the test in your business and your life.

THE RIGHT KIND OF SUPPORT

Getting on board and staying engaged in a practice-building program for an entire year can be tough, especially when you have a full and busy life. If you are disciplined and self-motivated, you will find that you can use this workbook by yourself and make significant gains.

If you are less disciplined, like most therapists I know (I include myself in this group), you may find it necessary and more pleasurable to have the right kind of support for your program. The right kind of support includes colleagues, a coach, or a facilitated coaching group who will celebrate with you when you succeed, commiserate (but not indulge you) when you have a tough time, help you stay consistently motivated, encourage you to do all the exercises, fieldwork, and reading, and hold you accountable for your goals. Your chances to succeed with my practice-building program double when you add in the right kind of support.

Getting support for using a workbook may not be your usual approach, but in the business world, support is the smart way to go. Consider getting support for using the workbook in one of these three structured ways:

1. Ask other like-minded colleagues who also want to improve their practices to do the year-long program with you. The ideal would be to meet twice a month, but once a month will work too. A group of 4 to 10 peers will work best, so that if everyone can't attend every meeting, there will be enough people present to offer energetic support and lively discussion. Decide on who will facilitate each month. You may want to rotate facilitation, so that each person takes a turn at leadership.

2. Become part of an existing, facilitated telephone coaching group. If you don't have the time or the inclination to create a support group, why not let me help? I have created a telephone coaching program to coincide with the publication of this workbook. The telephone groups meet regularly each month to help you stay motivated and proactive. You will be part of a real-time telephone conference call with other therapists like yourself, from across the country. Your facilitator will be one of my staff of therapist-coaches who are trained to supplement the workbook and deepen your understanding of each month's concepts, goals, and exercises. To find out more about the ongoing telephone coaching groups or to register for one, see the Web site: www.privatepracticesuccess.com.

3. Hire an individual coach, or ask a mentor or supervisor to coach you through the workbook so that you have someone to account to. This type of individual support can help you to stay on track and not get discouraged or distracted by minor setbacks. Any one of the associate coaches listed on my Web site (www.privatepracticesuccess.com) would be a good choice since they have trained with me extensively and are available for this type of coaching.

Other listings of coaches (not under my auspices) can be found at the following sites: www.coachfederation.org, www.coachville.com, or www.coachu. com. Please be advised that coaching is a new, unlicensed profession. Take the time to carefully interview your coach before hiring him or her, to make sure you find someone who will understand and support your goals and process.

Ready to start? Turn to Month 1 and begin by taking an honest inventory.

Part I
Becoming an Instinctive Entrepreneur

MONTH 1

Physical Preparation: Taking an Honest Inventory

In my early twenties, I worked for a year in an azalea nursery in Washington state. We grew Hershey Red azaleas, a flowering shrub with fire-engine red blossom that bloom for only 2 weeks a year. Imagine thousands of potted azaleas filling seven large greenhouses. The last day of each month we took inventory, to see what state the plants were in. When I first started the job, I thought taking inventory was incredibly boring. I moved through the first greenhouse in about 30 minutes, giving the plants a cursory look, then went to find my boss. "I'm done with the first greenhouse; they all look okay to me," I said.

He frowned and said I was moving too fast, that I hadn't taken an honest inventory. "How long does an honest inventory take?" I asked. He told me to follow him, and we went into another greenhouse. He held each plant, looking at it with a combination of curiosity and scrutiny. Sometimes he would stop and smile, showing me a particularly beautiful and healthy azalea. Sometimes his brow would furrow at a plant whose growth was stunted, as he would unpot it and look for the reasons for the damage.

I understood that taking an honest inventory meant slowing down and really seeing what existed, good and bad. After that, monthly inventory became a time of learning to see, moving unhurriedly through the sea of plants under the soft, filtered light, knowing that each plant's health relied on my ability to take a careful look.

The best way to start a coaching program is to take an honest and complete inventory of your business. Quantify your resources, your challenges, and your assets to get clear about your existing situation. The exercises, skill set, and fieldwork are designed to help you to have clarity about your current situation and marshal the energy you need to make changes in your life and your private practice.

My Monthly Prep Form

Answering these questions each month will help you to chart your progress and define your next goals.

1. What have I accomplished since last month that I feel positive about? What are my wins?

2. What challenges am I facing this month?

3. What opportunities are available to me right now?

4. What blocks me from taking advantage of these opportunities?

5. How could I make life or work easier or better for myself right now?

6. My goals for this month are:

When was the last time you took a slow, honest inventory of yourself, your life, and your business? What would you learn about yourself and your practice if you looked at your current situation with curiosity and scrutiny, really opening your eyes so that you could note both the good and the bad? This month, I want you to take that kind of an inventory. I want you to recognize what you already have in place, as well as what you lack, so that you can make good decisions about what you do and don't need to change. Begin by taking the Strong Start Survey.

EXERCISE: STRONG START SURVEY

Answer each question fully. Take your time.

1. Where do you get your energy from?

_____

_____

_____

_____

_____

2. Where are you most personally limited?

_____

_____

_____

_____

_____

3. What do you love about your work—being a therapist, coach, or healer? What are your unique strengths and talents? What is going well in your work right now? What are you proud of in regard to your work?

_____

_____

_____

4. What motivates you to take action?

5. What challenges and problems regarding your practice are you currently facing?

6. What challenges and problems regarding your personal life are you currently facing?

7. Of these challenges, which need attention immediately? Which are low priority that can be corrected over time?

8. What are the five business opportunities that you are currently not making the most or anything of?

_____

_____

_____

_____

_____

9. What are the 10 goals you want to accomplish in the next 90 days?

_____

_____

_____

_____

_____

10. If you have an existing support system (friends, colleagues, mentor, coach, peer group, etc.), what should they know about you in order to best understand the challenges you face now? How can they best support you (strong feedback, gentle encouragement, listening, direct suggestions, advice, accountability)?

_____

_____

_____

_____

_____

EVALUATING YOUR STRONG START SURVEY

I ask everyone I coach to fill out the Strong Start Survey because it helps me to quickly understand patterns and clues that explain each person's current situation in private practice. As I read over a Strong Start, I group the answers into four major topics: energy level, motivation, direction, and action.

Energy Level

The answers to questions 1, 2, and 6 help to understand your current energy level. Kathy, a psychotherapist who had a part-time practice in a rural southern town, sent me her Strong Start. In our first conversation, I heard a level of exhaustion in her voice, so I was very curious about how she answered these three questions that pertain to energy level.

Under question 1, Where do you get your energy from, she listed: walks in nature, time with husband, gardening, and sewing. She said that she hadn't taken time for any of these activities in the past three months. Under question 2, Where are you most personally limited, she wrote: "I don't have much willpower and I take rejections that occur in my practice personally. I get my feelings hurt a lot by things that clients say or not having phone calls by possible referral sources returned." Under question 6, regarding personal challenges, she wrote: "I am tired a lot at the end of the day, even though I am only working a few hours. My husband is recovering from a curable cancer and I am worried about him a lot." Together, we discussed these answers. Her work was draining her, she took too many things personally, and her husband's health was a great concern. She knew some sources of getting energized, but she had not felt motivated to pursue them.

Your turn. Look at your answers to questions 1, 2, and 6 and think about your current energy level. Is your work listed as a source of energy in your life? Are your limitations draining you? What are you doing, or will you consider doing, to build your energy as you get ready to build your business?

Motivation

The second group of answers I look at are questions 3 and 4, which explain a person's natural motivation, passion, and current success—important components for fueling further change. For example, if you feel passionate about baseball and are motivated by competition, I will want you to use that sporting energy to help you design a gamelike quality to your practice-building efforts, perhaps keeping score and competing against yourself so that you stay naturally motivated and passionate about your efforts.

Kathy, in question 3, wrote that she loved helping her clients to grow and change. In question 4, she wrote: "I am motivated by fear of going broke." I acknowledged fear as a big motivator for many people, but wondered with her about other motivators that were equally compelling for her in other aspects of her life. She expanded her answer to question 4 to include being motivated by a desire to learn. I would remember this when helping her to find and implement better strategies for her practice, and frame them as learning.

Your turn. Look at your answers to questions 3 and 4 to see what helps you to take action. Does your love for your work help motivate you to build your practice? If not, why not? Are you motivated primarily by fear? What positive motivators can you add to your list?

Direction

Questions 5, 7, and 8 are strategic questions that help formulate the direction for you to take in the short- to mid-term. These questions pinpoint what needs to get done now, including what opportunities are right in front of you that you tend to overlook.

Kathy had a long list of challenges that needed her immediate attention, including balancing her business checkbook, clearing up some accounts receivable, recontacting some past referral sources, and renegotiating her office rent with her landlord. She also had two good business opportunities that she had been slow to pursue. One of these was to partner with a colleague to present a workshop for a women's health fair, which later became a source of several referrals for her. She had a hard time prioritizing these challenges and seeing the opportunities.

Your turn. Look at your answers to questions 5, 7, and 8. What challenges and tasks do you need to attend to and clean up in the short-term to make more space for your bigger business goals? What do you think the short-term direction of your practice will look like? What opportunities are you ready to pursue this month?

Action

Questions 9 and 10 define your 3-month goals, the specific actions you will take, and the support you need to take them. Your support system (and how you utilize it) may make the difference between how fast and how well you achieve your goals, so pay particular attention to question 10.

I asked Kathy to make sure that half of her goals listed under question 9 would be actions that would increase her energy level, and she added goals such as playing golf, reading an inspirational book, and taking time to sew. She had little support for herself, so question 10 became a jumping off point for a discussion about creating a larger personal and professional support system. Kathy realized that she likes gentle, encouraging verbal support with no criticism, but many reminders, to help her keep going.

Your turn. Look at question 9, your list of 10 goals. Will these goals add to your sense of energy or do you get tired just looking at the list? If it's the latter, add and change that list so that you have some goals that create a feeling of energy within you, even if the goals are not directly related to building your practice. Your level of energy and desire will be contagious, and assist in your ability to achieve the harder goals. What support system do you have in place, or could you begin to put in place, to help you take action for your business? How do you best like to receive support?

➙ FIELDWORK

Evaluate your answers to all 10 questions, using the categories of energy level, motivation, direction, and action. Then look at your list of goals, question 9. Prioritize your list of 10 goals from easy to difficult. List the easiest ones first and commit this month to achieving the 3 easiest goals.

ASSETS AND LIABILITIES

Next I want you to list your assets and liabilities. *Assets* include:

1. your physical business belongings (property, furniture, money, equipment, client list, and anything else of a real, tangible nature);
2. your resources of people (network, referral sources, contacts);
3. your materials (programs, advertisements, manuals, written policies, newsletters);
4. your products (books, handbooks, audiotapes, workshops, seminars, talks);
5. your reputation (credentials, affiliations, connections, perceived value).

Liabilities include:

1. debt;
2. serious problems (including problem clients);
3. all unmet responsibilities;
4. any real, situational issues that must be dealt with for you to stay safely and ethically in business.

As you list your liabilities, think about what worries you the most late at night when you can't sleep. List those worries that are real and concrete here. They might include, for example: no cash flow, lack of equipment, inadequate billing system, money owed, issue with cotherapist, no plan for future, big credit card bill, not enough referral sources.

Assets	Liabilities

The next chart is for gains and drains. You did some of this exploration in the Strong Start Survey, but you can take these categories further by using this chart. *Gains* include:

1. all of your personal strengths;
2. everything about you or your business that could be seen as an advantage, benefit, or resource, even if you don't currently take advantage of it. (This is where you can list the intangibles, such as optimism or persistence. Include your level of physical well-being and overall resilience, if those are gains.)

Drains include:

1. intangible aspects (vague feelings, concerns, worries) about yourself or your business that reduce or restrict your rate of progress—intangibles may be existing or projected, such as "lack of self confidence" or "nervous that I will look foolish";
2. current circumstances or problems that sabotage your efforts—drains may be physical or situational, such as "dealing with chronic back pain" or "no time available in a too busy schedule for marketing."

Gains	Drains

EXERCISE: ACCEPTANCE

Once you have completed your Strong Start Survey and assets and liabilities and gains and drains charts, contemplate all three without judgment: just accept what you read. Use the following process.

1. Look at your Strong Start Survey and your charts and think about all that you have written with both curiosity and detachment. Remember the way I was taught to look at the azaleas in the greenhouses? Understand and accept your current situation, the good and the bad, and think: *How fascinating!*
2. Allow new insight and ideas to emerge. If you need help to stay open and detached, allow someone from your professional support system to look at your inventory with you.

3. After reviewing the charts, use this space for notes regarding new insights and ideas you have about your situation:

_____

_____

_____

_____

_____

EXTREME SELF-CARE

As the sole proprietor of a business, you may feel that you carry the weight of your business on your shoulders. Like a long-distance hiker with a heavy back-pack to haul, you need to be in good physical and mental condition to go the distance. Devote time to taking excellent care of yourself, your primary business resource. Fill out the following Self-Care Checklist.

EXERCISE: SELF-CARE CHECKLIST

Check the items that are true for you. A majority of these items checked indicates that you have ample care of self; checking less than half means that you will need to improve your self-care, to have the energy with which to enhance your business.

- ❑ I get good sleep each night to feel healthy and alert.
- ❑ I eat foods that promote my physical well-being.
- ❑ I exercise several times each week to stay flexible and resilient.
- ❑ I have quiet time each week for myself, doing things I love, so that I feel refreshed.
- ❑ I have friends and family that I can talk to whenever I need a sense of connection.
- ❑ I make time each week to engage in activities that give me pleasure.
- ❑ I live in a home that feels nurturing, safe, and pleasing.
- ❑ I get all my personal needs met outside of my practice.
- ❑ I am on a strong financial track.

❑ I get clinical supervision, peer support and business consulting/coaching as needed.

❑ I actively seek solutions for the complaints I have regarding my life and my work.

❑ I maintain a high level of personal and professional integrity.

❑ I know how to forgive and/or feel compassion for myself and others who have hurt me in the past.

❑ I let go of my guilt over my past mistakes.

❑ I keep clear, consistent boundaries regarding my personal and professional life.

❑ I rarely rush; I go through my day being on time.

❑ I have a reserve (more than enough) of money, time, friends, space, love, fun, and affection.

❑ I carry the insurance and protection systems I need to feel and stay safe and protected.

❑ I take action based on feelings of love instead of feelings of fear.

❑ I am part of a community that gives me a sense of purpose.

❑ I live a life based on choice and meaning.

➜ FIELDWORK

Find two items from the Self-Care Checklist that you did not check. Work on them this month. Define the specific action steps necessary to achieve each item. For instance, if you want to work on the item I rarely rush, what specific actions do you need to take this month to make this true?

Examples can be:

- I will allow myself 15 minutes of extra time.
- I will schedule my calendar with longer breaks between sessions to allow me to do everything I need to.
- I will organize my morning so that I can leave the house calmly and not worry about the traffic.

Use this format for identify and setting actions to increase your self-care:

Item: _____

_____

_____

Actions: _____

_____

_____

Item: _____

_____

_____

Actions: _____

_____

_____

MONTHLY SKILL SET: RECOGNIZE THE POWER OF POSITIVE SPEAKING

As you complete the steps of this inventory, you may notice that it is easier to focus on your problem areas than on the positive aspects of your practice. When I ask a therapist to talk to me about his or her practice, I often hear a litany of complaints and worries, even when parts of the practice are going quite well. Some therapists believe that noting achievement or speaking positively is boasting, and as a result they regularly downplay all business success. It's rare for me to hear a therapist tell a business success story, or state his or her strengths and talents with confidence and a smile. We know that positive thinking builds a person's energy and self-confidence—so does positive speaking.

Monitor the way you talk about your work to others. What do you say and how do you say it? Try emphasizing the positive by using words that signal confidence, satisfaction, and accomplishment. Minimize your verbal anxiety and negativity. Here are two specific skills that can help you develop the skill of positive speaking:

- Speak about your strengths.
- Share success stories.

Speak About Your Strengths

During a recent workshop I asked people to break into small groups and talk about their strengths and talents. I listened in on a group of four men and four women. They were sitting in silence; no one wanted to speak first. Finally Joan, a physical therapist, said, "Nothing is particularly special about me. I do what other physical therapists do. I am sure most of my colleagues are just as good as I am and many have a lot more skills than I do."

Sean, an addictions counselor, went next: "I feel the same way. I don't think I talk about my strengths, but let me try. I don't know if this is special or unique, but I am very good with helping extremely resistant addicts come to a quick acceptance about their situation and their addictions. It can be very difficult to get an addict to actually admit the degree of his addiction, but the patients in my groups do this well."

"What do you contribute to making this happen?" I asked.

He thought hard. "I think I signal acceptance in my nonverbals. I always find something I can respect in each person and I focus on that. I never put anyone down. I never feel better than anyone else. I give each person direct eye contact. I like to think I can see the spirit of each person, deep inside, and when I speak to an addict, I am actually speaking to that nonaddicted part of him, sometimes buried deep inside him or her. I find this to be an amazing process, getting someone to take the first step of sobriety, and I never get bored or feel ho-hum about it. I think that this quality in me, which is a combination of my training and also of my own recovery process, makes me a very good counselor."

We all looked at Sean and enjoyed hearing about his gifts. It helped us to know him, to respect his work, and to feel more connected to him professionally. It did not sound boastful. It felt intimate, as though he was giving us a chance to know him.

Now others in the group began to understand how to proceed. Joan asked to go again. "I am very good at finding out exactly where my patients hurt, and then educating them about what is happening in their bodies to cause the pain. While I work with them, taking them through what can be excruciatingly painful exercises, I talk to them. I engage their brains to help them manage the pain. They appreciate the fact that I am really trying to help them become an expert on their own bodies. I do know that not every physical therapist does this. Some are very silent, and I know their patients get confused and don't work as hard on the exercises. I think this is a strength I have that makes me unique."

EXERCISE: EVALUATE YOUR STRENGTHS AND TALENTS

Answer the following questions to evaluate your strengths and talents. If you need help thinking about this, review question 3 in the Strong Start Survey and your list of assets and gains.

What do you love about the practice you have built or the work that you do?

_____

_____

_____

_____

_____

Where are you professionally strong and talented?

_____

_____

_____

_____

_____

What is going well?

_____

_____

_____

_____

_____

What are you excited about in your work?

_____

_____

_____

_____

_____

⟶ FIELDWORK

Practice talking about your strengths in a conversational manner with 10 people this month.

Share Success Stories

Another way to talk positively and concretely about your work is to have a success story or two that you can share. When crafting a success story, make sure that you respect confidentiality, ethics, and your professional sensibilities.

1. Use a composite of several clients or an unrecognizable, unnamed client with a generic problem. Minimize any details that would break confidentiality.
    Several years ago I had a client come to see me who had a very difficult time with managing anger.

2. Highlight what you did specifically that helped.
    I put this client into one of my groups, which are a good environment for anyone who has anger issues. I helped my client learn how to identify when he felt angry, how to release his feelings safely without violence, and eventually how to see what triggered him. I encouraged the group to role play difficult situations, so that he would find constructive ways to appropriately relate to people, even when he was triggered.

3. Explain the good results in specific ways.
    After less than a year of being in group, my client made some important shifts in relating with others. His family deeply appreciated how well he listened and how much calmer he could be. At work he was accepted into a fast-track management training program, because he could stay calm under pressure and communicate well with others.

EXERCISE: CRAFT YOUR SUCCESS STORY

Craft a success story here to emphasize the constructive and positive elements in your work and the real benefits your services make to your clients.

1. Use a composite or an unrecognizable, unnamed client with a generic problem. Minimize or change any details that would break confidentiality.

_____

_____

_____

_____

_____

2. Highlight what you did specifically that helped.

_____

_____

_____

_____

3. Explain the good results in specific ways.

_____

_____

_____

_____

_____

→ FIELDWORK

Practice telling your success story in a conversational manner this month with others. If someone asks how your work is going, you will now have something new to share. Make sure that any success story you verbalize respects your confidential and ethical agreements with clients.

Monthly Review

This month you took an honest, complete inventory of your current situation to look at your resources, challenges, assets, liabilities, strengths, and successes. The fieldwork for Month 1 includes:

- Take the Strong Start Survey and evaluate your answers using the categories of energy level, motivation, direction, and action.

- Prioritize your list of 90-day goals from easy to hard, and complete the three easiest ones.

- Enhance your self-care by taking two action steps.

- Speak positively with others about your strengths.

- Share your success story with others.

MONTH 2

Mental Preparation: Honing Your Entrepreneurial Mind-Set

If you own a business, even a very small business, you fit the definition of an entrepreneur. But we commonly reserve the word *entrepreneur* to mean the kind of businessperson who naturally and assertively pursues business. This month, I want to help you adopt an archetypal entrepreneurial mind-set. Think of this archetype as an energetic response that allows you to move forward on behalf of your business without fear, take action effortlessly, welcome challenge, and seek opportunities. Most therapists in private practice need a large dose of archetypal entrepreneurial energy to balance their often interior, more reserved selves.

The first step in adopting an entrepreneurial mentality is to evaluate your existing business ability and then boost it. To evaluate your ability, use this abridged version of a pre- and post-assessment test that I have given to therapists for several years; it measures skills that will help you succeed in business. If any of the terms in this assessment are unfamiliar to you, refer to *Building Your Ideal Private Practice*—or keep reading here because these terms will also be explained in subsequent chapters of this workbook. You may start with a low score. No problem! This workbook will give you the knowledge and experience to help you check more items month by month, and you can return to this assessment as often as you want to measure your growing business acumen.

If you learn to think like a successful entrepreneur, you can become more mentally resilient and go the distance as a business owner. This month, analyze your business ability, learn to craft a business affirmation to overcome negative beliefs, and identify your ideal clients as you continue to prepare to build your ideal private practice.

My Monthly Prep Form

Answering these questions each month will help you to chart your progress and define your next goals.

1. What have I accomplished since last month that I feel positive about? What are my wins?

2. What challenges am I facing this month?

3. What opportunities are available to me right now?

4. What blocks me from taking advantage of these opportunities?

5. How could I make life or work easier or better for myself right now?

6. My goals for this month are:

EXERCISE: PRIVATE PRACTICE SUCCESS PROGRAM ASSESSMENT

Check off only what is true for you today. Give yourself 1 point for each item. Each section has seven items for a total score of 42 points.

Approach

To be successful in private practice you need to approach your practice as you would a business, not a hobby.

- ❑ I assess and remove all of the non-businesslike elements from my practice.
- ❑ I surround myself with other entrepreneurial colleagues who want me to succeed.
- ❑ I am becoming more pragmatic and optimistic in my thinking about business each month.
- ❑ I know how to construct and use a powerful business affirmation to clear away my negative business beliefs.
- ❑ I have created my own advisory board to surround myself with those who can offer me good business advice.
- ❑ I am accountable to others for achieving my monthly business goals.
- ❑ I am comfortable talking about the positive aspects of my work (my strengths and talents).

___0___ Section score

Business Vision

Your business vision brings meaning and direction to your private practice.

- ❑ I understand the concept of a building a business by design—that if I don't make choices for my business, circumstances will.
- ❑ I make the time each week to work *on* the business, not just *in* the business.
- ❑ I know how to spot trends and can list several future trends that may effect my practice in the next two years.
- ❑ I've identified my top three core values.

- ❑ I have a vision for my practice that is oriented around my core values, strengths, and talents, and set into a predictable future context.
- ❑ I have a written vision, purpose, and mission statement with a list of action steps.
- ❑ I have articulated my vision to other trusted associates in my circle of encouragement.

_0_ Section score

Marketing

At the heart of every healthy private practice is a steady flow of new clients. Knowing how to market your services is an essential skill that will keep your practice viable.

- ❑ I have an articulated basic message that I use as a professional introduction.
- ❑ I can list the benefits of my services and tell specific success stories.
- ❑ I can comfortably ask for referrals in a manner that reflects the integrity of my practice.
- ❑ I have a menu of options for new clients and have packaged my services in five different ways so that price is not a barrier to my services.
- ❑ My promotional materials focus on the solutions I offer to others, in language that highlights what clients really want, not what I think they need.
- ❑ I cultivate practice angels—influential people who are well connected and can make multiple referrals.
- ❑ I know several ways to market my services that actually work, and can pick and choose the ones that are most comfortable for me to use at any given time.

_0_ Section score

Money

A business must make a profit. As the business owner, you need to attend to making money while doing the work you love.

- ❑ I have reconciled the difference between profit and service, as it applies to my practice.
- ❑ I am well within the profit formula guideline for a therapy business.
- ❑ I know how many billable hours I will work this year and what my fee needs to be to meet my income goals.
- ❑ I have more than one profit center and revenue stream.
- ❑ I understand the hidden costs in my practice.
- ✓ I am very comfortable discussing fees, fee raises, how I handle missed sessions, cancellation policies, and other financial issues with my clients.
- ❑ I am building a practice to sell, not just to own.

_____ Section score

Ease

A successful entrepreneur regards operating a business as not only work, but also as pleasure.

- ❑ I understand the difference between a fear-based and a love-based practice.
- ❑ I educate existing clients how to get the most from therapy so that they can become my ideal clients.
- ❑ I organize my calendar to reflect a balance of work, spirit, and buffer time.
- ❑ I set monthly goals and enjoy achieving them.
- ❑ I model the strategies of other successful businesspeople.
- ❑ I collaborate and link with others to make operating my business more fun.
- ❑ My practice operates from a model of abundance, not deprivation.

_____ Section score

Practice Evolution

Growing your practice means helping it develop as you, the business owner, also change and evolve.

❑ I am familiar with the color-coded stages of business evolution and can chart where my practice is on its developmental path.

❑ I understand how to take my practice beyond a medical model.

❑ I have a list of services for clients at all of the stages of personal growth.

❑ I am a model of the personal growth or coaching services that I offer to others.

❑ I have a 5-year vision and am excited about my future direction.

❑ I know how to use circles of community to keep energy and opportunity flowing through my practice.

❑ I have strategies of self-motivation to use that help me stay active and focused over time.

_____ Section score
_____ Total score of all six sections

Scoring

35–42 points: You are really working on the business and have a strong sense of how to set up and maintain your ideal private practice. Congratulations!

27–34 points: You're definitely on your way. Use the workbook to motivate yourself to take the important next steps. Go for it!

19–26 points: Time to do some additional work on your practice and on yourself, so that you can meet your goals and learn to enjoy the business of therapy. Get the support you need to see results you deserve.

0–18 points: You can make some important changes and vastly improve your practice. Use this workbook to get started. Strengthen your business abilities by going through each month and completing all the exercises the field-work. Take in lots of support to make the process easier.

ENTREPRENEURIAL THINKING

How do you think about your business? Are you a worrier—dwelling on worst-case scenarios, feeling down about your lack of success, rejecting possible ideas because you assume they won't work? Are you a planner—making mental lists of what to do next, staying focused and motivated? Are you overly optimistic—

List activities plan for achievement. goal: Business vision is.

seeing many opportunities, not able to prioritize, needing direction? Are you a procrastinator—coming up with good ideas but never feeling ready to start?

How you think about business influences your ability to take action. Negative beliefs and critical self-talk hamper your efforts, while constructive, optimistic yet pragmatic thinking help you to take big steps. Developing an entrepreneurial mind-set—the combination of thinking, feeling, and sensing that is the hallmark of successful business owners—is the next step in your business education.

Therapists often have a part of this mind-set developed, but need to activate additional elements. For example, we are often very skilled at sensing, and can read subtle cues and unspoken signals. This is good and can be very helpful in business situations. But we must also learn to use the linear, unemotional thinking that is necessary in business. Successful entrepreneurs tend to display the following six qualities in their thinking:

1. Given a set of challenges, they see opportunities.
2. Given a problem, they are both optimistic and pragmatic.
3. They expect a lot from themselves and others. They want a lot for themselves and others.
4. Persistence is their middle name.
5. They enjoy making a profit.
6. They operate from a state of abundance.

EXERCISE: ASSESS YOUR ENTREPRENEURIAL QUALITIES

Look at the above list of six qualities and reflect on which are natural for you, and which are not. Then answer the following questions.

Which of these six qualities do I currently possess?

1

2

4 - med

How specifically do I demonstrate these qualities in my life and my business?

I get a sense of achievement from achieving a goal - if I set realistic goals I am to achieve them.

Glass half full person but also knew Rome wasn't built in a day - realism. Knew what you can change.

Which of these six qualities do I need to develop?

4 - get this to an extent. Not a do or die type person.
5 - not money orientated but knew I need to make a living
6 - not really sure what this means

What are the consequences for me, in my life or my business, of not having these qualities yet developed?

Not passionate enough to make the business work

Now let me break down these six qualities, with a way for you to begin to adopt and apply each one to your practice. Here are the first two:

- Given a set of challenges, they see opportunities.
- Given a problem, they are both optimistic and pragmatic.

Therapists face a lot of challenges and problems, just from being in a profession that is still regarded with considerable apprehension by some who most need its services. To deal with this, you need to see the opportunities inside each challenge, and keep an optimistic, yet pragmatic attitude. Taking right action when you are in a challenging situation means combining an optimistic and hopeful stance with realistic expectations and pragmatism.

EXERCISE: CHANGE YOUR CHALLENGES TO OPPORTUNITIES

Here are five common challenges about the therapy business, opportunities to overcome these challenges, and then a space for you to add your own ideas. Think about the challenges that affect your practice and the opportunities you see for taking action.

Challenge 1: Therapy Signals Weakness

Our culture is based on the notion of personal independence. People seeking therapy are seen by others as dependent and weak. Many people hate to ask for help, and prefer to be self-reliant, at all costs. This stops people in our society from seeking counseling or other forms of health care.

Opportunities for the therapist-entrepreneur:

- Reframe your role as one of mentoring or coaching.
- Adopt a collaborative position.
- Highlight your partnership position for your clients in your promotional materials.
- Be willing to offer yourself as a resource, not an expert.

The opportunities I see:

making this clear in my business information - online / flyers.
Raise profile locally in other @ centres - gym healthy body healthy mind.

Challenge 2: Therapy Is too Expensive

The cost of therapy stops many people, especially without insurance. Many people who need therapy define it as a luxury item. Luxury items are dispensable when finances are tight.

Opportunities for the therapist-entrepreneur:

- Offer a menu of your therapy services for clients, from most expensive to less expensive, and encourage them to design a therapy program with you that they can afford.
- Be able to help your clients get the most for their therapy dollars by becoming ideal clients (read further for an explanation of ideal clients).

The opportunities I see:

1/2 hr sessions. reduced costs

_____

_____

_____

Challenge 3: Therapy Is Mysterious

It's difficult to explain exactly how therapy works, even for those who practice it. Most mental health treatment falls somewhere between art and science. If you practice methods of alternative therapy that are unknown to the public, such as Rolfing, Reiki, or energy healing, you have an added job in terms of explaining your craft.

Opportunities for the therapist-entrepreneur:

- Educate others. You will need to have a concise way to explain what you are doing and why.
- Have a Web site and well-edited printed materials to give clients.
- Have a way for the public to preview your work, so that potential clients get a chance to see you and know you before actually booking a session.

The opportunities I see:

_____

_____

_____

_____

_____

Challenge 4: Therapy Is Taboo

Portions of our society actively discourage the use of therapy. Religious and cultural concerns about therapy include a belief that therapy is bad, mingled with the desire to keep emotional problems private, within the purview of the family or the church. Clients come to sessions secretly, not telling family members, friends, or ministers for fear of censure. Forms of therapy that rely on physical touch (massage), needles (acupuncture), guided imagery, or meditation can face an even larger barrier than talk therapy, based on the lack of public acceptance.

Opportunities for the therapist-entrepreneur:

- Be sensitive about cultural differences.
- Educate potential clients about the process.
- Suggest additional reading.

The opportunities I see:

_____

_____

_____

_____

_____

Challenge 5: Therapy Is not Convenient

Many people have trouble physically getting to therapy. The barrier may be your location, the hours you work, or that you are hard to reach and don't return calls.

Opportunities for the therapist-entrepreneur:

- Be reachable.
- Be flexible.
- Use technology—e.g., e-mail, voice mail, fax lines—to let your clients connect with you.
- Consider working from several offices or locating your office near public transportation.

The opportunities I see:

_____

_____

_____

_____

_____

↦ FIELDWORK

Of all the opportunities you have listed, which will you pursue this month to make your services more accessible? Write these down in the forms of goals on your prep sheet. Make sure that your goals reflect both optimism and pragmatism.

RAISING YOUR STANDARDS

One way to become more of an entrepreneur is to raise your standards about your business. Take all the hobby elements out of your business and take your work (and yourself as a businessperson) more seriously. Let's look at the next two entrepreneurial qualities that speak to this:

- They expect a lot from themselves and others.
- They want a lot for themselves and others.

What does *expecting a lot from others*—those who work with you, be they staff or clients—mean? It may mean having clearer boundaries around your requests with clients or staff. Express your needs and wants more cleanly and directly. Expect those around you to come from the best in themselves, and hold yourself to this expectation as well.

Wanting for others means that you can hold a big vision and goals for those around you. When one of my clients sets a goal, I support the achievement of the goal by staying interested, by brainstorming, and by celebrating when it is met, but I don't demean the client by reminding or nagging about the goal. I am there as a very interested party for my clients to report to, but not for babysitting goals.

What I do instead, which has more value, is hold a strong vision of success for my clients, even when they can't see how things will ever work out. I am amazed at how just holding this vision, week after week, month after month, even in the face of setbacks and challenges, can result in my clients' being brave and persistent, taking difficult steps, and accomplishing great things for themselves. I allow myself to express what I envision for my clients in clear, precise language, without any demand. I might say, "I see that it's possible for you to meet a man that you could love, who would love you back and be a good marriage partner" or "I see that it's possible for you to make six figures and still have a balanced life. I'd be happy to support you to see you reach that goal."

When you, as an entrepreneur, begin to feel that there is abundance in your environment, then it is easier to hold a big vision for your clients and yourself as well. You come to believe that there is enough in the world for each client you see to have a meaningful life, satisfying work, enough money to live well, love, and happiness. You come to believe there is enough for you to have all this as well. Read further to the skill set for this month to see how you can develop an attitude of abundance.

EXERCISE: LIST YOUR WANTS AND EXPECTATIONS FOR YOURSELF AND OTHERS

Fill in the blanks in the following sentences.

I want _time to develop my own practice._

_____ for myself.

I expect _that I will be able achieve what I want to achieve_ for myself.

I want _to _____ the law_

_____

_____ for others.

I expect _____

_____

_____ from others.

IDEAL CLIENTS

Another way that entrepreneurs raise their standards is to gravitate toward the concept of *ideal clients*.

As my expertise as a business coach for therapists began to grow, I became curious about the fact that certain participants got great results from a workshop while others progressed much more slowly. After tracking the progress of many participants over several years, I began to understand that those who grasped the material easily and reported the biggest wins shared four characteristics. Using this profile at the beginning of any coaching class or workshop, I could predict who would do well and who wouldn't. I call the person this profile represents my ideal client, because he or she gets the most out of my coaching program and because it is the most fun kind of client for me to work with. (One of the easiest ways to build an ideal practice is to quickly fill it with ideal clients!)

I decided to see if I could not only attract more ideal clients, but create more ideal clients from existing ones. I found that just by articulating the ideal client profile to therapists at the beginning of a coaching course, I could increase the percentage of ideal clients in each class. Soon more therapists were "getting it" faster, and the classes became more challenging and fun for all involved. See if you can let yourself move into the role of ideal client so that you can get as much as possible from this workbook. Here are the four characteristics that make up the profile:

1. *You are willing to take risks and try new things.* I will ask you to think about your practice in a new way and to take some actions that may be different from your usual method of behaving. (By the way, openness to change is a hallmark of a successful entrepreneur.)

2. *You can let me be the coach.* You may be an expert in your professional role as a therapist, but to get the most out of this book I'd like you to approach the material I offer as a receptive student. I encourage you to learn by reading and also by doing: to experiment freely and enjoy participating in the exercises and the fieldwork. Stay curious.

3. *You will adapt any or all of this material in order to make it fit best for you and your situation.* My ideal clients take the initiative to change, alter, or combine any parts of my program in order to get the best results they can in their practices. I actually count on you to do this. From my experience coaching so many professionals I know that this workbook will be useful for a wide range of therapists, physicians, healers, and body workers, if the practioner can adapted it to his or her practice. If the examples in a chapter seem geared to psychotherapists and you are an acupuncturist, please adapt the idea so that it can be useful to you. If I give you an idea that is not right for your particular style, adapt it so that it fits for you. Since I can't be with you to help you

redesign the material to insure a perfect fit, I have to rely on your creativity. (When I teach a workshop, I'm often delighted by the way my ideal clients take a coaching idea and change it in a way I never would have considered, so that it works perfectly for their practice.)

4. *You understand the 90/10 law.* Ninety percent of my value to you will be outside the time you spend reading this book. I will really be doing my job as your coach when you take the information and ideas and put them to the test in your own professional life. My ideal clients like to take the strategies I offer out into their world, use them, and then report back to me and others about their results.

Let's take the concept about ideal clients into your therapy practice. What qualities characterize the clients that you enjoy working with most? Chances are they will be clients who also get the most out of being in therapy with you, too. Notice that your ideal clients probably mirror some of your own characteristics. For example, my ideal psychotherapy client:

- *has a sophistication about the process of therapy.* He or she knows, or is willing to learn, the value of not missing sessions, paying on time, following through on assignments between sessions, and reading books I suggest, which makes us able to focus more on the issues he or she brings to therapy than on the boundaries.
- *is self-motivated and ready to make lasting change.* Since I have a small practice, I limit myself to working only with serious, committed clients.
- *values direct and honest feedback from me.* Since I integrate my coaching style into my therapy sessions, I work best with clients who have enough ego strength to tolerate direct interpretations, and let me know as directly when something I have said is not right or is off base for them.

To help existing and new clients to get their money's worth in therapy, I want to communicate this concept early on and invite new clients to become ideal clients for their own benefit. Because therapy can be such a different experience with each different therapist one sees, and because therapy is somewhat vague and mysterious in general, I don't assume that people who come to see me know how to be ideal clients, even if they have been in therapy before. It's my job as the business owner to educate them in this regard. And it's your job, too!

EXERCISE: CREATE YOUR IDEAL CLIENT PROFILE

Create your own profile of your ideal client. Limit it to just a few items, making the criteria inclusive, rather than exclusive. An ideal client profile invites someone into a relationship. Focus on attributes rather than on age or gender or symptoms.

My ideal client has these qualities:

Able to talk about themselves.
can work with thoughts and feelings
wants to achieve change.

My ideal client appreciates:

Things take time
It is a difficult process.
and is going to be challenging.

My ideal client values:

Trust
Honesty
openess.

My ideal client understands:

My role and my
boundaries and limitations.
The change is in them

My ideal client agrees to:

challenge themselves.
work with difficulty - baby steps.

➜ FIELDWORK

Communicate your ideal client profile. Educate new and existing clients. When articulated clearly, your ideal client profile will help people understand your approach as a therapist and increase the value others can receive from therapy.

MONTHLY SKILL SET: DEVELOP AN ABUNDANCE ATTITUDE

The last three qualities of a successful entrepreneur fall under what I call an *abundance attitude*—the belief that there is enough in the world for all of us to meet our needs. This means (for you) that there is enough opportunity, time, information, money, clients, and business for starters. Entrepreneurs who believe in a profusion of possibilities share these qualities:

- Persistence is their middle name.
- They enjoy making a profit.
- They operate from a state of abundance.

When you believe there is a lot out there, you don't mind being persistent in order to get your share. You begin to think pragmatically. Of course it takes effort to set up a thriving practice, identify and cultivate referral sources, fill a workshop, land a book contract. It's nothing personal when your goals take more effort than you thought they would. It's just that with so much flow and people and opportunities, it takes time and energy to make certain things happen.

To learn to operate from a state of abundance, you need two heavy-duty skills. You need to know how to: create and use a business affirmation and tap into an internal resource that I call meeting your inner entrepreneur.

Creating Your Business Affirmation

Business affirmations do two things: They soothe your anxiety and correct your negative, self-sabotaging beliefs.

Some therapists get dramatic results using a business affirmation. They work with an affirmation consistently and find that without any other behavioral change on their part, their business grows and opportunities surface spontaneously. Others have less dramatic results, but talk about a noticeable change in their emotions, saying that using the affirmation helps them to feel calmer and in control. Still others use the affirmation, but don't notice any immediate change. I fall into this camp; I do it for a while and forget about it. Months pass, and then I realize the affirmation I worked with briefly six months ago, *My practice is a pleasure to operate*, has become my reality. Try this process, keep some notes about your experience and watch what happens.

Step 1: Choose a Business Affirmation

Choose an affirmation that you will use for at least 10 minutes a day, every day for the next month. The affirmation needs to speak to your particular situation, affirming what you most need or want in your practice. Here is a list criteria for the affirmation:

I want to be working in private practice with 2 clients by end of May

- Use positive language.
- Keep it short.
- Use the present tense.
- Focus on changes in yourself, not others.
- Go outside your normal comfort zone, to your leading edge of growth.

Here is what I mean by this last point: Imagine you are standing near the edge of a cliff. If you are 20 feet back from the edge, you feel safe and secure. When you move closer to the edge of the cliff, you start to feel nervous. When your toes are hanging off the edge of the cliff, you are at your leading edge. An affirmation that just restates your present reality keeps you in your comfort zone. If you make your affirmation bold enough, you will notice that an immediate protest forms in your mind and negative beliefs quickly surface. This is a leading-edge affirmation.

A leading-edge affirmation feels grandiose. It stretches you to a new level of thought that seems impossible. This is desirable, because this exercise is designed not only to help you learn to state and hold onto large business goals *before* they become your reality, but also to elicit and then eradicate negative thoughts.

Sometimes adding the right adjective or adverb will turn a comfort-zone affirmation into one at your leading edge. If you make money at your practice but find it takes a lot of hard work, a comfort-zone affirmation is *I make money in my practice*. A leading-edge affirmation would be *I make money effortlessly*. If your practice always stays just a little below full, a leading edge affirmation is *My practice overflows with ideal clients*.

Here are some sample affirmations that meet the criteria of a leading-edge affirmation, listed above:

I manifest my vision for my practice.
I generate all the business that I need.
My practice is highly profitable.

I balance the success of my business with the rest of my life.

I have a practice that stays full so that I can do my best work.

I easily attract an abundance of ideal clients.

I enthusiastically let people know about my services.

I fulfill my personal definition of success.

Having prosperity in my life and work is easy for me.

I have a waiting list full of clients.

Step 2: Write the Affirmation

Now use a paper with two columns to write your affirmation. On the left, write the affirmation. The reason for making the statement succinct is that you will be writing it over and over. You can do it by hand, or on a computer, but the key to making this work is writing it, not just thinking it. (Page 55 is a sample form to duplicate and use.)

Once you have written the affirmation, listen quietly for any internal negative thoughts. Write down the negative thought in the right-hand column, opposite the affirmation. Then repeat this process, until the page is full. Use the same affirmation each time. Resist any inclination to change it. At the end of the exercise you will have a list that looks something like this:

Affirmation	Negative Thought
I happily do what it takes to have a full, vibrant practice.	No I don't.
I happily do what it takes to have a full, vibrant practice.	I can't do what it takes.
I happily do what it takes to have a full, vibrant practice.	That's for other people not for me.
I happily do what it takes to have a full, vibrant practice.	I'm not smart enough to do this.
I happily do what it takes to have a full, vibrant practice.	My practice never stays full.

Affirmation	Negative Thought
I happily do what it takes to have a full, vibrant practice.	I'm too lazy.
I happily do what it takes to have a full, vibrant practice.	That's not me.
I happily do what it takes to have a full, vibrant practice.	I'm scared of doing what it takes.

Your negative thoughts will read like a stream of consciousness, albeit a highly critical stream. Time after time, in the classes I teach, we read out these negative beliefs and everyone is amazed at how similar they sound, regardless of who is reading them and or what the affirmation states. As long as you are at your leading edge, it will tend to bring up a long list of your fears and anxieties. This means you are doing the exercise correctly.

Step 3: Clear Away Your Negative Beliefs

Here are the three Rs of countering your negative beliefs: run through them, refute them, or replace them. Pick one method to use.

Run through them. Exhaust them by using your affirmation to drain away their charge. Write the affirmation over and over again, day after day. Over time you will notice that your mind quiets, tires of protesting, and agrees with the statement. When this happens, begin to notice any changes in your behavior and your thinking about this issue. This may take a day, a week, or a month, depending on the affirmation you have created.

Refute them. Make a third column on your paper and use your intellect to answer back to the negative belief. Let's say your affirmation is *I generate all the money into my practice that I need* and the negative thought you first notice is *I am no good with money.* Think this through. Is it always the case, or can you think of times when you've managed money well? Even if you haven't managed money well in the past, you, like others, can educate yourself and learn. Write all this down in the margin next to the negative belief. It might look like this:

Affirmation	Negative Thought	Refutation
I attract ideal clients.	I'm not that lucky.	It's not about luck. I can learn the marketing strategies that attract ideal clients.
I attract ideal clients.	Ideal clients never stick with me for very long.	I may need to refine my retention skills, as a clinician and a businessperson, so that existing clients stay long enough to complete their therapy.
I attract ideal clients.	I'm nothing special.	My training is similar to that of many other therapists, but I have unique qualities and talents. I need to identify and claim them.

A good resource for refutation is Martin Seligman's book *Learned Optimism.* He gives many examples of how to use reason to overcome pessimism. Engage your neocortex to examine your negative reactions and eliminate unnecessary negative self-talk.

Replace them. Use visualization to give yourself a different picture, a message that counters the negative belief. For example, imagine a clear mental image of the affirmation and hold that picture in mind. Create a piece of artwork, make a collage from magazine photos, or draw a symbol that represents the affirmation. Look at it often. Meditate on the image. Again, the point is to help your mind create a new sense of what is possible.

EXERCISE: USE A BUSINESS AFFIRMATION

Make 30 photocopies of this blank chart. Each day, fill in one page. Write the affirmation and then write any negative thought that surfaces in response. Write the affirmation again, and repeat the process, filling up both sides of the chart. The object is to keep writing the affirmation until you clear away negative thoughts, so that at the end of 30 days you have no negative response when you write or think your affirmation.

Affirmation	Negative Thought

➜ FIELDWORK

Use a business affirmation each day this month. Use one of the three methods for clearing away negative beliefs that surface.

Meeting Your Inner Entrepreneur

A resource state is a state of mind that helps to shift you into a better mood. It promotes your ability to try a new behavior or to gain a deeper understanding of yourself. The following meditation will help you create a resource state of an inner, unflappable, wonderful entrepreneur who will be behind you, giving you energy and support, whenever you desire.

GUIDED IMAGERY: LISTEN TO YOUR INNER ENTREPRENEUR

Tape-record the following instructions and listen to them, or ask someone to read them to you in a slow, gentle voice, giving you plenty of time to complete each step.

Sit in a comfortable chair that has a firm back.

Close your eyes and relax your body, using your breath as a focal point. Imagine directing your breath into any areas of stress or tension in your body, breathing into them. Breathe in and out easily and effortlessly, letting your breath help you to relax and be comfortable.

Now imagine a person whom you actually know, have seen, read about, watched in a movie, or create in fantasy, who might be a man or a woman, or even a combination of several people, who represents the archetype of entrepreneurial energy to you—the energy that moves into the world without fear. This person has a high comfort level of self, takes action effortlessly and with pleasure, has enormous vitality, and moves forward into the world without fear. This is a person who takes risks, is expansive, welcomes public interaction, enjoys competition and challenge, radiates strength, and moves forward into the world without fear.

See this person in front of you. Note the color of his or her eyes, hear the sound of his or her breath, feel the heat from his or her body energy. Now imagine placing this person directly behind you, right at your back. Literally lean back into your chair, leaning back into him or her. Lean back and sense his or her strength, vitality, and energy. Lean back and see how it feels to move into the world without fear. Lean back and feel that level of effortless energy. Lean back and take in strength.

From this place of leaning back, think about any challenge you currently have in your private practice. Notice any new thoughts or ideas that come from thinking about this challenge, from this position.

Open your eyes and write down what you remember.

→ FIELDWORK

Revisit your inner entrepreneur once a week, to get a new perspective on a business problem or to help you to stay motivated. When you feel the need, just close your eyes, imagine your inner entrepreneur at your back, and lean into him or her.

Monthly Review

This month, you analyzed your current business ability level, learned to adopt six entrepreneurial qualities, and created a business affirmation to become more mentally resilient. The fieldwork for Month 2 includes:

- Shift your challenges about the business of therapy to opportunities. Choose several opportunities you listed and add them to your goals on your prep form.

- Establish your ideal client profile and communicate it to your new and existing clients.

- Use a business affirmation each day this month and clear away any negative thoughts.

- Revisit your inner entrepreneur once a week for new understandings.

Remember to use your monthly prep form to keep track of your wins and challenges to and define the next set of goals you want to accomplish.

MONTH 3

Emotional Preparation: Building a Reserve of Support

Owning and operating a private practice is not just a physical and mental process; it's emotional, too. The daily challenges of business can bring up old, unfinished emotional issues. If this happens to you, you may find yourself confronting feelings of insecurity, frustration, jealousy, hopelessness, anger—you name it. Having these feelings surface doesn't mean that anything is wrong with you or with your practice. What's important is whether you have a way to process your feelings so that you can move forward on behalf of your business.

The best antidote for difficult emotions that surface during the course of being in business is to have the right kind of support. Knowing how to ask for and receive the right kind of support to sustain your business efforts is not always obvious. If you are a person who works in isolation, doesn't ask for much help from others, or feels cut off from his or her professional community, this month's exercises and fieldwork will help you to put more support into your practice to reduce the emotional swings of owning a small business.

Many therapists I meet are hungry for inspiring and uplifting professional connection. When I conduct weekend workshops, I design the workshop to show therapists how to build professional support for themselves in the room, all day long during the weekend. It's typical to see therapists form alliances and collaborative partnerships by the end of the first day. Phone numbers are exchanged. There is laughter and lightness in the

Owning and operating a private practice can be emotionally draining; you need the right kind of professional support in place to minimize the ups and downs. This month, learn the best ways to develop a strong external and internal support system to create partnership and encouragement for yourself and your business.

My Monthly Prep Form

Answering these questions each month will help you to chart your progress and define your next goals.

1. What have I accomplished since last month that I feel positive about? What are my wins?

2. What challenges am I facing this month?

3. What opportunities are available to me right now?

4. What blocks me from taking advantage of these opportunities?

5. How could I make life or work easier or better for myself right now?

6. My goals for this month are:

room, as people share and normalize their business experience. Participants have brainstorming sessions during the breaks, discover business opportunities, and form professional support groups that last for years.

When facing a serious downturn in your practice, having solid professional support can be the difference between resilience or collapse. Anne, a social worker, has been in solo practice for 15 years. She is bright, competent, and hard-working. She is also quiet, reserved, and shy; she works in relative isolation from her peers and her community.

In 4 months this year, Anne's practice took an unexpected drop from 23 clients a week down to 12. The drop-off in clients was the convergence of several factors: moving her office unexpectedly, losing her two main referral sources, who both retired, and attrition—a number of clients happened to finish their treatment at the same time. Summer came and went, Anne took her usual weeks of vacation, and no new clients called for appointments.

Anne was frightened; a loss of 50% of one's income and workload is hard to handle. She did what was natural for her: She retreated inside herself, tried to think through what was wrong, and tried to calm down. She began to feel depressed. She called a few close friends and told them what was going on and they listened and commiserated. She went to a professional meeting, but no one else was complaining of a drop-off of clients, and Anne felt embarrassed to talk about her problem. When November came with no change in client count, and a growing credit card debt, she found herself doing something she hadn't done in 20 years: She looked through the want-ads for an agency job.

Contrast Anne's story to that of Jill, also a social worker, whose practice also took a sharp drop this year. Jill belongs to four professional support groups. Two support groups are made up of therapists who meet weekly for case consultations. The other two support groups are made up of business owners—one is a group of women business owners; the other, an entrepreneurial club sponsored by her chamber of commerce.

When Jill's practice fell off, she talked about her concerns in all of her support groups. "Right away I got professional support. My therapist colleagues assured me that they had gone through this from time to time, so I didn't feel like a pariah. They offered some good ideas, and they wanted to know each week how I was doing. The business groups took it as a personal mission to keep me motivated. Some asked me to call them each week and just let them know how I was doing with my marketing. They became a cheerleading squad for me. No one could fix the situation—that was up to me to do—but I found the support invaluable to help me stay upbeat. The women's business group also turned out to be a source of some referrals. Two women in the business group began to send several clients to me. I had never really tapped into these groups for marketing because I had been full previously. Who knew?"

Jill's practice bounced back quickly, because she had so much energy to put toward her practice and she did not suffer any loss of self-esteem or financial crisis. The support acted like fuel and kept her business engine running.

Being a small-business owner means that you carry the emotional weight of your practice on your shoulders. Having support can make the burden lighter. During the last decade, with its economic downturn, a top survival strategy for all types of business was connection: finding ways to link, affiliate, collaborate, partner, share, network, or merge with like-minded concerns. Let's look at how you can bring this strategy into your small business by increasing and solidifying your professional support system.

YOUR SUPPORT SYSTEM

Professional support systems tend to fall into three areas:

1. *People you hire*—staff, consultants, supervisors, or coaches who help you to reach outcomes or accomplish specific tasks.
2. *People you attract*—peers, colleagues, friends, or family members with whom you may or may not actually do business, but who offer support, advice, coaching, and brainstorming.
3. *People you are attracted to*—mentors and models of excellence you seek out so you can shift to a higher level of accomplishment or awareness.

Hiring others is an easy way to feel supported when you feel overwhelmed, overworked, or under pressure. Sometimes you need to hire staff—a full- or part-time bookkeeper, secretary, receptionist, or others to whom you can delegate—to ease the pressure. Most therapists in successful practices delegate some aspect of billing, administration, public relations, web-site design, accounting, or promotion. Some also hire outside consultants—business coaches, financial planners, marketing experts—to assist with operational planning, goal setting, or future development. I love hiring people who know more than I know, or who can do simple tasks more easily than I can. Whatever business problem you have, chances are you can find staff, consultants, or experts to help you resolve it. You will need to manage your staff, but it may be a workable trade-off for having additional support.

Attracting people for collaboration can generate new opportunities and referrals for a practice. Three years ago I joined two professional support groups to increase my connections to my community, since I am naturally an introvert and tend to keep to myself outside of working hours. These groups have provided a lot of emotional support for me, as well as new business opportunities that I would have never expected. As you attract others with similar goals or a shared enthusiasm for entrepreneurship, you build a circle of encouragement for yourself. You may decide to pursue business endeavors with this circle of peers, or just use the time with them to share support and ideas.

When you *connect with mentors* or those whom you admire, you can shift to a higher level of accomplishment or increased awareness. This might mean giving yourself permission to hang out with others who are much further along the path than you are. There are many ways to do this: going to workshops, conferences, or seminars, getting supervision from the most senior, respected clinicians you can find, reading books by your favorite mentors, or joining organizations where you will be in the same room with those you admire. I let myself feel a sense of connection with mentors, even when the connection is tenuous and long-distance. You can recognize this type of connection and feel a sense of support from those whom you admire.

EXERCISE: EVALUATE YOUR SUPPORT SYSTEM

List your current support system in each of the three areas, and ask yourself if it is sufficient for you.

People I hire and why:

N/A

_____

_____

_____

People I attract and why:

_____

_____

_____

People I am attracted to and why:

____

____

____

Is my support system sufficient for my current needs?

____

____

____

Which areas do I need to increase and how will I do this?

____

____

____

→ FIELDWORK

Increase your professional support this month by adding additional people into your life in at least two out of the above three areas.

BRAINSTORMING

One benefit of support is the added brainpower. The old maxim about two minds being better than one is true when strategizing business problems. In isolation, we see our problems from one narrow perspective. It's good business to talk and share ideas with others. When you are in private practice, you need to make continual decisions about lots of business issues, such as:

- the hours you agree to work;
- the direction of your practice for the next year;
- your arrangements regarding billing, payment, or insurance;
- which clients are best for you to see, and which aren't;
- strengthening your policies, such as changing a weak missed-session policy;

- charging what you deserve;
- getting adequate training and supervision;
- taking on too much, versus taking on too little;
- finding skilled administrative help;
- overcoming boredom or anxiety about your work.

What is the right way to solve these problems? There is no one right way. There are many, many ways to set up and operate a practice. Ultimately you want to find *your* right way, so that you build a business that is based on your passion, vision, plan, and specific goals. Because I talk to so many therapists each year, I get to hear the many creative ways that therapists find to be successful in practice. When you realize that so many therapists can make a practice work in so many different, yet valid, ways, you see that freedom and flexibility are possible for you.

Have you ever asked others to brainstorm with you about your practice? Here's how: Make a list of your top complaints or problems and then listen, without defensiveness, to the solutions offered by others. The solutions you hear often need to be adapted to work for your practice, but don't reject them simply because they aren't exactly right. Watch for your resistance: *I can't do that because . . .* or *I thought of that and rejected it because . . .* or the classic *That won't work for me because . . .* These statements are signals of defensiveness.

Instead of defending against ideas, strategize. Adapt, adapt, adapt all solutions offered to you. Then, with this list of adapted solutions, all of which *could* work, decide which ones actually to use. Which ones should you choose? If you want an easier practice, pick those that feel most natural. Listen in on a brainstorming session from one of the small groups that formed during a weekend workshop:

Complaint from the therapist: I hate to work evening hours, but most of my clients can't schedule appointments during the day. Working nights means I am away from my family for four out of five weekday evenings each week.

Brainstorming solutions from the group:

- Target your services to those who can see you during the day—retirees, self-employed people, college students, housewives, professionals with flexible lunch hours.

- Give your clients examples of how those who see you during the day set it up at work. Many clients take lunch hours from as early as 11:00 A.M. to as late as 3:00 P.M. to come to daytime therapy appointments.
- Work Saturday mornings and Sunday afternoons to replace all weekday evenings.
- Run one or two groups on a weeknight evening and put all evening clients in group.
- Stop offering evening hours so you won't be tempted to work at night and see what happens.
- Offer sessions by phone for those clients who can't get to your office during the day.
- Offer half-hour sessions to see more clients in the morning before work or at lunch time, and supplement with an additional longer session once a month.

Adapted solutions by the therapist: I will offer early-morning sessions and start an evening group to leverage my time, to see more clients in an evening. I won't work weekends, but I will block out several evenings each week and as clients leave therapy, I won't refill those hours.

EXERCISE: BRAINSTORM WITH OTHERS

Use the following form to help you brainstorm with others.

My top three complaints about my practice:

_____

_____

_____

Three people I will ask to brainstorm with me:

_____

_____

_____

Their advice:

____

____

____

My adaptation of their advice (what I will actually do)

____

____

____

→ FIELDWORK

Follow through your brainstorming with others. Curb your tendency to say, Yes, but. Just listen. Reject nothing. A poorly thought-out solution may still contain the seeds of a great idea. Think: 80% of this solution won't work, but 20% can be helpful. How can I identify and adapt this 20% to use it in my business? Finally, select or synthesize a solution based on the ideas offered, and take action.

INTERNAL SUPPORT

In his book *Search for the Real Self*, James Masterson defines early abandonment depression as a condition when, due to trauma or situational stressors, the "self leaves the self." I think about this definition when faced with the stresses and strains of business, because it is so common, as business owners, to respond to stress by abandoning ourselves.

You abandon yourself when, due to business problems, you dissociate, feel hopeless, get obsessed, or forget who you are and what is really important to you. If you need a way to come back to yourself when you are under pressure, to remember your worth as a person and a professional, and to soothe yourself internally, use the following exercise to create a list of healing activities.

EXERCISE: RECLAIM YOURSELF

Answer each question fully.

1. What is most important to me in my life? What am I doing to honor this each day?

   Having a good balance
   between work and living

2. What meaning and purpose do I ascribe to what is happening to me? What is the most personally compassionate or generous meaning I can make out of this for myself?

3. How do I express my creativity? When was the last time I engaged in this activity?

   Sewing. making something
   - started to make a
   quilt + set one aside
   to do this

4. What does my intuitive sense suggest that I need to do, be, or think right now?

What are my priorities to get to where I want to get to. what is my end game.?

5. What spiritual practices do I need to include each day to keep me grounded and calm?

meditation
mindfullness.

6. How can I be more loving to myself when I am under stress? What will I commit to do this month on a daily basis? What is my monthly plan for enhancing a stronger sense of self?

mindfulness for self compassion.
Daily diary

SYMPTOM VERSUS SOURCE

Business problems are similar to physical or psychological symptoms. If you seek their source, you may find that the source of the problem is—you guessed it—inside you, the business owner. Think of this as the good news. You know where to start when solving the problem. If you identify the source of a business symptom as being something in you, you can correct it and improve your business just by working on yourself. Symptoms and their internal sources can be tricky to identify. Here is a list of common symptoms and their deeper, personal sources that therapists attending a workshop compiled:

Business Symptom	Possible Internal Source
not enough clients	fear of putting self forward
paperwork in disarray; procrastinating	way to avoid deep-seated anxiety and fear of failure
goes over the clinical hour; lateness	poor personal boundaries
therapist overworks	weak personal life, nothing to go home to
charges too little for services	acting out childhood negative beliefs about money
gossips about colleagues or clients	envy or insecurity about own work
gives services away for free	lack of self-confidence
takes on too many projects	fear of getting serious
business in continual crisis	uses adrenaline as fuel

EXERCISE: LIST YOUR SYMPTOMS AND SOURCES

Make a list of your top five symptoms and the corresponding internal sources:

Symptom	Possible Source
1. _____	
2. _____	
3. _____	
4. _____	
5. _____	

⇀ FIELDWORK

If you have trouble figuring out your source issues, brainstorm with others. Stay open to what you hear, don't defend. If the possible source resonates for you, write it down. Pick two internal source issues to address and correct this month. Heal the source problem so that the business symptom can disappear.

SUPPORTIVE GOALS

It helps to set goals. But how do you set goals that support instead of burdening you? Setting goals with support can give you the sense of having a strong backbone that allows you to move freely, instead of feeling like a weight that drags you down.

The solution is to create a relationship between yourself and the goal. Relating to a goal makes the difference between achieving it easily or not. If your goal is to double your client count, first think: *If I do meet my goal, how will I feel about myself? If I don't meet my goal, how will I feel about myself?*

If you answer *good* or *bad*, you are overidentified with the goal, a sure recipe for unhappiness. You need to relate differently to the goal, seeing it as separate from you, and forming a relationship with the goal. The next exercise shows one way to do this:

EXERCISE: RELATE TO YOUR GOALS

Consider a goal you really want for your practice. Then fill in the following blanks:

Goal: _____

Does having this goal feel supportive (energize me) or burdensome (tire me out)? _____

Why? _____

_____

_____

Would achieving it help to promote the best of me and my practice?_____

_____

How? _____

_____

_____

What is my relationship to this goal? How can I improve the relationship?

_____

_____

_____

Do I want to achieve it for my own purposes, or do I think I should achieve
it to meet someone else's judgment? _____

_____

_____

If it's the latter, how can I reformulate the goal so that it supports (energizes)
me?_____

_____

_____

➡ FIELDWORK

*Look at your list of goals on your monthly prep form. Using the above questions,
think about your relationship with your goals. Make all your goals ones that support
you and your practice, not ones that feel burdensome.*

MONTHLY SKILL SET: ACCEPT COUNSEL

We therapists know a lot about how to give advice and counsel to others. We
spend most of our working hours in the role of the expert, counseling our
clients to improve their lives. But learning to request, accept, and then utilize
advice and counsel from others, especially as it pertains to our business, can be

an unknown skill set. The formalized process of getting first-rate advice and counsel for your business is to create an advisory board.

If you've spent any time within a large corporation or nonprofit organization, you're probably aware of the important role of the advisory board. Ideally, a board functions as the brain trust of an organization. The CEO selects the best and brightest people he or she knows from a variety of fields, from within and outside the organization, to provide advice and direction. In a perfect world, the board operates without any personal or political agenda, save one: It wants what is best for the organization.

Create a formal advisory board to guide you on the direction of your practice. Ask the best and the brightest businesspeople you know to sit on your advisory board. Communicate with them on a regular schedule, individually or as a group, by phone call, memo, or in person. Let them advise you on your business direction, specific problems, business plan, marketing plan, or your vision, purpose and mission statements. Let each member of your board offer his or her expertise. Listen, make notes, follow through on the best suggestions, and express your open appreciation for the members of your brain trust. Add or subtract new members as your business develops.

Some therapists who want to create a formal advisory board ask, "What is in it for the board members?"

Most successful business people feel a natural desire to give back in some way by mentoring others. The successful business people you ask to sit on your board need to be people who like you and want to see you succeed. They should also see their participation on your board as a way of mentoring you. Because you are in the business of helping and healing others, those business people may also take the perspective that by making sure your practice stays viable, they are indirectly assisting those who will benefit from your services.

Or, if you liked the exercise about brainstorming this month, take the brainstorming concept one step further and create an advisory *circle*, which is a blend of an advisory board and a brainstorming session. Here's how to proceed with an advisory circle:

EXERCISE: CREATE YOUR ADVISORY CIRCLE

Follow this format to create your own advisory circle.

1. *Who.* Select four to six people for your advisory circle, including yourself. Who should be a member of the group? It will help if everyone is in business. You might include some therapists, but also consider having a lawyer, an accountant, or a management consultant. Each person should be someone you respect, whose advice and experience will be relevant and someone you would like to give your support to, in turn. When advising, everyone agrees to speak from a place of the highest good, without personal agenda. (For this reason, you may not want to have your spouse or close friends sit in on this professional support circle, unless you are sure you can both remain loving and objective for each other professionally.)

Who will be in my circle:

_____

_____

_____

2. *When.* If the group has six members, everyone agrees to meet once a week for a minimum of six weeks. Each meeting will take an hour.

When we will first meet:

_____

3. *How.* The format of each meeting is simple—a different person takes center stage, each time. This person takes 30 minutes to present his or her professional situation and answers any questions other members may have; then the group gives their best advice for the remaining 30 minutes. During the advice-giving 30 minutes, the center-stage person must sit quietly. The key word here is *quietly.* Breathe. Take in. The members of your circle will now give you advice, direction, and suggestions, based on wanting the best for you personally and professionally. They will talk about your situation among themselves, while you just listen.

Our format:

_____

_____

_____

_____

_____

4. *Why*. The value of advice is hearing it cleanly (with detachment, without resistance). You will hear many ideas that you may want to downplay or resist. Listen with an open mind and reject nothing at this time. Take notes. You are free to accept or reject whatever you like later, but first consider all the possibilities without excuses or explanations. When the time is over, thank your circle for their efforts. The next time you meet, it's somebody else's turn and you become part of their advisory circle.

How I will stay open to advice given and remain detached:

_____

_____

_____

_____

_____

5. *How long*. Keep the circle meeting as long as it is useful to the group. Include a method of accountability, for follow-up. Make time in each subsequent meeting for each person to briefly report on changes and progress. Some therapists who formed these circles tell me that over time the circles shift and change structure, becoming less formalized and more like a support group. When one member faces a difficult situation, they revert to the process for giving clean advice (advice that is accepted openly by the listener, without resistance).

My plan:

_____

_____

_____

_____

_____

Monthly Review

This month, we looked at several ways for you to greatly increase the internal and external support you have in place, so that you can feel more resilient and motivated in the process of building your practice. The field-work for Month 3 includes:

■ Increase your collaborative efforts at hiring, attracting, or being attracted to people who support you.

■ Ask three people to help you brainstorm solutions for your top business problems.

■ Pick two business symptoms and possible source issues to address on your own.

■ Make sure that you have a positive way to relate to the goals you focus on each month.

■ Create your advisory board or advisory circle.

MONTH 4

Spiritual Preparation: Orienting Your Practice Around Values and Vision

Your sense of spirituality shows up when you build a business that reflects your integrity, values, and vision. A spiritual business signals *right livelihood*, a Buddhist term meaning employment with high standards, good boundaries, and service to others. Is the integrity of your business intact? Have you built a business based on principle, not just profit? Do you behave with compassion and responsibility toward your staff, clients, and yourself? Do you operate your business so that it stays solid and balanced?

When I drive across the Bay Bridge, a large span of concrete and steel that connects the Washington, DC area with the Chesapeake Bay, I rely on the bridge's integrity to keep me safe. I don't consciously think about the bridge's solidity each time I drive over it, but I would definitely notice if it was lacking. If the bridge buckled under the weight of the cars, or if I saw steel columns that needed repair, I wouldn't be able to relax and concentrate on the task at hand—driving safely. I certainly wouldn't enjoy the view of the water and the shore. To drive at my best, I need to know that the integrity of the bridge is unbroken.

Similarly, when a client enters your practice, you want him or her to sense that the integrity of your practice is whole. You want your values, standards, policies, and business vision to be in place so that a client can internally relax and get to work. This month, as we

To infuse your business with spirituality, orient your private practice around your passion and your core values. This month, define your business vision using a value-based approach and examine the integrity of your practice. Then, with your vision, purpose, and mission statement in place, you can move forward with a clear direction.

My Monthly Prep Form

Answering these questions each month will help you to chart your progress and define your next goals.

1. What have I accomplished since last month that I feel positive about? What are my wins?

2. What challenges am I facing this month?

3. What opportunities are available to me right now?

4. What blocks me from taking advantage of these opportunities?

5. How could I make life or work easier or better for myself right now?

6. My goals for this month are:

explore the spiritual aspect of your practice, I want you to evaluate any integrity breaks that might need your attention. Integrity breaks are the small, but noticeable cracks in the foundation of your practice—inconsistencies, contradictions, or irregularities that signal that something is wrong on a deeper level.

EXERCISE: INTEGRITY BREAKS CHECKLIST

Check the items that are true for you at this time, or write in your own.

- ❑ I forget to return phone calls from clients and/or colleagues.
- ❑ I quote different fees to different clients for the same service, without well-thought-out reasons.
- ❑ I am behind in my important paperwork—taxes, treatment reports, letters, etc.—and I have no idea when I will get to it all. ✓
- ❑ I make repeated mistakes with clients, like double-booking sessions or making errors on their bills.
- ❑ I am not clear about my policies regarding missed sessions or cancellations, so I end up being inconsistent.
- ❑ I haven't been able to pay myself a salary or take money out of the practice for my own use in months.
- ❑ I am not making a profit.
- ❑ When asked how my practice is going, I find myself telling white lies because I feel embarrassed at my lack of success.
- ❑ My office space is a mess.
- ❑ I am terrified when clients talk about leaving therapy, and I make them feel guilty or defensive when they say they are done.
- ❑ I have dual or even triple relationships with certain clients.
- ❑ I barter for my services with others.
- ❑ Clients call me anytime, night or day. I am always on call.
- ❑ I can't take a real vacation, because my clients can't handle my being gone.
- ❑ I have relationships with clients that my colleagues (if they knew) would think were inappropriate.
- ❑ I don't bill on time and many of my accounts are months in arrears.
- ❑ I have no idea what direction my practice will be going one month from now, much less one year from now.

❑ I have no plans for the future, other than hoping I survive in this business.

❑ Talking about my work is a drag.

❑ I feel like falling asleep during sessions, I am that bored.

❑ I don't know what my practice earns or what I really make. ✓

❑ I don't rely on anyone else to advise me about business. I prefer to keep my own counsel in all matters.

❑ I'm exhausted, I work too much, and have too little to show for it.

❑ I have goals, but I don't follow through on them.

❑ My family, friends, and colleagues are tired of hearing me complain about the same issues in my work.

❑ I know my practice needs help, but I do nothing about it.

Other integrity breaks not listed above that I need to address:

_____

_____

_____

_____

_____

INTEGRITY REPAIR

All businesses are vulnerable to integrity breaks from time to time. It's important to keep on top of these breaks, because these are the ways that your spiritual energy leaks out of your business.

Some integrity breaks create resentment in the business owner, such as when you have no boundaries around your time so that clients can reach you night and day. Feelings of resentment are an immediate signal that some aspect of your business is on shaky ground. Other signals are feelings of secretiveness, shame, or embarrassment about any aspect of your practice. When I coach therapists, I keep my antennae out for integrity breaks, and make correcting those breaks a priority. Evaluate your practice and repair all integrity breaks, even when they show up as hairline cracks.

Gerry, the owner of a small acupuncture clinic, had a full-time secretary, but needed an additional typist. When one of his favorite acupuncture clients mentioned that she was looking for secretarial work during a session, he decided to try her out and offered to barter his acupuncture sessions for her typing services. Gerry wasn't sure if bartering services with a client was a good business practice, but he secretly liked the fact that it wouldn't cost him any money to hire her.

As this client began to do more administrative work for him, he let his full-time secretary go. The client was now his only administrative help and she was getting daily acupuncture treatments as payment. Gary loved saving money, but began to complain to others about his client/secretary.

"I can't tell her anything to do without her getting an attitude. She acts like she is doing me a favor to work here," he complained to his accountant. "You wouldn't believe how bossy she gets with other clients, too." The accountant urged him to stop his practice of bartering, but Gerry said, "It's not uncommon in alternative healing practices to barter for services with clients. I'm saving a bundle and I'll just have to make the best of it."

His accountant referred him to me for business coaching. During our first session, I asked Gerry to tell me all of his concerns about his client/secretary. "There are several problems and I don't know what to do about them," he admitted. "I feel embarrassed having to own up to all this. She's not very good at numbers. She makes errors all the time. But I understand her so well, being her acupuncturist, and I know her personal issues and problems, so I feel that I can't really demand too much because she has such a difficult life and she's doing the best she can. Plus, the price is right—it's free administrative help."

We looked at what this "free" administrator was actually costing him. She made errors on his billing and with his bank deposits, so he had extra work to explain the problems to clients and smooth over their annoyance. He felt angry after these errors and needed to take time to calm himself down. He tried to check her work each day, and she accused him of not trusting her, but then she broke down in tears and he felt sorry for her. He realized that the business relationship was quite personal: She was much more to him than a secretary; she was a client that he cared about and he was caught in a dual relationship.

One afternoon Gerry left a memo for the secretary stating that he was having concerns about her errors and that he wanted to talk to her that evening after work. She didn't wait for the appointed time. Instead she read the memo and had a tantrum in the office, yelling and upsetting clients in the treatment area and waiting room who watched the drama unfold. She announced that she was quitting, and "by accident" erased his computer hard drive on her way out. It took many weeks for Gerry to undo the damage to his computer and deal with his feelings. He felt guilty, angry, embarrassed, and saddened.

I asked Gerry if he had any guilt about the lack of care he had shown to his business. He had undermined the very real needs of his practice by giving it unprofessional administrative help. This was a new concept for him to think about: giving his practice what it deserved, instead of what he thought he could get by with. I asked him to raise his standards about his practice by giving it his complete respect and utter care. I also requested that he tell me all the other things he did in the guise of saving money, to check for more integrity issues.

There were more integrity breaks, from the way he paid the part-time acupuncturists, to the fact that he was in arrears for 6 months on a lease agreement for equipment. When he corrected these issues he reported a distinct shift in the way he felt about his practice. "I feel a greater respect for my practice and for myself. I am sleeping better at night. I hadn't realized how much these integrity breaks and low standards were really costing me," he said.

→ FIELDWORK

This month, check your practice for integrity breaks. Look at anything that bothers you, anything that feels wrong or "off." You may need to let someone from outside the system help you spot integrity breaks—someone in your advisory circle, a coach, a colleague, supervisor, or even a business-oriented friend. Don't settle for feeling just okay about your practice and your policies. Make whatever changes you need so that your practice has high standards and then notice how you feel and what energy is restored to you.

BUSINESS VISION

A business works best when it is guided by vision—your awareness, inspiration, and foresight—instead of your anxiety, reactivity, or fears of survival. To increase the integrity and spiritual component of your practice, design a business vision and hold to it.

Whether you are new to private practice or a 20-year veteran, using a business vision makes everything else you'll need to do to build an ideal practice much, much easier. A business vision gives you direction, helps you make big and small decisions, keeps you on track, and when aligned with your heart, provides you with energy and passion—the fuel that drives your day-to-day activities.

Although many entrepreneurs credit having a business vision as central to their success, few therapists have one in place, because they don't consider their practices enough of a business to need a vision. As a result, therapists often miss the wealth of benefits that having an articulated vision can bring. This month we will change that in your practice.

Even if you have never taken the time to create a business vision, it doesn't mean that your practice functions without direction. All businesses follow a path of some kind. What is yours? You can see your path by taking a moment to draw your business history. Even if you have only been in practice for a short time, try this exercise.

EXERCISE: DEFINE YOUR BUSINESS PATH

In the empty box at the end of the exercise, draw a line that represents the path your practice has taken, from its origins to today. Put in all relevant details that help to describe your business journey.

For example, my practice path looks something like this:

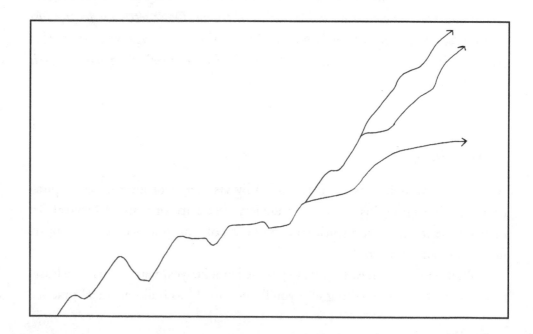

My sketch begins with my starting a small practice working with children, which had a bumpy start and then began to go quite well. The drop my practice took when I decided to stop working with children and families and instead began to rethink how to work with adults, is shown next. Then my path shows my move to a larger home office where I started to run groups, work with adults, and get more serious about business. The line is not straight; again it shows some ups and downs as I learned to grow my business, took some false turns, corrected, and kept going. The line begins to rise as my practice became more successful. Then the line splits, showing the diversification that took me in a second direction, that of business coaching. Then it splits again to show a further diversification into writing.

My drawing represents the diversification of my services over time, my perception of my rising or falling success at different stages, and the general forward movement of my practice. I could have added words, colors, or symbols to show how I felt about the different stages, when the practice was most energizing or most difficult, how satisfied I felt, or how much of my passion was present. I also might have noted at what stages I was working based on having a business vision, and when I was building a business based on presenting circumstances.

You can use other markers to represent the current path of your practice, including revenue, profit, services offered, rate of referrals, type of work, setting or location, or major shifts and changes. However, the marker I would ask you to keep in mind as you do this exercise is the level of your personal satisfaction, as the business owner.

Your level of satisfaction is a key factor to analyzing your efforts in practice building. Your business needs your best efforts and enthusiasm at all times. Your business may be making progress in many areas, but if you are not feeling satisfied, something needs your attention. The hard truth is that if you don't consciously make choices for your business, circumstances will. Without giving much thought to the direction of your practice, you will often follow the path that's most expedient, instead of the one that reflects your desire.

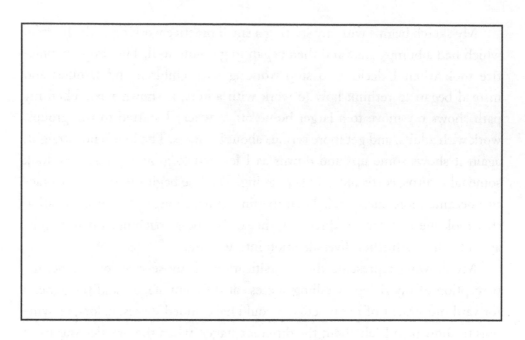

Now draw your business path.

Without a business vision, you tend to feel unfocused, easily burned out, and unsure of what to do next. You have little energy to invest in the daily tasks a business requires. The ability to have an *ideal* practice, one that brings you both satisfaction and profitability *at the same time*, is the hallmark of a practice with a vision.

THE ALIGNED VISION MODEL

In quantum physics, space is understood to consist of fields. Think of any energy field, such as gravity or electromagnetism. These are forces that can't be seen, but can be felt. We know that the field exists, based on observing its undeniable effects. Think of *vision* as an energy field—one that surrounds you and your business—as opposed to thinking of vision as directed toward end point that you continually try to reach. If you conceive of vision as a field of energy that permeates and infuses your practice, you can begin to live and behave as though your vision was already being realized. Your current actions, not just your list of goals, can reflect the trends you spot, your natural strengths and talents, your core values, and your overall vision, purpose, and mission statement.

John is a couples psychologist in a western state with a very successful fee-for-service practice. He has a 5-year plan for his practice, based on a business vision that he lives by. His core values are: commitment, genuineness, and compassion, and these inform his vision. When you first call his answering machine, you hear his voice saying hello and explaining briefly the nature of his practice: "I work with couples. If you are feeling stuck, unhappy, considering divorce, or in a difficult place with your partner, I want you to know that I am committed to helping people just like yourself."

When you walk into his office, you see a number of very fascinating articles about couples therapy, some that he has written, some that he collects. He hosts weekend workshops for couples with out-of-town speakers, so he brings the best and brightest therapists he can find to his client's doorsteps. He only sees 25 couples a week, but they get significant time and attention from him and they know it. On his evaluations, which he asks clients to fill out every 6 months and, with permission and anonymity, which he posts on his Web site after the clients have finished therapy, the words *commitment* and *caring* are often cited in describing the experience of working with him.

Ask John about his vision and he will say, "I don't have plans to expand, I have plans to deepen my work with existing and new couples. I am totally committed to the work I do, and see this as my path for now and into the future." John uses his vision as an energy field, and lets it permeate his office so that his clients feel and respond to it, consciously or not.

How can you develop a vision that is part of an energetic field? The aligned vision model can help. This is a five-step process for creating a business vision as a field. The vision process changes with time as you, the business owner, change. You may want to go through this process every year. Here is the five-step model for you to follow:

1. trending up;
2. strengths;
3. values;
4. visioning;
5. vision, purpose, and mission statement (VPM).

Step 1: Trending Up

Having a business vision requires that you see into the future, beyond your immediate reality, so that you can place your idea of a future business into a context that makes probable sense. What you can (or can't) determine about the future of your profession, the local region in which you practice, or society at large, will directly affect your ability to create a viable, future business.

The way to see into the future is to spot trends. Trends are not wishes about reality. Trends are an extension of current reality. Look at what is already happening around you and mentally follow it to a logical conclusion. How will this present reality look in six months or one year from now? Trends are not fads. A fad is a momentary interest in something new, a flash in the pan that won't last. Trends are broad movements, sometimes subtle at first, but eventually they pick up momentum and shape our daily life. The question for all of us is, Which of the millions of details we observe as we go through life constitute a trend, and which of those trends will have an impact on the future of our practices?

Trending up is a way of spotting trends and expanding what you see, until you see a pattern, a large cultural movement. When my coaching clients are discussing trends that carry a lot of emotion, I often tell them to trend up until the trend no longer feels personal. Trending up helps you detach from emotion and opinion, so you can notice the important patterns.

For example, when I asked Kathleen, a social worker in a small midwestern city, to tell me the trends affecting her practice she said, "Managed care." She was a new therapist in practice and everyone told her she needed to get on the managed care rolls, even though she knew it meant problems for her to operate within that system. By asking her to trend up, she began to think about it less personally. Yes, the shifts in insurance coverage were part of a large restructuring of an industry, which is still going through major changes. No, there was no point for her to rail against the ongoing restructuring. Instead, she needed to look at how she wanted to position her small practice, inside or outside of the managed care landscape. Look at the landscape, I told her, see the overall patterns forming, and pick your spot.

She decided to take a risk, and not get on managed care rolls. "I see how useful it might be, but I am in a position not to need any income from my practice for the first 6 months. I am planning a very niched practice. I only need a small corner of the market. I will take that time and try to go in the direction of fee-for-service, using all the strategies and efforts I can offer to set up my spot in the landscape, and see how I do at the end of that time, reevaluate."

Connie, a professional counselor in New York City, went to a professional association meeting to hear a marketing specialist speak, whose advice was to follow a trend of society at large and define a niche for one's business. The marketing specialist suggested that professionals niche their services based on specific populations they worked with or services they offered. Connie complained that she couldn't define herself so narrowly.

"I work well with teenagers, women, families, and geriatric patients. I run groups and see individual clients. I use an eclectic mix of methods. I like to have variety in my work. Am I doomed to fail because I can't or won't find a niche?" she asked.

I encouraged Connie to trend up, to see the biggest implications of the trend of niching. She could see that the trend was based on the flood of information affecting everyone in society. People were overwhelmed with information and needed help sorting and remembering details. By trending up, she could see that niching was one way that people could sort and remember information about a business, but it was only one way. From this larger perspective, Connie could see that other strategies might offer similar results. "I could make my practice memorable in other ways," she said slowly.

She thought about the common thread that defined her practice, her ability to work well with a general population, and one thing that made her practice unique, her willingness to work evenings and weekends. She decided to create a tag line that she would use on her business card, in her brochure, and during presentations that would make her practice memorable. "Evening and weekend therapy sessions for all." Connie loved her "un-niched niche"; she had found a way to differentiate her business without reducing the variety she loved.

Think of trends in each of the following three areas:

- your profession;
- your regional area of practice;
- society at large.

EXERCISE: CONSIDER WAYS YOUR CAN TREND UP

Fill in the following blanks.

Trends I spot about my profession

Trend: _Social bullying_

Trending up: _Being able to carrel people who are or have experienced this and how to sign post._

How I can make this useful for positioning my practice: _Put it in how I can help section on my profile info_

Trends about my regional area:

Trend: _____

Trending up: _____

_____

_____

How I can make this useful for positioning my practice:_____

_____

_____

(handwritten margin notes: interaction / culture / telephone. / more / flexible / available.)

Trends about society at large:

Trend: _Social media._

Trending up: _social media bullying_

_____

_____

How I can make this useful for positioning my practice:_____

able to offer help to

people who experience this.

_____

→ FIELDWORK

Spotting trends can be a hard task to do alone, so consider getting some support around this exercise. Ask others to help you to spot the trends occurring now, see the big picture, and make it useful for yourself. Need more help? Refer to Chapter 4 in Building Your Ideal Private Practice *to see dozens of examples of current trends in our profession.*

Step 2: Strengths

To be aligned with your heart, your business vision needs to reflect the best of you as a professional—your strengths and talents. By strengths, I don't mean a resume of the places you have worked, the types of clients you work with, or even the methods of therapy in which you are trained to practice. Your strengths and talents are not so much about *what* you do as about *who* you are while you are doing it. In Month 1, you practiced speaking about your strengths as part of your skill set and fieldwork. Review that skill now and do the following exercise.

EXERCISE: LIST YOUR STRENGTHS AND TALENTS

List your strengths and talents in the following categories:

My professional strengths and talents:

*calming, adaptable to
each client. mentally + physically
in a good place.*

What is distinctive about me as a therapist:

*various life experiences
than mean I can provide
empathy per various
presenting issues.*

What I do best:

*none judgmental -
this is something I have
always considered of
myself prior to counselling
Able to talk about areas
of Therapy to in a understandch
way.*

What my clients say they most appreciate about me:

*easy to talk to.
none judgmental.*

Step 3: Values

I want you to put the principles and values you hold most dear at the core of your aligned business vision. Core values are not the principles you think you *should* hold; they are the values you *already* stand for, the ones that give your life and work meaning.

For example, if honesty is one of your values, you are honest, regardless of whether anyone else notices or cares. You are naturally drawn to speak the truth. Your honesty is reflected in all your relationships and the way you try to live your life. No one has to tell you to be truthful; you already are.

The happiest, most effective business owners I know are those whose businesses are centered around their core values, and as a result their business practice is filled with integrity. Sometimes simply defining your values can help you see where you have gone wrong in your practice and how to get back on track.

EXERCISE: KNOW YOUR POINTS OF INTEGRITY

Here is a list of words that signify principles and core values. Circle the three that are most central to the way you live your life. If a value that is core for you is missing from this list, feel free to add it and circle it

health	strength	fun	sexuality
sensuality	love	kindness	grace
understanding	beauty	adventure	courage ✗
risk	leadership	inspiration	change
honesty	patience	fairness	compassion
freedom	spirituality	service	sacredness
security	home	family	community

(continued)

partnership	growth	enlightenment	happiness
joy	support	contribution	advocacy
respect	power	influence	honor
trust	creativity	invention	openness
imagination	planning	building	challenge
discovery	learning	self-expression	feelings
nature	action	rules	persuasion
encouragement	mastering	winning	accomplishment
peace	quiet	calm ✗	inner strength
intuition	intellect	play	truth
nurture	wholeness	safety	vitality

loyalty

Answer the following questions.

What would a practice based on your three values look like?

a calm space, loyalty to my clients that I work for their best interest. clients having the courage to make changes they are willing to take.

What would need to change about me or about the way I operate my current practice to create a practice based on these core values?

not yet in practice, so starting off being able to consider how I can do this from the start.

How would I benefit from making these changes? How might my clients benefit from my making these changes?

_____

_____

_____

_____

_____

STEP 4: VISIONING

The next resource that you need in order to create your aligned vision is one that is often forgotten in business—your creative imagination. Although we are building a practical vision, I want you to first examine it and have a mental dress rehearsal by using guided imagery. The great benefit of bringing in your imagination at this point is that it lets your creative mind begin to fill in the missing pieces. Your intuition will be the true architect of the vision. As a result, when your vision takes form, its details and actual appearance may surprise you. The following exercise, which includes both a guided imagery and a few questions to answer, is designed to stimulate your creativity and expand your awareness of what may be possible for you in your practice.

EXERCISE: PICTURE YOUR ALIGNED VISION

I suggest that you follow the exercise exactly as it is written. You may ask someone to read it to you, while you close your eyes, or tape-record your own voice reading the instructions. Give yourself enough time to relax before you begin the imagery. Breathe easily. Then close your eyes and let your senses take over. You may see a clear picture of the vision, or you may have a felt sense of it. You may experience auditory clues or emotions as you construct the vision. Be nonjudgmental. Simply allow the vision to form in your mind. This is a natural thought process. Once you have finished, take some time and write your impressions on the worksheet. Try not to edit or critique what you experienced. Any time you want to return to the vision for more information, just close your eyes and go through the exercise again. It is helpful to revisit this vision from time to time, to see how it may be shifting to adapt to your personal changes.

Let yourself begin to imagine a picture of your ideal practice. If you don't see a picture, allow a felt sense of your practice to come to mind. Start by imagining your practice in the future, a year or two from today. To create a picture of the future, think of the trends that you see today, and carry them forward in time. Place your practice in a future that makes sense, according to what you think is highly probable. Position your practice well, so that you can see it flourish within that future setting. As this vision evolves, let it take its own shape and form. What you see may surprise you. It is fine if this happens. Let your imagination work for you here.

Is your practice located in the same place as it is now, or is it in a new setting? Are you working by yourself, with other partners, with new alliances? Are you using new methods, or do you offer different services as you visualize your practice of the future? Do you have more clients or less? More free time or less? What has changed and what has stayed the same, as you see your practice one, two, or more years into the future?

See or sense your practice as an observer, looking at it from the outside. You may see specifics or just have an overall impression. Either one is fine. Take the time to allow a clear awareness of your future practice occur to you.

In this vision of your practice, see that your practice flourishes because your true strengths and talents are evident, to yourself and others. Your practice allows your strengths and passions to shine through your work. As a result, your practice attracts those clients you most want to work with.

See that your practice is based on the most important points of your personal and professional integrity. Allow those points of integrity to be at the core of your vision.

Your practice fits within your best understanding of the future, reflects your unique strengths and talents, and is oriented around your points of integrity. As you imagine this vision, let it be big and compelling enough so that you feel very drawn to it. Let your vision encompass all of this, imagining a practice that is profitable and extremely energizing for you.

Now I want you to experiment seeing or sensing this vision with your eyes open. Open your eyes and still retain a strong awareness of this vision. Now close your eyes and take a better look. This time I want you to walk into the vision and notice how it feels to be inside it. Adapt and adjust anything necessary so that you resonate with the look, feel, and sound of being inside your practice.

Notice where you have located this vision in your imagination. Is it out in space, far away from you? To the right or to the left? Is it in your mind's eye? Imagine relo-

cating it and placing it close to your heart. Notice how it feels to have it at the center of your chest. Hold the vision in your heart. Now open your eyes, still holding it in your heart. This is how it feels to have a vision aligned with your heart.

Answer the following questions.

What did you see or sense in this visualization?

_____

_____

_____

_____

_____

What pleases you about this vision?

_____

_____

_____

_____

_____

What disturbs you about this vision?

_____

_____

_____

_____

_____

What surprises you about this vision?

_____

_____

_____

_____

Step 5: Vision, Purpose, and Mission Statement (VPM)

Having a written vision, purpose, and mission statement can keep your business focused. The first part of the statement, the vision statement, is at most a brief sentence or two that sums up what you see as being possible. The purpose statement recognizes that you will need to change yourself to become the person who can manifest this particular vision. The mission statement specifies the actual steps you need to take to fulfill the vision and purpose. Here are some examples of VPM statements:

Vision: I am working in a holistic healing center that promotes well-being and community (my core values). It is housed in a large building that I own with others, one that houses about six therapists. We all contribute energy, time, money, and expertise to make the business a vibrant, successful community-based healing center.

Purpose: I need to become a therapist who is more connected to other therapists in the community. I need to become financially sound, so that I have money to invest in a building. I need to develop a stronger reputation, and that includes overcoming my fears and lack of self-confidence about my skills.

Mission: (1) Find five other like-minded colleagues who want to create a healing arts center by the end of the year. (2) Consult with a financial planner and my accountant to get my finances in better order. (3) Schedule some therapy sessions to confront my fears and lack of self-confidence so that I can move forward with this vision. (4) Find a way to begin to reach out more to the community around me. Join some local community associations to develop a presence.

Vision: I see that in two years I will have written a book about my work with couples. I will be giving more presentations locally and nationally. I will be doing less clinical work and more presenting and writing.

Purpose: I need to become more comfortable as a public speaker and overcome some of my shyness. I need to become a stronger writer and stop procrastinating about writing my methods in book form.

Mission: (1) Take classes in public speaking and join the National Speakers Association for support. (2) Find opportunities for speaking locally and at conferences this year. (3) Schedule eight hours of writing time each week. 4) Write a book proposal by the end of the year. (5) Find three book agents to send my proposal to.

EXERCISE: WRITE YOUR VPM

Now it's your turn. Using your visualization exercise from before, review what you see as possible, consider who you would need to become to make the vision a reality, and decide on your first steps. Complete these three statements using short, simple sentences.

Vision: (What I see is possible for my practice)

I am working with veterans to help them over come their experiences while on operation and enable them to feel it is okay to have counselling

Purpose: (Who I need to become to fulfill this vision)

I need to be more involved in military organisations or other military services to be able to promote my service.

Mission: (The specific steps I will take to make my vision and purpose a reality)

1. Find local services that help veterans
2. Offer to work per them to extend my knowledge in this field.
3. Ensure when people are looking for this service I am easy to locate

MONTHLY SKILL SET: DEVELOP PURPOSE

In the VPM that you just completed, the purpose statement asks you to consider who you need to become in order to make your vision possible. If you were already the person who could make your vision happen, chances are you would already have the vision in place. The fact that it is a vision, a wonderful, compelling image just beyond your immediate experience, signals your need to stretch, go beyond your comfort zone, and become different from who you currently are in order to manifest it.

Are you up to the task? I hope so, because this is the gift inside each business vision. If your vision is based on your becoming a presenter and you are tongue-tied and shy, your stretch will be to overcome your fear and anxiety and learn to love to speak publicly (not just tolerate it, but love it). If your vision is to expand and work with others in an affiliation of services and you have never worked as part of a team, your stretch will be to learn about teamwork, attract others to your cause, and raise your understanding and ability to be a leader. If your vision is to run a profitable practice and your experience with money has been dismal, your stretch is to learn how to relate differently with money, and become a "money master." If your vision is to do a different kind of work, you have the opportunity to stretch into new skills and learning.

EXERCISE: CARRY OUT THE VISION

Complete the following sentence.

I am purposeful when *I feel what I am doing adds value.*

I show focus regarding *goals and aims, when I truly believe in them*

I am resolute about *being a counsellor to help veterans*

When I feel determined, then *I get things done and achieve my aims.*

Persistence is easy for me if *I believe what I am doing is a benefit*

I will apply the above qualities to reaching my vision by *ensuring I have the right goals to achieve them.*

↬ FIELDWORK

Become more purposeful, determined, resolute, and focused this month by stretching into new behaviors that will make your vision take shape. What resources do you need? Who can help you? What is your budget? How long will it take? What specific action steps can you design? Go for it!

Monthly Review

This month you prepared yourself spiritually to build an ideal practice by checking and correcting integrity breaks and creating an aligned business vision. The fieldwork for Month 4 includes:

- Evaluate your integrity breaks and correct them so that your practice operates with a high level of integrity.

- Let others help you to spot trends in your profession, your regional area of practice, and society at large, and use those trends to position your practice for the future.

- Work with and refine your vision, purpose, and mission statement.

- Become purposeful by stretching into new behaviors to become the person who will manifest your business vision.

Part II
Taking Steps to Create an Ideal Practice

MONTH 5

Articulation: Communicating Your Value as a Professional

The first 4 months of the workbook dealt with preparation, to help you get ready to build a strong practice. The next 4 months focus on the building blocks—articulation, marketing, security, and profit. All of these areas are important, but the one strategy that I teach that has consistently proven to be the most powerful in transforming a therapist's practice is this month's—articulating your basic message, saying who you are and what you do, and doing all of this with poise, passion, and simplicity.

Whether I work with veteran therapists or those who are new to private practice, this skill is often at the forefront of our individual coaching sessions. We therapists are notoriously inarticulate when trying to explain what we do in a way that attracts interest, much less referrals. Many of us are shy, nonpromotional, and our educational experience did not teach us the skills of speaking easily and clearly to the public about our professional value.

I talked to a therapist recently who is bright, personable, and talented, but not able to attract many clients into her practice. "Let's discuss some basics," I said. "I'm curious, how would you respond when someone at a social setting asks you what you do?"

"I tell them I am a licensed professional counselor with training in marriage and family therapy from the Ackerman Institute and additional training in the field of Jungian analysis."

"Where does the conversation go after that?"

Now is the time to put the building blocks in place for your ideal private practice. The first step is to determine your basic message—the essence of who you are and what you do as a therapist. This month, you articulate your basic message and explore strategies to expand its reach. Develop your speaking ability further and learn the important skill of enrolling—how to persuade potential clients to become paying clients.

My Monthly Prep Form

Answering these questions each month will help you to chart your progress and define your next goals.

1. What have I accomplished since last month that I feel positive about? What are my wins?

2. What challenges am I facing this month?

3. What opportunities are available to me right now?

4. What blocks me from taking advantage of these opportunities?

5. How could I make life or work easier or better for myself right now?

6. My goals for this month are:

"Nowhere. The person looks at me with no response. I think the person simply doesn't know what to say back."

"Do you ever try to say more, to keep the conversation going about your work?"

"Yes, but I get pretty technical, I guess, because either the person's eyes start to glaze over or she takes it as an invitation to begin to tell me her problems, as if announcing my profession means that 'the doctor is in.' I have pretty much decided to say as little as possible about my work in social settings."

"Do you think this inability to speak confidently about your practice relates to your difficulty in attracting clients or referral sources?"

"It probably does. I was at a party filled with lawyers, physicians, and other therapists last month, just the types of people I wish knew about me and referred to me, and once again I felt tongue-tied."

In the early years of developing The Private Practice Success Program, I spent months trying to formulate the best way to help my colleagues do this seemingly simple task—talk about themselves in a lucid, positive, and energetic manner that invites conversation and builds a professional relationship. I finally found a formula that helps a lot of therapists do this well.

One of the most interesting benefits of this exercise is how the discipline of compressing one's philosophy and value-based message into a sentence or two creates a new level of professional focus and clarity for the therapist. If you work your way through this exercise to its completion, I guarantee you will have to think about yourself and your services in a new way. When you find the right words to say, your basic message may become the easiest and most effective step you need to attract quality clients to your practice.

With an articulated basic message, you will finally know how to talk about your work publicly. Instead of getting the usual bored or puzzled looks, you may hear your listeners say; Tell me more. This is the first step to effortlessly generating a referral every time you say hello.

CREATING YOUR BASIC MESSAGE

I want you to create a short, verbal introduction that sums up the essence of who you are and what you do as a therapist in an engaging and attractive manner. Think back to last month's exercises about your core values, your strengths and talents, and your vision, purpose, and mission statement to help you remember who you are and what you are trying to create. You want to have a basic message that helps propel you in the direction of your vision.

Here's the criteria of a well-crafted basic message for the nonprofessional, public situations you encounter (you may wish to craft a second one to use for professional settings):

- *No more than three or four short sentences.* This is an introduction you are going to memorize, so keep it brief and easy to remember and hold in your mind at all times.

- *No jargon words or technical terms.* If you use a technical term in your introduction, your listener will tend to stop at that term and not hear the rest of the introduction. If you must use a technical term, anticipate that your introduction will do little more than explain the term. My advice is that you drop all jargon and let the introduction be about who you are and what you do, rather than the techniques you use.

- *Keep your language upbeat and positive.* This is an opportunity to attract others, not discourage them. I want you to project what excites you about your work, not what you find difficult.

- *Target only one aspect of your work.* You may have a diverse set of skills, but this is a short introduction. You simply can't say it all. I suggest you target the aspect of your practice that you want to build—an area where you want to generate referrals. Are you trying to fill a new group, reach a specific clientele, attract an ideal client type? You will have more impact if you let this introduction speak to just one component of what you do.

- *Learn to love to say this introduction.* The most important part of this introduction is loving to say it. The sole purpose of the basic message is to become a container for your passion about your craft. The words are just a vehicle to express your underlying feelings and enthusiasm. When you can speak about your work with love, people will naturally want to move closer to you. Passion is attractive.

MESSAGE STYLES

I have found four basic-message styles. Pick one to work with, to help you structure your message. Under each style I have given you several examples that come from my classes. Don't just borrow one of these, because it won't carry your particular essence. Do the hard work and compose your own.

All styles should begin with this first sentence:

My name is _____ and I am a _____.

The first blank is your name. The second is your professional title. Some therapists have trouble deciding which title to use—the most generic, the most technically correct, or the title that reflects their key training? I suggest that you use the title that is simplest and easiest for the public to understand. Make sure to select one you most like to say, so that you are able to smile, not frown, when speaking.

Style 1

I specialize in _____. What I enjoy (value, appreciate, love, cherish) about my work is _____.

This is a straightforward, conversational introduction, one that you can use to highlight your niche, philosophy of service, and enthusiasm about your work. Here are two examples:

Psychotherapist: I specialize in working with adults who are going through difficult times in their lives—divorce, job loss, depression, maybe the loss of a family member. What I love about the work I do is that although I initially see people at a low point in their lives, as we work together they find the courage, skills, and resilience to keep going and make life worth living.

Movement therapist: I specialize in helping people who suffer from chronic physical pain relearn how to move their bodies. In some cases, just by learning to walk, sit, and stand with better coordination, my patients are able to correct and heal old problematic injuries that have caused them years of distress. I really enjoy watching people relearn a basic skill that sets them free.

Style 2

I support _____ in their desire to _____ by the means of _____.

This style is very useful if you are trying to break down the process of why people come for therapy and what you have to offer.

> *Psychologist:* I support couples in their desire to make their marriage a success from the start. I do this by offering premarital counseling classes and weekly couples therapy sessions, both of which give couples the confidence and skills they need in order to make a new marriage really work well.
>
> *Family therapist:* I support adolescents in their desire to become responsible and independent young men and women, and I do this by helping them identify their true potential.

Style 3

You know how _____? Well, I _____.

This style is especially effective if you have a complex message because it sets up an analogy which speeds understanding.

> *Family therapist:* You know how it is possible to get lost when you are in walking in a dense forest and don't have a compass or a map to use as a guide? Well, I help families who are feeling lost and confused by functioning as a guide for them, and together we develop reference points such as how they can set house rules, talk to each other, and resolve conflicts.
>
> *Life coach:* You know how a personal trainer helps you get your body in better shape? Well, I work with people who want to get their lives in better shape. Instead of meeting at the gym, we will meet each week by phone and have a focused coaching conversation that will help you to set your priorities, stay on task, and take the necessary steps to get your life where you want it.

Style 4

If you _____, I'm the kind of (therapist) who can help you to _____.

This style lets you define the type of clients you like to work with and get more specific about the benefits you have to offer them.

Psychotherapist: If you are a person who has been in therapy before and is ready to try it again in order to make lasting change, I am the kind of experienced therapist who can help you to understand and resolve your issues at a deeper level. Many of my clients find that by working in a deeper way, they develop the possibility of creating real transformation in their lives.

Addictions counselor: If you are an addict and you are really serious about wanting to stop using and turn your life around, I'm the kind of addictions counselor who can lend a hand. I've been there, I've helped others, and if you'll let me, I believe I know how to help you, too.

EXERCISE: WRITE YOUR BASIC MESSAGE

Pick one style and write your basic message. Take your time and be prepared to do several drafts. Remember, the words you choose are important primarily as a vehicle to hold your passion and enthusiasm for your work, so pick words and phrases that you like to say. People will remember the feeling they got from hearing you long after they remember exactly what you said. Begin with

1. My name is _____ and I am a _____.
2. I specialize in _____. What I enjoy (value, appreciate, love, cherish) about my work is _____.
3. I support _____ in their desire to _____ by the means of _____.
4. You know how _____? Well, I _____.
5. If you _____, I'm the kind of (therapist) who can help you to _____.

→ FIELDWORK

Practice your basic message in front of the mirror, with friends, family, colleagues, and new acquaintances. You don't need to memorize it entirely, but you will need to retain key phrases. Even though you are writing the message like a script, allow your delivery to be conversational, so that your message sounds like you. *Its fine to add words, change words, or tailor it to your listener. Get feedback from at least five people you trust. Rehearse saying it out loud until you can deliver it calmly, conversationally, and with a natural smile.*

EXPANDING YOUR REACH

Once you have crafted your basic message, you are ready to expand its reach to build your practice. This month we will concentrate on your speaking skills by exploring four progressive strategies that can help you become more competent when speaking about your work. Then we'll look at enrolling, an important but rarely discussed strategy for converting potential clients to paying clients.

Strategy 1: Speak About Your Need for Referrals

In business, letting other people know about your business needs is considered a normal interaction. Most therapists shy away from asking for help in building their businesses, especially when it means asking for referrals, because any promotion feels unprofessional. But therapists in private practice are business people; we need a way to communicate our legitimate business needs, such as our need for referrals (the life blood of our business), in a way that matches our sensibilities and ethics.

The most straightforward way to ask for referrals is to add a simple declarative statement onto the end of your introduction that lets the person you are speaking with know that you are interested in seeing more clients. The sentence I like to use is: "I have some openings in my practice that I am interested in filling."

Other statements that work well include:

- "I am building my business and I would appreciate if you could become one of my referral sources."
- "I welcome any potential clients that you think would be good for me to work with."
- "I prefer only to see people who have been referred to me by someone I know and trust, and would like to have that kind of referral relationship with you."
- "My practice is built on referrals and I would greatly appreciate getting referrals from you."

EXERCISE: WRITE YOUR REFERRAL REQUEST

Decide how you will speak about your need for referrals and write your statement here:

> I am just starting up in private practice, if you knew someone who would benefit from counseling I would appreciate you passing on my details.

➟ FIELDWORK

Practice saying your introduction with the referral request to at least 10 people this month.

Strategy 2: Sponsor Yourself and Speak on Message

Some therapists find public speaking to be their best way to generate referrals, and others find it absolutely useless. After interviewing therapists for whom it does offer good results, I found that one factor in attracting referrals is speaking "on message," in other words, speaking with passion. Therapists who stick to their basic message actually give the same talk each time, although they often use different titles and make small changes to keep the talk fresh. They know their commitment and passion about their message will reach like-minded others and they relax and let their message carry them.

Many therapists would like to do some public speaking, but they don't have a sponsoring organization, track record, or much experience, so they back away from speaking. You can start with small steps and build your expertise as a speaker over time by using the strategies presented this month. If you don't have a sponsor, sponsor yourself.

Lisa, a psychologist, decided to sponsor herself by giving a series of talks in her own office space to small groups to keep expenses low. She put up some flyers in her office, ran a small ad in a local newspaper, and sent out notices to her small (less than 100 names) mailing list of friends, colleagues, and selected existing, past, and potential clients. She advertised her talks at $15 per person for a 90-minute evening presentation.

Lisa recognized she was on her learning curve as a speaker and tried to make the talk easy to deliver. She picked a topic that reflected of her basic message. Because she was talking about her basic message, Lisa said she would gladly speak to 1 person or 100, so that the number of people who actually attended the first time didn't matter. Four showed up. Lisa soothed herself by remembering that building an audience takes time, and she committed to giving a second and third talk on the same topic, each spaced two months apart, to try to interest more people and have some impact in her community.

I asked Lisa to make her talk a "high-touch" talk. High touch means that, like the old commercials for the phone company, you reach out and touch someone, but in this case you touch someone *emotionally*. I cautioned her not to give a dry, informational lecture on the topic; I asked her to make it experiential and demonstrate it. "Don't just say that you are a therapist. Be a therapist, the entire time you give the talk."

As a therapist, you provide an emotional experience for your clients. You must allow your audience to have an emotional experience as well. A high-touch talk, where you make sure that people get to see you at the front of the room being a therapist, can build enthusiasm, which can translate into referrals.

EXERCISE: PLAN A SELF-SPONSORED HIGH-TOUCH TALK

Answer these questions to plan your high-touch talk.

What is a good title for a talk that reflects my basic message?

_____

_____

_____

_____

_____

What will I do to make the talk not just informational, but high touch—experiential?

_____

_____

_____

_____

_____

When and where will the talk be given?

_____

_____

_____

_____

_____

How often will I repeat it to build an audience?

_____

_____

_____

_____

_____

What is the smallest number of people I am willing to speak to? The largest? What is my ideal number?

_____

_____

_____

_____

_____

How will I advertise this talk? What is my budget (time, money, energy) for marketing this? Who can help me?

_____

_____

_____

_____

_____

Strategy 3: Get Sponsored and Speak on Message

The next step in public speaking is to find organizations to sponsor you. You may not be paid for these talks initially, but you also will not have to carry the expenses of renting space, sending direct mail, or advertising. You will have access to many more people than you might reach on your own. Over time, as you build a track record, you can charge a satisfying fee. This is my favorite way to speak, with the support of a good sponsor.

To interest a sponsoring organization, you need to do some preparation. It helps to do some research on the organization and their membership, so that you have a sense of what topics they would be interested in learning about. You should have a speaker's sheet of basic information to give them, that includes your name and title and perhaps a picture of you at the top, a brief bio to credential yourself, and a list of previous sponsoring organizations and topics. All of the topics should reflect your message and be compelling.

I helped a therapist create a list of titles of topics she could give to retirement homes, her targeted market. Her first title was "Feeling More Energetic as You Get Older." Not compelling enough, we decided. She retitled it "When Your Mind Says Yes but Your Body Says No." This was a hit and several retirement venues signed her up.

To get started, approach local organizations and associations and ask, "Do you hire outside speakers?" Get information and be prepared to tell them if you can offer to deliver a keynote speech (an opening speech that starts a meeting or conference and appeals to the whole membership), a breakout talk (a brief talk given during the course of the conference, usually an hour long, on a topic that may not appeal to the broad population), a half-day presentation (3 to 4 hours), or a full-day workshop (6 hours).

What can you charge for a presentation? Start by asking the organization what their budget is. Some have no budget, but you may want to present anyway for the exposure; others may pay you for the talk and your expenses. The range for speaking varies greatly. Nonprofit organizations often have honorariums of less than $500 for a keynote or hour-long address; larger associations pay from $500–$2,000 for a keynote or 90-minute presentation; corporations generally pay in the $2,500–$10,000 range.

You want to be able to get repeat business, so plant some seeds even before your speaking date: Tell the meeting planner (your contact person at the organization) about other programs you have to offer. Make the meeting planner a hero for hiring you by tailoring your talk to those attending. You can do this by informally interviewing attendees prior to your talk to make sure you are on the right track, or spend time questioning the meeting planner about the needs of the audience. You can also offer to help the sponsor promote your talk. Will you be available for an interview with the local paper or radio station? Will you offer the organization access to your mailing list? Will you do a Friday evening hour-long free preview before a paid weekend workshop? If so, let the meeting planner know.

Work with the meeting planner on the logistics for your talk. Ask to preview the space, to make sure there are no surprises. (In one city on a recent tour of Australia, the room I was to speak in had a large column right in front of where I was to stand. It took some fast thinking on the part of the sponsor to reorganize the seating arrangement and make the room usable.)

Also ask for a copy of the evaluations. Ask ahead of time if you can get the names of attendees for your mailing list. When the engagement is complete and if it goes well, don't hesitate to ask the sponsor for a testimonial letter.

EXERCISE: GET SPONSORED TO SPEAK

Answer these questions in order to get sponsored to give high-touch talks.

What are the 10 sponsoring organizations I want to target?

_____

_____

_____

_____

_____

Who can help me gain introduction to these organizations? How will I make my first contact—phone call, letter, face-to-face meeting? How will I follow up?

_____

_____

_____

_____

_____

What are the titles for talks or presentations that I have given successfully in the past? Do the titles need to be revised to be more interesting or targeted to the organization? If so, what are my new titles?

_____

_____

_____

_____

_____

What will I do to make the talk not just informational, but high-touch—experiential?

_____

_____

_____

_____

_____

Are my materials ready—speaker's sheet with picture, bio, list of past presentations/ sponsors, and selection of topics? Do my business card, brochure, and speaker's sheet look professional and reflect my message?

_____

_____

_____

_____

Can I arrange with the sponsor to speak to their organization on a regular basis?

_____

_____

_____

_____

How will I capture the names and information of attendees for my mailing list?

_____

_____

_____

_____

What is the smallest number of people I am willing to speak to? The largest? What is my ideal number?

_____

_____

_____

_____

What will I charge for this presentation?

_____

_____

_____

_____

_____

How might I help the sponsor to promote this talk?

_____

_____

_____

_____

_____

➜ FIELDWORK

If you want to do more public speaking, decide on a plan to sponsor a talk yourself or find a sponsor who will host you this month.

If you are sponsoring yourself, budget for:

- promotion and marketing;
- administration time;
- a series of repeat presentations over the course of the year.

If you are looking for sponsors:

- Prepare your materials.
- Keep a list of organizations and people you contact.
- Design a tickler file—a follow-up file of the results of your phone calls and meetings and how to recontact sponsors over time.

Strategy 4: Become a Professional Speaker

Some therapists find that they love public speaking and want to turn speaking into a separate profit center. Public speaking is a big business, and you will be competing with people who do nothing but speak for a living. You need to be well prepared to compete in this market.

If you have a very strong message, a compelling niche, a product line (a book, audiotape, and/or publications) and a track record of sponsoring organizations who have given you good evaluations, you can compete for speaking engagements.

To leverage your time, plan to target both specific organizations as well as the middlemen who book speakers—meeting planners and speakers' bureaus. Bureaus work on a commission basis and find speakers for large organizations. Any time you get an engagement, part of your fee goes back to the bureau, sometimes as much as 25%. For this reason, most speakers' bureaus will not work with a presenter unless he or she charges at least $2,500 per engagement plus expenses (there is not enough profit for them otherwise).

You need to have professional materials. This is the time to spend some money on your packaging and hire a good printer to help you develop polished print materials. You will need a promotion kit, including:

- a speaker's sheet—a single page that you can easily fax, in lieu of a brochure, that includes a good photo of you, your bio, a list of recent sponsors or clients, and your most popular talks with great titles and testimonials;
- a professionally produced video demo that is no more than 15 minutes long—it should begin with you talking to the camera as though addressing a meeting planner, giving a short explanation of who you are and what you do (as a speaker), followed by footage of you delivering your talk, audience reaction shots, some live testimonials from audience members, and glowing words from the meeting planner or any other important contact from the sponsoring organization;
- written endorsements from sponsoring organizations;
- copies or excerpts of your book, manual, or articles you have written, all clearly reproduced;
- any promotional interviews from newspapers about you;
- a pricing structure (your fees);
- a professional Web site with more details about your credentials.

As I said, public speaking is a big competitive business. Well-known motivational speakers earn $5,000 to $15,000 per presentation. Celebrity speakers get from $20,000 to $50,000. You can tap into the many associations and resources that cater to professional speakers to learn more. Look into the following Web sites:

- *Toastmasters.org*   Toastmasters is the national organization of speakers that offers training and regular meetings for the practice of speaking techniques.
- *Nsaspeakers.org*   The National Speakers Association is the best-known professional organization for emerging and experienced speakers.
- *Igab.org*   The International Association of Speakers Bureaus (IASB) is a worldwide trade association of speaker agencies and bureaus. IASB member bureaus subscribe to a code of ethics, take part in ongoing professional development, and adhere to a high level of professional standards.
- *Mpiweb.org*   This is the world's largest association of meeting professionals.
- *Speakers.com*   The Speaking Platform lists professional speakers and their fees for conferences, meetings, seminars, and other events. Going through their lists can give you a good idea of the current market, topics that sell, credentials of your competition, and fee ranges.
- *Schrift.com*   Sandra Schrift, a coach for speakers, has a very comprehensive Web site with links to the important organizations, training centers, and speakers' bureaus around the world.

MONTHLY SKILL SET: LEARN HOW TO ENROLL

Enrolling is a sales term that means getting people to sign up to buy your product. For therapists, coaches, and healing professionals, enrolling means persuading potential clients (such as people in your audiences) to become paying clients. This topic is rarely discussed in the professional literature, because it is considered to be too coarse, too "business-y," much too promotional. But many therapists wonder how this is done and despair when they do the hard work of planning and giving a talk, get good evaluations, but don't get any new paying clients.

I got very interested in the enrolling techniques that are taught to sales-people and wondered if I could adapt them for use within our profession. I developed a method of enrolling that borrowed important elements of enrolling from a sales perspective, but modified them to reflect the ethics and sensibilities I adhere to and believe in as a therapist.

I tested the method informally by asking all the therapists I coach to try it when giving a talk or presentation. Based on several years of their results (new clients signing up after talks, significantly better responses at all presentations where this was used), I now think that enrolling can and does work well within our profession.

The method of enrolling I suggest is a much more subtle process than salespeople use and it requires a very different positioning or posture for the therapist. Your positioning is to show up as a therapist, in your professional role, from the start of the talk. In your role as a therapist, focus on forming a "real" or authentic relationship with members of the audience. Be experiential and show, not just say, what you do. Experience is much more powerful than explanation. Don't just facilitate the experience, add to it by the processing your do with your audience. By *processing*, I mean taking time to debrief people following the exercise, particularly regarding their feelings and thoughts. Talk with various members of the audience as you would talk to an individual client—asking challenging questions or making therapeutic interventions or comments. Try to focus on one specific person at a time and process his or her experience; this style will give other members of the audience a direct sense of how you work as a therapist. Processing with members of the audience during your talk allows you to remain firmly in your role as a therapist. (Very often it is this processing time—a chance to see you interact as a therapist—that is a turning point for those in the audience who are trying to decide whether or not to hire you.) Then build a bridge from the experience to the services you offer. Your audience will feel connected to you, understand that you have something important to offer them that matches their needs and wants, and clearly comprehend how to engage your services.

Sound simple? It is, but not all simple things are straightforward. Let me break this skill down for you and explain it with a real-life example.

There are three steps:

1. Create a deep or "real" relationship with potential clients (your audience) by starting and staying in your role as a therapist during a talk or presentation.
2. Show what you do, don't just say it (be experiential).
3. Build a bridge from the experience you create to that services you offer, using your improved skills of articulation, staying mindful of potential clients' wants and needs.

1. *Create a deep or real relationship.* To enroll successfully, you have to be willing and able to work deeply and authentically beginning with the point of contact. This is where most therapists go awry in public speaking. They are comfortable doing this in their offices, but the moment they get in front of an audience they take on the role of a teacher, trainer, information provider, or facilitator, which are valid but more superficial roles. These roles will not yield "enrollments."

Think about it this way: The primary motivation for people to hire a therapist is the pain or discomfort they feel; something is wrong in their lives. If you approach your presentation as a quick fix, you remove their primary motivation for hiring you and undermine your role in the process. But this is what many therapists do when they get in front of a room. They become anxiety-dispellers with a lot of suggestions and ideas to immediately fix a serious or compelling problem.

2. *Show what you do.* As you may have experienced in your life, the best therapists, coaches, and healers don't see it as their job to necessarily remove or reduce anxiety or fix anything in the first contact. That would be disrespectful to the client, the situation, the issue, and the relationship. Often, great therapists need to heighten anxiety, because they must open up important, tough issues or frame old issues using a new perspective, or try to get to really know the person who is sitting in front of them. Great therapists offer the potential of something bigger than anxiety-reduction for potential clients. They offer transformation, vision, healing, or change.

Can you handle showing up in your role as a therapist when you are a speaker, perhaps heightening the anxiety in the room as you stay in that role, and not trying to just fix the problem or give solutions right away? Since the first step of enrolling requires you to quickly form a real, deep relationship with audience members, you will need to practice starting and staying in that role.

3. *Bridge from the experience you create to the services you offer.* You will need to ask for referrals in a way that feels appropriate for the setting. Don't be vague out of embarrassment. Get comfortable about the fact that this talk is part of your marketing efforts. Help people in the audience understand specifically how to take the next step in working with you.

Jill, a therapist in practice for 10 years, gives talks on stress reduction for people who are battling chronic, serious illness. She gives these talks as a way to market her services, hoping for new clients. She speaks to associations, hospitals, clinics, and nonprofit volunteer groups. She gives four to six talks a year. She gets great evaluations. She does a long guided imagery during the talk and people leave the hour feeling much calmer and better. Even though Jill assumes that the audience will automatically make a connection from their experience of feeling better to eventually calling for a session when they feel stressed again, she does not expressly make that link, and so they do not follow through. The talks have never yielded a single new client.

I asked Jill how much time she normally spends hearing why people have come to the talk. "About five minutes," she said.

I asked her to spend 20 minutes, one-third of her time, on that section.

"That means we would be doing nothing but talking about their chronic aches and pains. I want to get to what will help them, not dwell in the pain," Jill said.

"What if someone comes into your office," I asked her. "Do you rush over their initial complaints?" She said no, she spends a lot of time listening to clients talk in depth about the details of presenting symptoms and issues. Jill's first error was being afraid to show up at a talk as a therapist. "Show up at the talk in your role as a therapist and behave more like you do in the office," I said. "Let people hear you being a therapist and a healer, not just a teacher."

Jill normally spent 45 minutes demonstrating a long guided imagery. I asked her to do no more than 15 minutes of that, and take 20 minutes to process the results with the group. She was to pick a small piece of imagery to show the group, in effect giving them a "taste" of stress reduction, instead of the whole meal. She was to take 20 minutes to process the experience, again standing in her therapist (not facilitator) role.

Then I asked Jill to take the last 5 minutes to bridge the experience to her services, by explaining that there was much more she could offer with more time, and all that people needed to do was to come up to the front of the room at the end of the talk to get more information about how she might help them in their specific situation.

Jill tried this method of enrolling at her next talk. She reported that the opening 20 minutes were a very special, touching experience. Not everyone shared, but those who did voiced the fears, worries, and concerns of all. Jill encouraged them to speak fully, and she mirrored back and enhanced what they said. The atmosphere in the room quickly became compelling and deep.

After the "taste" of stress reduction, Jill reported that the group seemed hungry for more. This is the right response for an hour-long talk, as opposed to hearing that people are satiated. Then she processed with the group and more emotional, touching sharing occurred. She bridged her services, articulating her basic message and letting her words convey her passion for her work. After the talk five people came up to get her card and four ended up booking sessions. Another dozen wanted to chat further, but Jill, having been coached, did another bridging technique. She listened carefully to each one and then said, "I think a problem of this nature deserves the respect of more time and attention. I have methods and skills that can really help with the problems you describe. If you want to schedule a session with me I would be happy to work with you." Two of these people called her the next week. She got six new clients from this one talk.

Stan, a psychologist in a well-known university town, has an opportunity to enhance one aspect of his practice—peak-performance coaching. The university track team coach invites him to spend a morning with the team each semester. Stan gives the runners tips on staying mentally alert and focused. He would like to enroll some college runners into his private practice for peak-performance coaching, but so far this has not happened as a result of his talks.

Stan told me that he considers the morning with the team as a class; he becomes their teacher. He prepares a lecture with handouts and diagrams. He lectures students about the brain, neurology, and their physical performance. His experience is that the students are interested in what he has to say, but his efforts do not translate into any new coaching clients.

I asked Stan to stop being a teacher and become a peak-performance coach. At his next session with the runners, he is to put away his handouts and diagrams and, instead, coach the runners to peak performance. Stan was understandably nervous about this shift in roles, but willing to try something new. When the next college semester started, Stan spent a morning with the running team, and then reported back to me.

"In the past, I spent the morning with the runners in a classroom. This time I asked the runners to meet me on the track. I explained briefly who I was and why I was there. Then I asked each student to think about how he most commonly got mentally distracted during a race. Each one shared a small anecdote about distraction. There was a lot of head-nodding as the students commiserated with each other over common distractions, and some laughter at the more absurd anecdotes. It felt good to do this. More like I was leading a coaching group, instead of teaching a class."

Stan did well in step 1 of enrolling, showing up in his role as a coach, not a teacher. I wanted to know what happened next.

"I had them line up and timed a short run, during which I asked them to be distracted by thoughts of an upcoming exam. Their times were not good, as I had expected. Then I taught a focusing exercise and the students repeated the run and vastly improved their times. They could see exactly what I was talking about, in terms of focus. They got excited."

I validated how well Stan had handled the second, experiential step in the enrolling process and then I asked how he concluded the session.

"Well, then I kind of blew it. They were excited and really ready to know more, but we were out of time and I got nervous. I just thanked them for their time and put my cards out on one of the bleachers in a nonassuming way. I didn't explain how I could take them further, or that I have so many other techniques for them to use, or let out any of the passion I really feel about my coaching practice. I've got to work on that part."

I agreed that Stan needed to rehearse the final stage, making a bridge from the experience to his services. Stan needs to feel at ease with asking for the referral, by letting the students know specifically how and why to hire him as a coach. This final step of enrolling is essential in order to see the ultimate results of having new clients.

→ FIELDWORK

This month, use this method of enrolling. Apply this concept to your initial sessions and/or your talks. Stop rushing to fix problems or entertain when you speak. Work deeply from the start, stay in your role, be experiential, process sufficiently, and help people build a bridge from their deep experience to your helpful services.

Monthly Review

This month you articulated your basic message, learned how to become more adept as a public speaker, and how to enroll potential clients. The fieldwork for Month 5 includes:

- Practice your basic message in front of a mirror or with friends, family, colleagues, and new acquaintances. Get feedback from at least five other people you trust about how you come across.

- Add a referral request to your basic message when you use it as an introduction. Try out this longer introduction on at least 10 people this month.

- Decide on a plan to either sponsor yourself for a high-touch talk or to find a sponsor to help you extend the reach of your message.

- Apply the concept of enrolling to your practice and speaking engagements.

MOnTH 6
Marketing: Generating a Flow of Quality Clients

Marketing may be the most hated word in private practice. Most of the therapists I meet tell me that they can't stand marketing their practices. For them, any marketing is synonymous with push marketing—shameless advertising, overpromising, promoting, or seducing, the direct opposite of good therapy, and they don't want any part of it.

Their instincts are basically on target, because push marketing is rarely an effective strategy for a relational business such as therapy. Here's why: It's hard to use push marketing tactics and not feel like a salesperson. Most of us have had some experience being on the other end of push marketing and know it is not pleasant to be someone else's prospect.

Push marketing ignores the complexity of the beginning phase of a therapeutic relationship. Since push marketing tends to be linear in process, you look and sound like you are after only one thing—making the sale, instead of helping a person.

One therapist in private practice expressed the most common objections I hear about marketing. For her, marketing meant failure. "If my practice were full, I wouldn't be doing this, so having to sell my services via marketing is a statement of my inadequacy as a therapist," she said. Marketing also meant self-promotion to her, which she took to be a crude hawking of her wares. She continued, "I believe in the 'Field of Dreams' school of getting clients: If I do good work, they will come. I'd rather put my energy into being a better therapist, going

A flow of quality clients is the lifeblood of a private practice, and your ability to market your practice may determine whether or not you can keep it healthy. This month, explore the marketing strategies that work best for therapists. Then, add to your strategies with a targeted reading list so that you have an abundance of marketing ideas, and then learn to create and follow a marketing plan.

My Monthly Prep Form

Answering these questions each month will help you to chart your progress and define your next goals.

1. What have I accomplished since last month that I feel positive about? What are my wins?

2. What challenges am I facing this month?

3. What opportunities are available to me right now?

4. What blocks me from taking advantage of these opportunities?

5. How could I make life or work easier or better for myself right now?

6. My goals for this month are:

to workshops and learning some new techniques. Also, I am shy. I get tongue-tied when I talk about myself and my practice."

A different way to think about marketing is to consider pull marketing, also called marketing by attraction. Attracting clients means knowing how to convey both the best of yourself as a therapist and the distinctiveness of your private practice as you build relationships within an expanding community. When done well, marketing by attraction works like a magnet, allowing those clients who need your services to naturally gravitate toward you. To do this kind of marketing, you need to bring several elements about yourself and your business into alignment, including: your skills as a business owner, your awareness and articulation of your strengths and services as a clinician, and a marketing plan based on your preferred style of outreach. Attraction marketing is nonlinear and tends to grow you as a person and a business owner.

A third way to understand marketing is to see it as a process of developing awareness. Marketing can mean making the public aware of your existence and the value of your services. But first, you must enhance your own internal awareness of your practice. Working on your basic message last month was an effort to help you heighten your internal awareness of what you do. Using your work from last month as the jumping-off point, this month you will continue to build your marketing plan in an organic way.

WRITING

In addition to public speaking, writing is another effective marketing strategy. Two approaches to writing for the purposes of marketing are:

- writing a newsletter based on your basic message;
- writing a personalized referral request letter.

Writing a Newsletter

Some therapists find that they can generate interest in their work and a steady flow of clients just by composing and mailing or e-mailing a good newsletter. An effective newsletter is one that you author, not a prewritten one that you purchase from another company. It lets clients know who you are and includes your best thinking. It's written from your heart and contains something of value for your readers. It stays on message, so that you continue to articulate your basic message.

Are you unsure about what to include in your newsletter? Keep it simple. Have you read an important book or taken some training that is inspiring you in your work? Write about that. Are you finding a new technique or a thematic topic that occurs in sessions that fascinates you? That would be a good thing to include. Your newsletter can be as simple as one typewritten or e-mail page. Make it valuable to others, not promotional. This is not a flyer, advertising your services; it's a way to extend your reach and express the essence of who you are and what you do.

EXERCISE: WRITE A NEWSLETTER

Answer these four questions to see if writing a newsletter would be an effective marketing strategy for you.

1. *Do I need to stay in touch with potential clients or referral sources on a regular basis?* If you have a mailing list that you ignore, a newsletter with a quarterly publication date will force you to stay current. The rule of referrals is that people come to therapy when they are ready. That can be a long wait. There is nothing you can do to rush another person's process of getting ready. It helps simply to stay in touch. I have had many people contact me after several years of hearing my name or getting a mailing. They waited until they were ready. Staying in touch with them via my newsletter is one way to help them feel connected to me and makes it easier for them to call when the time is right.

   ❑   Yes
   ❑   No

2. *Do my referral sources or potential clients need a tangible experience of me?* A marketing guru I talked with told me that the major value of a brochure or a newsletter is the security value that attaches to a tangible item. People like to hold something in their hands. It's nice to have a newsletter, instead of or in addition to a brochure, to send out when people ask for more information about what you do. It offers

you the opportunity to say more about your basic message in an attractive manner.

❑ Yes
❑ No

3. *Could I use some new opportunities?* Newsletters yield spin-off, just as books and articles do. My clients tell me that they get radio interviews, speaking engagements, and teaching positions as a result of their newsletters. You may find your e-newsletter articles being carried by other Internet sites and developing an international response.

❑ Yes
❑ No

4. *Do I like to write and desire to be published?* Most of us need to grow into the writing process. Give yourself a learning curve by publishing yourself, via a newsletter. Start small and stay on track. E-mail newsletters may cost the least to produce and send, allowing you to reach large groups of people without mailing costs of any kind. Edit your articles thoroughly and strive for brevity—especially with your e-mail newsletter articles, as people at a computer like to scan, not read. Make sure that your content reflects your style, and that it sounds like you.

❑ Yes
❑ No

Last month we explored the importance of enrolling, a three-step process that creates a deep, immediate relationship with others, is experiential, and uses your articulation skills to bridge their needs and wants with your services.

If you are using writing as a marketing tool, you need to consider enrolling as well. If you see your role as a writer just to present information and solve problems, your readers may feel no need to consult you further. As with speaking, if you want to enroll with your writing, first and foremost you need to write as a therapist. Write deeply, provocatively, and with the intent to help others begin to feel emotion, heighten awareness, or access innate issues. Don't just solve problems. Create questions. Doing this may increase tension for a reader; anticipate this as part of the therapeutic process. Don't see your role as a writer as soothing, advising, or answering problems. Your professional role is more than that.

The Pencil to Paper Paralysis

As the time draws near to complete the newsletter or white paper, you may begin to demonstrate signs of procrastination or resistance. The newsletter needs unending revisions. It is partially written, but then writer's block sets in. It gets completed, but never printed. It's beautifully printed, but not mailed. The root of this resistance is usually a fear of exposure. It's common for therapists to feel this particular fear since most of us are, at heart, introverts. But the fact that we share this common fear doesn't mean that we need to become a victim to it. In her classic book *Feel the Fear and Do It Anyway*, Susan Jeffers asks readers to place themselves on a "pain-to-power" continuum in order to see how incapacitated they are by their fears. Sometimes the pain-to-power path requires a shift in one's vocabulary, from a fearful "I can't" to a powerful "I won't" or from a fearful "it's terrible" to a powerful "it's a learning experience."

By charting your experience of pain versus power in regard to your writing, you can increase your comfort zone for taking a risk and chart subtle shifts as you become less fearful. Use the following exercise, adapted from the one Jeffers offers in her book, to increase your tolerance for the feelings of fear, anxiety, or discomfort as you write, by carefully noting the degree of fear you have at any given time, seeing if it shifts in the direction of power, and then becoming more comfortable staying on the power side of the chart.

EXERCISE: MOVE FROM FEAR TOWARD POWER

Follow the steps to make your experience of writing less difficult.

$\longleftarrow\!\!\!\!\!\longrightarrow$

Fear   Power

1. Begin a writing project. Put a dot to indicate where you are on this fear-to-power continuum, with respect to your writing. As you write, track your feelings from day to day. Does your position move? Notice what you are doing when your position moves toward feelings of fear, and what shifts you toward feelings of power.

2. Think: "Is the act of writing moving me to a more powerful place? Would my letting others read this move me to a more powerful place?" If the answer is no, you will be filled with resistance. (If you don't want to move in the direction of *power*, substitute a word that is right for you, e.g. *enlivened, joyful, successful*.)

3. Each day, notice if you are moving on the chart toward power. You'll find it easiest to move in this direction if you write from the heart. Write about what you know, what you believe in, and what you have to give. Offer your knowledge freely, without reservation, as a gift to others. Give away your best ideas, your best efforts, and send out your writing as an act of service to others. Then notice the shifts on your continuum. Having the correct intention in place is the easiest way to move from feelings of fear to feelings of power and joy.

➺ FIELDWORK

Write or improve your existing newsletter this month. Include the concept of enrolling. Write from the heart and let it move you from pain to power. Find someone—a colleague, friend, or coach—who will be an initial reader, to give you feedback to see if you have accomplished your goal of writing, on message, as a therapist.

Writing a Personalized Referral Request Letter

Many therapists send out a letter asking for referrals, but few write it well enough to see results. The standard letter reads like this:

Dear Doctor,

I want to introduce myself. I am a psychotherapist with ten years of clinical experience working with adults dealing with depression and anxiety. My training includes cognitive therapy and EMDR. I have enclosed some cards and hope you will think of me if you have clients who could benefit from my services.

Sincerely,

For better responses, write a personalized request letter. Send your letter to new and existing referral sources. Send it alone or as a cover letter with your newsletter or another article you have written. In order to establish a meaningful relationship with the recipient, you need to personalize the letter so that it makes reference to what you know about the recipient, including his or her needs. This requires preparation: Find out more about the referral source, be it a doctor, minister, or human resources director. What is important to her in her practice? What are the needs of her patients, clients, or members?

A personalized letter needs to do four things, building on skills you have already learned:

1. Define a meaningful relationship with the recipient.
2. Articulate the essence of who you are and what you do as a therapist.
3. Build a bridge from the recipient's needs and wants to your services.
4. Ask cleanly and clearly for the referral.

Here's one example:

Dear Doctor,

As an internist in private practice who specializes in chronic illness, you know that the prevalence of depression and anxiety is on the rise, even in our community (as reported by the Cleveland Plain Dealer health section last month.) Medication, while effective, is not always the complete treatment for certain at-risk patients. Many patients will also benefit from psychotherapy.

As a psychotherapist in private practice, I specialize in helping adults who are struggling through difficult life situations begin to take control of their situation. Using a solid, solution-focused cognitive approach, I offer my clients a calm, understanding presence and the experience of over ten years as a clinician in a variety of settings, to help them sort out problems and find a way to cope and resolve their important concerns.

I know that you want your patients to follow through on any referrals you make, and I am able to help in that regard since I am located within a mile of your office. We have never met, but I have sent several of my clients to you in the past year who report that they are very satisfied with your care and appreciate that you are a compassionate and resourceful doctor.

I'd like to let you know more about who I am, my professional experience, the clients I work best with, and my credentials so that I can be a referral for you as well.

This letter is my initial attempt to create a referring relationship between our two practices. I will call you this week to see if we can either meet or chat briefly by phone.

I have included the most recent copy of a newsletter I make available to all my clients as well as a reprint of the article I referenced earlier about the rise of depression locally, so that you can better understand my approach.

Sincerely,

This letter, which was personalized for each recipient, took time to prepare. It yielded the therapist a good responses: 10% responded positively, as opposed to the 1% to 2% response that direct mail companies equate with success, and several doctors sent immediate referrals.

EXERCISE: DRAFT A PERSONALIZED REFERRAL LETTER

Make a list of five new or existing referral sources. Then, answer the following questions based on the above approach, and write a letter to one of them.

My list of potential referral sources:

1. _____

2. _____

3. _____

4. _____

5. _____

What do I know about this referral source, his or her clients, and the needs of those clients?

_____

_____

_____

_____

_____

What do I want him or her to know about me, including my basic message?

_____

_____

_____

_____

_____

How will our work benefit each other's practices so that this is a mutually constructive relationship?

_____

_____

_____

_____

_____

How can I bridge the gap and create a meaningful connection in this initial letter?

_____

_____

_____

_____

_____

What language will I use to ask for the referral?

_____

_____

_____

_____

_____

→ FIELDWORK

Compose and send two personalized referral letters this month, and send the remainder in future months. Set up a tracking system so that you can keep track of when you sent the letters out, and how and when you will follow up. Each referral source needs to hear from you on a regular basis—by a letter or phone call of no more than once every two months, no less than once a year.

NETWORKING

Networking is a highly effective method of marketing. It can be as simple as meeting colleagues for lunch, or you may have a more formal plan that you follow. Networking opportunities abound, no matter where you live or whom you currently do or do not know. I have helped clients network successfully even when they lived in tiny communities where, they insisted, "There is no one here to meet who can refer to me."

You too can learn to network, even if you are very introverted and find it painful to meet new people, have recently located into an unfamiliar town, or are in a profession that is untraditional and a hard sell. I usually ask people I am coaching to increase the quantity of people they know each year by 100%. Marketing is often a numbers game: More is more. Usually only one out of every four potential clients who contact your practice will become a paying client. For this reason, you want to have a good flow of potential clients coming toward your office. You need abundance—more than enough referral sources and people who know about your work and feel positively about you.

EXERCISE: DEFINE YOUR NETWORKING STRATEGY

Check those that are true for you now and try to check them all as soon as possible.

- ❑ When networking, I focus first on creating relationships, not selling myself.
- ❑ If I join an existing group, I plan to attend meetings regularly. If asked to volunteer to be on a committee, I select one that allows me to get to know the whole membership personally, face to face.

- ❑ I know how to work a room. Working a room means that I can come into a room alone, if need be, go up to one person or a group of people, wait for a break in the conversation, put out my hand, smile, say hello, and use my basic message as an introduction.
- ❑ I follow up appropriately with new contacts. I don't flood new contacts with my materials (that's push marketing). Instead, I find ways to further a real relationship and make new friends.
- ❑ I opt for mutuality. I try to refer back to my referring sources whenever I can.
- ❑ I double the number of people I know each year.

EXERCISE: PREPARE TO NETWORK

One reason why so many people in business hate networking is that they are underprepared. Here are four questions to answer to see if you feel equipped for networking.

1. *Have I identified my ideal client profile, so that I know the type of clients I want to attract?* In Month 2, I introduced you to the concept of having an ideal client profile. Review that now so that you are ready to talk about the clients who are right for you and so that those you network with can begin to reference who they know fit whom would this profile.

   ❑   Yes

   ❑   No

2. *Do I have several success stories I can talk about?* In Month 1, you developed several success stories that would highlight the benefits of your services and the results that you are able to deliver. Review your success stories now so that you can relate the positive outcomes of your practice to others.

   ❑   Yes

   ❑   No

3. *Do I have a well-crafted basic message that I can use as a professional introduction and a referral request that reflects my integrity?* In Month 5 you crafted your basic message and found a phrase to help you conversationally ask for referrals. Review both of those now and make sure that you practice both before you attend a networking meeting or event.

   ❑ Yes
   ❑ No

4. *Have I identified my current referral network—by listing my existing and past clients and who originally sent them to me?* Do you know who is in your current referral network and how long it has been since you last contacted them? Instead of making new contacts, you may need to simply reconnect with those tried and true referrers. Take some time to review your client list so that you target your networking energy where it will be most effective.

   ❑ Yes
   ❑ No

EXERCISE: IMPROVE YOUR NETWORKING MATERIALS

Your networking materials—your brochures, business cards, and other public relations packets you send to others—need to reflect the best of who you are and what you do. Use this simple checklist to evaluate and improve your materials.

❑ My brochures and advertisements identify the benefits and solutions I offer, not just the features of my practice (my academic degrees, the types of training I have, the issues or populations I work with).

❑ My brochures, flyers, and advertisements reflect my basic message and ask clearly for referrals, where appropriate.

❑ I use everyday, understandable language in my materials that indicate what I hear my clients say that they want, versus the technical terminology that signals the way I (or my profession) diagnose.

❑ I niche my services not just by population or issues I address, but by the outcomes I consistently deliver.

- ❑ I really like the way my business card looks and what it says.
- ❑ I measure the results of my work with clients by conducting surveys, research, studies, evaluations, or exit interviews. I include references to my consistent results in my materials.
- ❑ I like the professional look of all my materials including the colors, use of graphics, professional layout, and design elements.

The networking materials that need more attention and improvement from me are:

_____

_____

_____

_____

_____

Leveraging Your Networking

Since you are just one person and marketing is not your full-time work, leveraging your marketing time is important. Leveraging means that you choose strategies that will help you meet the most people with the least amount of personal time and effort. Three strategies are

1. Meet "practice angels."
2. Build a Rolodex.
3. Help colleagues refer.

1. *Meet and cultivate four "practice angels."* Practice angels are influential people who are well connected in their community and can make multiple referrals. These may or may not be professional contacts within your field.

The rule of thumb is to find those key people within a community who know a lot of other people intimately, often hear about the psychological or health problems of others, and could offer your name as a referral. The most obvious sources are doctors, ministers, human resource managers, or employee assistance program directors—often the first point of contact when someone wants to find the name of a therapist. But I have heard of other good referral sources, including alternative health professionals (massage therapists, nutritionists, acupuncturists), self-care professionals (hairdressers, manicurists, sports trainers, personal shoppers), educators (teachers, school counselors, school secretaries, principals), and organizers (committee chairs of social organizations and business organizations).

EXERCISE: IDENTIFY "PRACTICE ANGELS"

Fill out the following questions to help identify and connect with influential people.

Five "practice angels" in my community, even if I don't yet know them personally:

1. _____

2. _____

3. _____

4. _____

5. _____

How can I get an introduction to these people?

_____

_____

_____

_____

_____

What is my true agenda with each one?

_____

_____

_____

_____

_____

What do I have to give? What do I want to get?

_____

_____

_____

_____

_____

How will I express appreciation for each person's efforts on my behalf?

_____

_____

_____

_____

_____

2. *Build a Rolodex.* If you don't have a big Rolodex, now is the time to begin building one. Do this by becoming a referral source or a resource for others. Get to know 50 top professionals in your local community who provide services your clients might need (in the process you expand the network of people who know about your services, too). You can become a professional resource for your clients, by finding out who is the best at everything within your community.

EXERCISE: ENHANCE YOUR IMPACT

Use this exercise to increase the number of people you know to whom you can refer clients and colleagues.

1. On a separate sheet of paper, create 50 categories of professionals (think broadly, from accountants to zen masters).

2. Make this a "getting to know you" game that you play over the course of a year. Get to know highly qualified people, such as a really fine accountant, lawyer, financial adviser, nutritionist, body worker, internist, meditation instructor, printer, hair stylist, etc., to fill in your list of 50 categories with 50 names.

3. When you are interviewing someone to add them to your list, most likely he or she will also want to know about you. Use your basic message and your referral request. Before you know it, you will be well connected to your community.

3. *Help colleagues refer.* Want more referrals from your colleagues? Maybe you need to help them, by not only telling them what you do, but also showing them. It's hard for colleagues to refer to you unless they have direct experience of your skills. Invite a small group of colleagues to join you for a chance to learn something new and teach them something that you do well. What do you know that you could teach to your colleagues?

One licensed counselor had good skills helping teenagers to manage their anger. To build a peer referral network, he invited a circle of colleagues for coffee and bagels on a Saturday morning and taught them two effective techniques that help angry teens calm themselves. The group discussed the techniques, brainstormed about ways to adapt them for broader clinical use, and socialized. This boosted his reputation and referrals from those who attended. A body therapist taught colleagues a lovely, gentle meditation. A social worker facilitated a formal book club with a reading list of clinical texts. A massage therapist showed his peers how he combined deep breathing exercises with muscle relaxation.

You don't have to be brilliant or have a revolutionary new method to make this strategy effective—just be willing to give away your best ideas for free. Some therapists think they need to fiercely guard their hard-won knowledge. I find, however, that creativity works best when it flows freely. The more good ideas you give away, the more good ideas will occur to you to replace them.

EXERCISE: DEVELOP COLLEGIAL REFERRALS

Use this exercise to help you identify colleagues and specify skills to share:

List three specific skills you would like to demonstrate to others:

1. _____

2. _____

3. _____

List the colleagues you would like to share these skills with:

_____

_____

_____

_____

_____

How will you set up your demonstration logistically (when and where will it take place?)

_____

_____

_____

_____

_____

What is your budget for this project (time, money, energy)?

_____

_____

_____

_____

_____

How will you make this gathering highly enjoyable for everyone?

_____

_____

_____

_____

How will you further collegiality (the sharing of ideas and new relationships) in the room?

_____

_____

_____

_____

How will you stay open to new opportunities that can arise from this experience?

_____

_____

_____

_____

_____

➥ FIELDWORK

Pick a strategy to use this month to increase your leverage when networking: Meet practice angels, develop your Rolodex, or host a gathering of colleagues.

RESOURCES FOR MARKETING

I like those I coach to have an abundance of information, tips, and ideas about marketing, so that they can select only those strategies that feel easiest and most interesting to use. I suggest that you have a personal library of books you can consult just for marketing ideas. When your practice drops in numbers and you feel anxious about where your next business will come from, it's nice to have a book on hand so that you can immediately find a strategy or action that feels easy and doable, add it to your monthly marketing plan, and take action.

A word of caution: There are many, many ways to market, and they can all work for different people in different situations. Don't let the large number of ideas overwhelm you. Don't select actions that are distasteful to you. *Do* select ideas that feel most natural to you, so that the way you market your services feels as natural as possible. Choose what fits well with you right now—take the easy path in marketing. Refer to Appendix B for a recommended reading list for marketing.

MONTHLY SKILL SET: USE A MARKETING PLAN

The biggest obstacle to successful marketing that most therapists face is that they don't take the time to create an actual written plan, with dates, times, a budget, a tickler or follow-up system, and external support. I know some of you will look at this section of the workbook and be tempted to skip it. Although you don't like marketing, you might be willing to do it piecemeal— but don't like the idea of having to actually formalize a plan.

Using a plan makes marketing easier, and can determine whether or not you will see marketing results. You need a blank page and your calendar. On the page, create a written plan for this month and the next that includes the points in the following exercise.

EXERCISE: CREATE YOUR 30-DAY MARKETING PLAN

Respond to the following questions.

What are my objectives? (To set your objectives, go back through this month and select the strategies that are most important and make most sense for you to put in place. Or do some additional reading [see Appendix B] and then set your objectives.)

Who do I need to contact and in what way?

_____

_____

_____

_____

_____

Do I need to join an organization? How will I do that?

_____

_____

_____

_____

_____

What materials do I need to prepare?

_____

_____

_____

_____

_____

How often will I follow up with each person?

_____

_____

_____

_____

_____

What will I do each week, and each day?

_____
_____
_____
_____
_____

Do I need to budget more time, money, energy, or support to make this happen?

_____
_____
_____
_____
_____

Other ideas for my monthly plan:

_____
_____
_____
_____
_____

➥ FIELDWORK

Who will you be accountable to? Give this supportive person a copy of your written marketing plan so he or she can follow along, make suggestions, check in on you, commiserate when things didn't go as well as hoped, and celebrate all small or big successes. That's all it takes to succeed.

Monthly Review

This month we focused on marketing, specifically the strategies of writing and networking and how to create a marketing plan. The fieldwork for Month 6 includes:

- Write or improve your newsletter this month and remember to use the principles of enrolling.

- Send out two of your five personalized referral letters this month, and set up a system to keep track of when you sent the letters, and how and when you will follow up.

- Select one of the three strategies that increase your leverage when networking, meet practice angles, develop your rolodex, or host a gathering of colleagues, and begin to contact people this month.

- Create a written marketing plan and find someone to be accountable to, and follow through on your plan week by week.

MONTH 7
Security: Establishing a Solid Client Base

Therapists in private practice often feel insecure, because in a small business it's hard to predict the future of your client count, anticipate annual earnings, or in general feel assured that your business is always on solid ground. While a degree of uncertainty is part of the package of owning and operating a private practice, you, as the business owner, have more options than simply worrying and hoping. You can take steps to secure your practice by learning how to solidify your client base.

Having a solid client base is, in part, a clinical issue: Your skills and style of work will determine how well you retain clients. But it is also a business issue. From a business perspective, a solid client base means that you have a foundation of clients who

- *stay with you* long enough to complete their therapy,
- *return to you* when they need further services, and/or
- *refer to you* based on their satisfaction with their experience.

With a solid client base you can better weather the inevitable ups and downs, build a practice that stays full with less effort, and above all, relax a little. You can become more flexible in the way you plan your work and your life. You can take a vacation and not worry about whether you will still have a practice to come back to; you can branch out and try new methods without fearing that your clients will leave; you can add new services, such as

To feel more secure about your business, use this month's plan for solidifying your client base. Establish a strong client connection and turn your practice into an added-value business that builds client respect, trust, and endorsement. Then learn how to support all termination, because good endings create goodwill.

My Monthly Prep Form

Answering these questions each month will help you to chart your progress and define your next goals.

1. What have I accomplished since last month that I feel positive about? What are my wins?

2. What challenges am I facing this month?

3. What opportunities are available to me right now?

4. What blocks me from taking advantage of these opportunities?

5. How could I make life or work easier or better for myself right now?

6. My goals for this month are:

groups or workshops, and feel confident about filling them. Best of all, with a solid client base you can sense the loyalty, advocacy, and enthusiasm from your existing and past clients, which helps you as the business owner feel more confident and secure.

Why do some therapists have trouble building a strong client base and others find it easy and natural? The answer is complex. If you find yourself challenged in this area, you are certainly not alone. It's important to consider any therapeutic factors that may hinder your attempts, but sometimes the problem isn't based on a lack of clinical skill or personality problems of the therapist. Sometimes the business is just not set up in a way that fosters a strong client connection.

This month we look at a strategy that I developed to help therapists create a strong business connection with clients based on a familiar psychological theory—attachment theory. If you think of your client connection as a form of business attachment, it will be easier to see how this works.

Kay, a competent and outgoing therapist who has been in practice for over a decade, says, "I have a part-time practice and I want a full-time practice. I get a few new clients and see my numbers go up and think, great, I'm going to be full-time soon, but then several clients leave unexpectedly and I drop back down to part-time. Getting to a full practice of 25 clients or more feels like my glass ceiling. I sense it's possible to expand, but I don't know how to break through. It feels like I am doing something wrong or missing something that other therapists who maintain a full practice know how to do."

Kay could better understand her dilemma by thinking about how she does or does not form the right kind of business connection with her clients over time. Attachment theory is useful for understanding the natural, biological, and emotional process of relating. As a business owner, your client connection is based on how well you relate with your clients in three distinct stages.

Thinking about your business connection with clients and then comparing it to attachment theory may seem confusing, so let me briefly review the stages of attachment and then show you how it dovetails into the client connection model. *Attachment theory* follows three phases:

1. *Proximity*—the caregiver provides full attention, safety, and nearness so the child can feel protected in his most vulnerable, dependent state.

2. *Safe haven*—the caregiver gives the child space to explore, providing reassurance and comfort so the child can leave and return to the loving parent again and again.
3. *Secure base*—the caregiver encourages further exploration and delights in the child's continued growth and development.

Contrast these early attachment stages to a business model of *client connection*.

1. *Loyalty*—clients establish an initial bond with you to feel safe and in good professional hands as the process of therapy begins.
2. *Advocacy*—clients have confidence in you and your services and can explore (themselves), distance (from you), or even leave (the practice), knowing that they can return.
3. *Enthusiasm*—clients differentiate further, recognize their gains, and want to share their experience with others.

Read further to understand each stage of the client connection as it relates to attachment, and complete the exercises to develop skills that can help you to solidify your client base.

LOYALTY

The first stage of attachment, proximity, signifies the nearness, bonding, and availability of the parent. For secure attachment, the parent must be safe, reliable, caring, and dependable. If the parent is distant and uncaring, the infant suffers from feeling abandoned; if the parent is too needy or overinvolved, the infant senses anxiety and can't relax.

In the first stage of client connection, loyalty, the client is often at his or her most vulnerable state, in need of immediate help. The therapist must be available, reliable, and attentive, without being too anxious, needy, or overprotective. When a healthy connection is in place, the client bonds with the therapist and develops an initial sense of loyalty to the process and respect for the provider, which fosters client retention.

Thomas Lewis wrote in his book about attachment theory, *A General Theory of Love*, that the first step in therapy is being emotionally known, having someone with a keen ear catch one's "melodic resonance." How do you catch the melodic resonance of a new client? As therapists, we are trained to be good listeners, but sometimes our clinical expertise gets in the way of really hearing what our clients say, and we don't connect well as a result. As a businessperson, your ability to hear and communicate is essential to creating the first stage of client connection.

At times, as Lewis inferred, connecting is a matter of resonance or dissonance. For example, if I have a new therapy client who says, "I get extremely nervous in social situations. I speak abruptly and inappropriately to people at work and, as much as I hate to admit this, even to women I date. I need more confidence," my clinical interpretation may be that he needs much more than confidence. He suffers from social phobia and needs to learn to tolerate external stimulation and reduce his impulsive anxious responses. I may also wonder about the history of this behavior and whether he has anger issues with women. But when I tell him this brilliant interpretation during the first session, he looks startled, and insists, "No, you don't understand me. I just need more confidence."

Unless I can bridge the language gap between "social phobia, impulsive anxiety, and anger issues with women" with "more confidence" he will not feel understood. If I do this repeatedly, I will not have achieved the respect and connection necessary to achieve this first stage, either as a therapist or a businessperson.

Listening well, turning clinical or technical language into everyday language and creating the melodic resonance that Lewis spoke of is an important business skill.

EXERCISE: TRANSLATE CLINICAL LANGUAGE

The right column below lists technical language that therapists sometimes use to determine client goals; the left lists the more common language that your client probably speaks. Fill in the blanks on the client's side to translate your diagnosis into everyday language, and the blanks on the clinician's side to identify your favorite diagnoses. There are extra blank spaces for you to fill in.

What a Client Says He (She) Wants	What You Think He (She) Needs
"to be happy"	to resolve depression
"to stop worrying"	manage anxiety
"to get my act together"	
_____	_____
	self-discipline
_____	work through past trauma
	overcome negative self-devaluation
_____	
"to get rid of my stress"	_____
"to stop beating myself up"	_____
"to speak up"	_____
"to have a better relationship"	_____
	_____
_____	(your favorite diagnosis)

→ FIELDWORK

This month, notice and correct any dissonance in your language with new clients. Improve your ability to resonate with everyday language. Make sure that you are pacing new clients well (mirroring and reflecting back what they say) so that they can establish a strong initial bond with you.

Boundaries

During the first stage of attachment, caregivers must provide safety for an infant to feel securely attached. As a business owner, you need to provide safety for new clients too, by having clear boundaries in the practice that are firm, yet responsive. Boundaries signal a well-run practice and translate into a feeling of safety and professionalism for new clients. Check your business boundaries next to see if they contribute to loyalty, the first stage of client connection.

EXERCISE: BUSINESS BOUNDARIES CHECKLIST

Check the following statements that are true for you. Checking a majority of these items means that you have strong business boundaries. Checking only a few signals a need to identify and strengthen your boundaries.

- ❑ I have clear policies about the way I work (time, fees, cancellation, missed sessions).
- ❑ I don't see everyone who calls. I have limits based on diagnosis, symptoms, preference, my skill set, and my ideal client profile.
- ❑ I have a solid referral network so that I can refer clients I don't want to see or can't see to others.
- ❑ I practice confidentiality, do not engage in dual relationships, adhere to the highest standards of my profession, its ethics, and my licensure.
- ❑ I know how many hours I am willing to work in a week, the settings in which I will and will not work, and don't go beyond these boundaries.
- ❑ I am aware of the policies, boundaries, and procedures that, if followed, allow me to do the best work I possibly can. Those are the ones I put and keep in place.
- ❑ Exceptions I make to my boundaries, policies, and procedures that weaken my connection with clients are: ____________________
- ❑ Exceptions I make to my boundaries, policies, and procedures that strengthen my connection with clients are: ____________________

→ FIELDWORK

This month, examine the last two items on the checklist. Correct any boundaries, policies, or procedures that don't strengthen your first stage of client connection, and don't promote client loyalty, respect, and retention.

ADVOCACY

As infants develop, they seek the second level of attachment with a parent, safe haven. They need the parent to be a constant presence, but one that allows them room to explore. As they become more independent, there is tension in the relationship (think about a 2-year-old's temper tantrums and delight in saying no). The child needs to explore and individuate, but can only do this if the parent is available for continued reassurance and comfort.

The second stage of client connection, advocacy, has similar tasks for the therapist/business owner, in that clients seek a more individuated level of connection after working with a therapist for a while. The client may be less dependent, needing to differentiate. Clients at this stage need to leave and return, either metaphorically (psychologically distancing themselves) or literally (taking a break.) The therapist/business owner who can gracefully balance this stage of connection is rewarded by the client's feelings of advocacy.

One organizational consultant whom I coach put it this way: "At a certain point in my consulting work on a long-term project, things always get tricky. A program doesn't go as planned. Someone on the corporate team gets upset with me. The CEO wants me out, rather than make a necessary big change. I always know it's going to come, it's a part of the process. It's hard on everyone, and the important thing is for me, as the consultant, to stay calm in the midst of the storms that brew and help my client stay calm too, by educating the client about the continued value of what I am doing for him and helping him understand why the storm is so intense and rough at the moment. He also needs to know that even if he tells me to leave, he can reconsider and hire me back again. As long as we have left each other well, I will be glad to come back in."

As a business owner, you can help your clients stay calm and continue in their work, despite the tension and stormy weather than happens during the "working through" stages of therapy. Two strategies can help during this stage:

- Continually educate clients about therapy.
- Support all termination.

Continually Educate Clients

You can build a solid connection with clients during the advocacy stage if you have a way to help existing clients remember the value of the ongoing work, the gains they have already made, and the process that they are engaged in. Do you talk with your clients about the results you see occurring over time and the nature of the process of therapy?

Too often therapists don't have this kind of discussion with clients until the termination process begins, as a way of evaluating the course of treatment. But this kind of discussion is needed throughout the second stage of client connection, to provide a holding space or a container for the changes that the relationship goes through.

Identifying results gives clients a way to chart their progress. It's easier for your clients to feel trust when they are clear about their results. Make the process of therapy less mysterious. Help your clients to articulate their gains and how and why the process is working, on an ongoing basis, so that they really understand the effectiveness of your services.

EXERCISE: MEASURE YOUR GAINS

Pick one or more of these strategies to help your clients articulate and measure the value of therapy.

1. At the end of sessions, leave time to debrief. "What was most important in our work today? How specifically might you make it count in your life this week? Was there anything that happened that you don't understand?"

2. Have a 3-month verbal progress update with clients to evaluate results and gains from that time period.

3. Have clients complete a written result/survey form every few months.

4. Find a process of measuring client gains that fits your therapeutic style. Help clients both articulate ongoing gains and better understand the therapeutic process that they are in.

My plan for measuring gains:

_____

_____

_____

_____

_____

➡ FIELDWORK

Put your plan in place this month, so that your clients continually understand both the process they are in, and the value of the work they do with you.

Support All Termination

If a client decides to leave your practice, as a business owner you want to set things up so that when and if they are ready, he or she can comfortably return. Businesses call this creating "lifetime" customers—those customers who will stay with a company over the long term, repeatedly purchasing services and products, coming and going as need be.

You can consider a client a lifetime client, whether they are an active (someone you currently see) or inactive client (a past client who could return) if you can find ways to keep a line of communication open and hold a space for them in your heart and mind. The skill that is essential to developing lifetime clients is the ability to end therapy well, so that a client can easily return.

Helping clients to end well furthers the advocacy and trust that are the goals of this second stage of client connection. It can be hard to let go of clients gracefully, when you don't think the work is completed, when each client represents a portion of your weekly income, or when you don't have a waiting list. Even when you have mastered your feelings of anxiety, not every client will leave well. Some insist on leaving with anger, abruptness, and in a hurtful manner. But you can do your best to try to have good endings with those who are ready. Here's a checklist to help you put the steps in place.

EXERCISE: END WELL WITH YOUR CLIENTS

Check the items that are true for you. Circle the items that would help you to promote better endings with clients, that you have not yet included in your policies, and then complete the fieldwork assignment that follows.

- ❑ I help clients leave with an absence of guilt, embarrassment, or shame.
- ❑ In the first session with a new client I say, "I want you to know that one of my policies is to support all termination, for whatever reason. When you are ready to leave, I would like to help you to leave well. Here are my suggestions to make that happen."
- ❑ I have my policy of supporting termination written in my client policy sheet.

❏ I educate clients about their role in making a good ending.

❏ Although a client has announced that he or she is ready to leave, I take the time to anticipate, with the client, what the next piece of work would be, if he or she chose to stay longer.

❏ When a client has decided to leave, I do not look for new issues to explore. I allow the process to begin to wind down.

❏ I spend the final session talking about how far the client has come, what he or she got from therapy, and what didn't get accomplished this time. I allow time for both me and my client to express appreciation for working with one another.

❏ If I feel anxious about my finances when a client leaves, I practice all the anxiety-reducing techniques I know and use a business affirmation from Month 2.

❏ If I am worried about my client base, I review Months 5 and 6, and take action to generate new referrals and do more marketing.

❏ I consider appropriate ways to stay in contact with old clients, such as keeping them on my mailing list or sending them my periodic newsletter.

➙ FIELDWORK

Note the items that you circled and begin to incorporate these policies into your prac-tice immediately to support all termination. Let new and existing clients know that you want to support them in ending therapy well. Add your thoughts about leaving to your policy sheet, or find a way to educate all new clients about how to leave.

ENTHUSIASM

In the third stage of attachment, secure base, the child becomes even more autonomous. While still feeling a strong sense of affection and connection, the child needs to move farther away from the parent, both physically and psy-chologically. Children who are given this degree of space, with limits, develop into strong individuals with deep affection for their parents.

Therapy clients in the third stage of the client connection model, enthusiasm, feel excited about their gains. They are more autonomous, yet still need connection, but of a slightly different nature. If the first stage of client connection responds to a client's dependence, and the second stage reflects his emerging independence, you might understand this third stage as interdependence.

At this stage, you as the therapist/business owner allow yourself to connect to your client the way a ballroom dancer might hold a seasoned partner: not too close, not too tight. You want to position yourself for more give and take with your client at this stage, to respect the maturity of the connection.

When this level of connection is working well, clients often become openly enthusiastic, endorsing you and their therapy. And you as business owner will tend to feel appreciative as well. The hard work of therapy may continue to proceed, but you can view your connection as one in which you provide a rich environment for future growth. The skill set this month, *adding value*, assures that you have a lot to offer clients who continue to work with you or return at a later date.

MONTHLY SKILL SET: ADD VALUE

If you have been in business as a therapist and your practice is thriving, with a continual flow of referrals and a strong client base, you are probably adding value to your practice already, consciously or not. Building an added-value practice means that your practice offers more, all the time, each year. You may already have elements of this in place, but they may not be explicit for your clients.

For example, many therapists continually spend time and money to train and improve their skills. That's an added value for your clients. Do they know about your current training and how it benefits them?

Other therapists read continually and stay current on the literature: That's another added value. Do your clients know what books you studied on their behalf this year?

Here's a list of additional services you can offer to keep your clients feeling highly enthusiastic about your practice.

■ *Teach a system instead of a class.* There is an old maxim that says: Give a man a fish, feed him for a day. Teach him how to fish, feed him for a lifetime. It's more valuable for clients to have a program or a system they can use for life and can refer back to when needed than to take a one-day, one-shot workshop targeting a specific problem. To turn a workshop or a class into a program, include these elements: a manual, self-tests, exercises, progress reports, follow-up exercises, occasional additional sessions, a stand-alone network to connect to, or an ongoing support system you provide to keep the program in place.

How I can make this work for me:

_____

_____

_____

■ *Create methods of self-evaluation.* Your clients can benefit from any type of evaluation that they can use on their own, to help them extend the value of therapy sessions. Create checklists based on therapy outcomes that your clients can have and keep to help them chart their progress over time.

How I can make this work for me:

_____

_____

_____

■ *Publish a list of resources (be a turnkey solution).* Compile your best ideas and resources and make them available to your clients. You might create a list of inspiring books, soothing music, great self-help audiotapes, or a top-ten list that you have written.

How I can make this work for me:

_____

_____

_____

- *Expose your clients to other wonderful teachers and therapists.* Host workshops of other therapists and teachers whom you admire. Allow their ideas and methods to inspire your clients to work more deeply. Use your regular therapy sessions with clients to explore the ideas that surface following their exposure to the guest teachers. You can't be an expert on everything; bringing in others with talents and skills you don't possess can add value to your practice and your clients' lives.

How I can make this work for me:

_____

_____

_____

- *Write a workbook.* Have a lot to say to clients? Give them a workbook to augment their therapy. One yoga teacher is in the process of documenting and illustrating all of the exercises she uses in her classes. She gives this out to her clients, free of charge. This is an added value that lasts, and can help clients remember and review all the good work she does with them. A workbook takes time and effort, but may dramatically increase the results from traditional services. That's added value!

How I can make this work for me:

_____

_____

_____

- *Help clients enlarge their community.* If you choose, you can help your clients expand their connections into the broader community. Offer information, resources, or suggestions of how to connect to others.

Help clients build a minicommunity within your classes and workshops.

How I can make this work for me:

_____

_____

_____

- *Write a Q & A column.* If you find yourself getting asked the same questions repeatedly, take a hint from Ann Landers and write a question-and-answer column, using short questions. Questions you want to answer might include How does therapy work? What should I do when angry feelings surface during my work day? Incorporate the Q & A into your newsletter, offer it to a publication within your profession, or just make it available for clients by posting it on your waiting room bulletin board.

How I can make this work for me:

_____

_____

_____

- *Know the stages of personal growth.* In Month 12 we will look at the stages of personal growth. Have one added-value service that is appropriate for your clients for each stage of development.

How I can make this work for me:

_____

_____

_____

FIELDWORK

Pick one or more of these added-value ideas or create one of your own to put in place each year. Schedule it on your business plan. Decide how to start the process of adding this into your practice and articulating it for your clients.

Monthly Review

This month we looked at how you could create a solid client base by adopting a three-stage client connection to promote retention, return, and referrals. The fieldwork for Month 7 includes:

- Notice and correct any dissonance in your language with new clients. Improve your ability to resonate with everyday language.
- Correct any boundaries, policies, or procedures that don't strengthen your first stage of client connection; also correct those that don't promote client loyalty, respect, and retention.
- Continually educate your clients so that they understand both the process they are in, and the value of the work they do with you.
- Support all termination. Let new and existing clients know that you want to support their ending therapy, as well as you did their beginning.
- Pick one or more of the added-value ideas or create one of your own to put in place each year.

MONTH 8
Profit: Making Peace with Making Money

More than 2,000 years ago Socrates asked the question, "What is the good life?" Today, we still try to understand the answer. For many of us, it means not only having a life of safety, security, love, and work that is satisfying, but also an ability to provide well for our material needs. We want to work at our craft of helping and healing, yet still be able to own property, take care of our families, and partake of a diversity of pleasurable experiences that cost money. In order to live the good life, therapists need to make their peace with making money.

It's not just therapists who are conflicted about money. Many high-functioning people who are mature in every other area of their lives struggle with money. But you need to resolve this struggle to succeed in business. As an entrepreneur, your developmental task is to develop an adult relationship with money.

Money is the topic most therapists find the hardest to examine, so the first step this month is for you to "come clean" about yourself and money, to inventory your current money situation. Then I want to educate you about the basics of money management and give you a lot of ideas for becoming more immediately profitable. Lastly I want to show you how to create a plan for building a business to sell, so that you become more profit-oriented both now and in the long term.

First things first: Identify your money attitude and any negative beliefs that may be playing out in your practice.

Show me the money! This month, take steps to ensure that you have a highly profitable practice. Examine your thoughts and feelings about money and profit, check your profit picture against a reliable formula, evaluate your current fee structure, see how to raise fees successfully, and build a business not just to own, but to sell.

My Monthly Prep Form

Answering these questions each month will help you to chart your progress and define your next goals.

1. What have I accomplished since last month that I feel positive about? What are my wins?

2. What challenges am I facing this month?

3. What opportunities are available to me right now?

4. What blocks me from taking advantage of these opportunities?

5. How could I make life or work easier or better for myself right now?

6. My goals for this month are:

EXERCISE: IDENTIFY MY YOUR NEGATIVE MONEY BELIEFS

Check the following negative attitudes or beliefs that apply to you, as well as the ways that they play out in your practice. Use the blank spaces to add additional comments.

Deprivation Attitude

Maybe you grew up with money deprivation. There was never enough money for your basic needs as a child. You still believe money is in short supply and watch every penny, reluctant to spend on anything "unnecessary." As a result, you fail to give your business the resources it needs to flourish.

You believe:

- ❑ I can't make money.
- ❑ I am just one step away from being on the street.
- ❑ I can't charge what I am worth because no one will pay my full fee.
- ❑ Money doesn't grow on trees.
- ❑ Other: _____

How your belief plays out in your practice:

- ❑ I won't attend major conferences because they cost too much.
- ❑ I annoy my colleagues who share office space with me because I am so cheap.
- ❑ I don't join associations because it's not cost effective; who needs them?
- ❑ I fail to give my business the equipment, advertising, or other resources it needs to flourish.
- ❑ I miss networking opportunities and skimp on training that would benefit my work.
- ❑ Other: _____

Dissociated Attitude

Maybe you grew up believing that money was mysterious, because no one in your family understood how to make it or save it. You ride an emotional money roller coaster: When your practice goes through a slow time, you are down and self-critical; when it's up, you feel great. Mostly you are confused, because there is so much about money you don't comprehend.

You believe:

- ❏ Nice people don't talk about money.
- ❏ I only care about my craft, money isn't important.
- ❏ If I don't pay attention to money, it comes when I really need it.
- ❏ Money isn't everything, in fact it isn't anything.
- ❏ Other: _____

How your belief plays out in your practice:

- ❏ I don't discuss money issues with clients, even when they act out financially.
- ❏ I don't bill on time.
- ❏ I carry the debt of uncollected accounts when I do bill.
- ❏ I don't know what I make, what I owe, and why I am so broke.
- ❏ My practice swings from positive to negative cash flow.
- ❏ Other: _____

Demonized Attitude

Maybe you believe money is inherently wicked. You watched anxiety on your parents' faces when they talked about money, so you feel scared or impure when *you* have to deal with it. You hate to raise your fees, negotiate with a landlord, or hold your boundaries about your established policies. You find all aspects regarding money unpleasant and suspect.

You believe:

- ❏ Money is the root of all evil.
- ❏ I can't have money and have integrity too.
- ❏ Only greedy people think about money all the time.
- ❏ Money is dirty and corrupting.
- ❏ Other: _____

How your belief plays out in your practice:

- ❏ I don't raise my fees when justified.
- ❏ I don't hold my boundaries about my established policies.
- ❏ Clients take advantage of me.

□ I sacrifice (unfair split-fee arrangements, managed care agreements, sliding scale for most clients) so that I don't have to deal with my money anxieties.

□ Other: _____

→ FIELDWORK

Resolve any beliefs and behaviors that impede your business development. Use the affirmation process from Month 2 directed toward money, or resolve your old beliefs with the help of your therapist, coach, peer support group, or mentor. Additional reading that can help resolve beliefs can be found in Appendix B.

RECONCILING PROFIT AND SERVICE

Most therapists can trace their problems with profitability to the fact that they have not reconciled two seemingly opposite concepts: profit and service.

The concept of service to others stands in opposition to the concept of profit. Service means helping, assisting, aiding, benefiting others; profit means to take advantage, make money, achieve financial gain from someone else. And yes, as a therapist in private practice, you do both.

For some in the field of service, service is seen as the "better" of the two concepts. Service is pure and good; profit is tainted and evil. For some within the field of business, profit is the natural order of transactions between people; service to others is considered charity and, while a worthwhile endeavor, one that is far removed from business.

But what if your work is primarily service-oriented? Your work is your livelihood and, by that definition, a business endeavor for you. Now you have the making of an internal conflict, one that can put very good, well-meaning people into a state of internal war that takes years to reconcile, if ever.

If you are in a private practice, you are, by definition, profiting from your clients. You may think: How can I be a person who helps others and, at the same time, take money from them? How can I take money from them if their resources are low, simply because the services I offer are so crucial to them? This internal dialogue becomes a personal, internal battle, one that I hear continually from therapists, doctors, life coaches, teachers in private practice, clergy, and counselors of all kinds.

How do you reconcile profit and service? There is no one right way to unite these two concepts. But you need to have a way that makes sense to you, in your heart and your mind. Possible ways to reconcile these concepts are:

- Separate the caring and affection you may have for your clients from your skills, recognizing that you charge for the skills, not the caring.
- Think about the time and value you provide, and the viability of your business (if your business doesn't make a profit you will no longer be able to provide services).

EXERCISE: RECONCILE SERVICE AND PROFIT

Write a brief explanation of how you reconcile the concepts of service and profit for yourself.

_____

_____

_____

_____

_____

YOUR PROFIT FORMULA

Still unclear about reconciliation? It might help you to understand more about profit.

Profit equals your gross income minus your expenses. Your gross income or revenue is all of the money that you earn in your practice. After you look at your gross income for a year, you deduct your expenses—the costs you incur from doing business.

A therapy business is considered an expensive business to operate. Whether you are a sole proprietor or part of a group practice, whether you work from home or out of a fancy downtown office, your expenses will always be a substantial percentage of your gross income, and that makes this an expensive business to run. It may not seem that way when you have a small practice, because there is relatively little start-up expense, especially with a home office. But when you look at your expenses as a *percentage of gross income*, you see the true picture.

Here are some business terms we will be using when we talk about profit.

- *Gross income or revenue*—refers to all of the money that you earn in your practice.
- *Expenses* are the costs you incur from doing business. There are two types of expenses I will look at with you: (1) *Direct expenses*, the essentials that must be in place to allow you to run your business (office space rental, utilities, telephone, licensing, supervision, billing, accounting, postage, supplies, malpractice insurance, self employment tax, etc.); and (2) *indirect expenses*, the expenses that you may write off to the business that are nonessential, but helpful (travel, publications, office decoration, meetings, conferences, etc.). Some therapists have low direct expenses (they work out of their home, employ no staff, don't advertise, have few equipment needs) and others have more overhead (high rent and utilities for multiple offices, advertising budget, direct-mail campaign, staff, a billing service, subcontractors to pay, equipment). For a more complete list of direct and indirect expenses, see the sample business budget form in Appendix C.
- *Net income* or *profit* is what's left of your revenue after you pay your direct and indirect expenses.

The product that you bill for is *your* services, and for most therapists that means billing for contact hours spent with clients. You can't send in a lower-paid "substitute therapist" to deliver therapy. You also can't mass produce your sessions and have 60 hours of sessions a week. Your time and energy is limited—there are only so many client sessions you can conduct each week. Based on this limitation of time and delivery of service, a private practice can't easily match the high profit ratios of a manufacturing or consulting business. You simply can't produce as much product to offset the expenses.

Even though I suggest ways that you can boost your income by leveraging your time or diversifying your services, if your primary revenue stream is generated by delivering hourly sessions, your profit potential will always be capped. Your ratio of expenses to profit will always be relatively substantial, because you have some set expenses that must be in place in order to operate.

In order to be as highly profitable as possible, you need to carefully consider how to charge for your time and how to control your expenses.

It can help you to evaluate the profitability of your practice by having a general profitability formula that you can use to check your figures against each month. How much profit can a therapy business make? Each practice is different, but there are some general guidelines, or formulas, that can help you see how you measure up. Let's look at a sample *profitability formula* for a one-person therapy business:

100%	gross income (all the money you make from your practice)
−30%	direct and indirect expenses
−15%	self-employment taxes
−5%	business reserve (cash reserve held back for emergencies)
50%	profit (includes your salary)

A 50% profit looks big, until you remember two things:

1. Operating a therapy business with direct and indirect expenses of only 30% means you are working with a very lean budget, carefully controlling all your costs (see the business budget in Appendix C for a listing of these expenses).
2. You haven't taken your compensation, or a salary, yet. Your compensation comes out of this profit. This profit amount will also be subject to additional federal, state, and local taxes. Since your salary comes out of profits, if you want a salary of $40,000 a year and your expenses run 40%, you need to bring in a gross income of $66,000. If you want to follow the above profitability formula and allocate funds for a cash reserve, you will need a gross income of $80,000.

Your hourly fee must be set so that it covers your total expense of doing business. When you see the sample business budget in Appendix C, you may note that you have additional expenses that are not covered in that budget, which would raise your overall expense total, or you may need to reapportion the expenses listed there to reflect the ones you occur in your specific practice. The sample business budget gives you some recommended guidelines for tracking your expenses as a percentage of your total revenue.

EXERCISE: TRACK YOUR PROFIT

Use the following chart to look at your end-of-year figures from last year, and then your profit from this year to date, and see how you compare in profitability. You can take these figures from your taxes or your worksheets. Don't have access to these figures? Get an accounting program in place so that you can see your budget and the profit picture of your business at a glance.

My profit formula for last year

$_____ (100 %)   gross income
$_____ (___ %)   direct and indirect expenses
$_____ (___ %)   business reserve (cash reserve for emergencies)
$_____ (___ %)   profit (includes my salary)

My profit formula for the current year to date

$_____ (100 %)   gross income
$_____ (___ %)   direct and indirect expenses
$_____ (___ %)   business reserve (cash reserve for emergencies)
$_____ (___ %)   profit (includes my salary)

SETTING FEES

From a business perspective, your fee is not just a dollar amount that reflects the time you spend with a client. Your hourly fee must cover your total business expenses.

If you bill clients for contact hours (therapy sessions) and some secondary services (such as phone consultations, court testimony, testing, or writing reports), your fee will need to cover the actual time you spend with clients, as well as the unbilled services you perform, as well as all of your direct and indirect expenses.

You will also want to have a cushion built into your fee to absorb things that come up in the normal course of doing business. Since your hourly fee is your only source of income, it has to contain all of your many expenses and be able to buffer your practice against the normal ups and downs of a small business.

As we've discussed, a therapy business is expensive to run, and the fees are the proof. The private-pay fee for therapy sessions generally falls in the range of $70 to $250 per hour for therapists. According to recent surveys in several national association newsletters:

- Psychiatrists, executive coaches, and therapists working in consulting positions command the highest hourly fees ($150 to $350, and more, per hour).
- Mental health therapists, such as psychologists, social workers, and licensed counselors, change in the middle range ($75 to $175 per hour).
- Alternative healers, including acupuncturists, massage therapists, and energy healers, tend to charge at the lower levels ($45 to $90 per hour).

How many hours do you work and bill for? National surveys show that therapists in full-time private practice see an average of 25 to 30 individual clients per week and those in part-time private practice see an average of 10 to 12 client per week.

Let's look at your billable hours. The billable hours chart in the next exercise starts with an average of a 40-hour workweek, 52 weeks a year, as a way to compute how many hours you actually have available for billing in a year. A 40-hour workweek is a conventional norm in our society and a useful starting place, even if it does not represent your situation. For example, your work week may exceed 40 hours if you work in multiple locations and have a very diversified practice, with consulting and assessment services, written reports, as well as any direct client sessions. Or, your workweek may be less than 40 hours if your only service is client sessions and you operate a less-than-full-time practice. As you saw above, national surveys show that therapists across the nation consider full-time work, in the therapy profession, to be 25 to 30 client hours per week. Most therapists I have questioned about the hours that they work say that the nature of conducting therapy sessions, whether the sessions are psychotherapy, massage therapy, or other types of counseling, prevent them from working a conventional schedule of 40 hours a week: The work is too taxing on the therapist's ability to provide 8 session hours a day, 5 days a week, 50 weeks a year.

Use the next exercise as a guide for defining the total number of hours you can bill for in a year. It will help you to understand further the natural limitations of this business; if you, as a sole proprietor can bill only for a limited number of hours in a year, probably less than 40 hours per week, you will see another reason why therapy is an expensive business to operate.

EXERCISE: FIGURE YOUR BILLABLE HOURS

How many hours are you currently working? How many do you want to work? Fill in this billable hours chart and see how many hours you want to or can work each year.

2080 hours	average work week of 40 hours, 52 weeks a year
−___ hours	vacation
−___ hours	training time
−___ hours	popular holidays I don't work
−___ hours	sick leave
−___ hours	other (child care, personal time)
_____	subtotal
−___ hours	marketing time (unbilled time to network and generate referrals)
−___ hours	administrative tasks (unbilled office operations)
−___ hours	downtime (those hours that don't fill)
____	subtotal
____	total hours I work (___ hours per week, ___ weeks per year)

➜ FIELDWORK

Look at your budget, profit formula to date, and your billable hours. Analyze your financial data by answering the following questions. Then discuss your answers with your circle of advisors, your coach, coaching group, mentor or trusted colleagues.

How much money can I anticipate making this year?

_____

_____

_____

_____

_____

What will I spend on expenses?

_____

_____

_____

_____

_____

What services produce the most profit for me?

_____

_____

_____

_____

_____

Which are least profitable?

_____

_____

_____

_____

What financial cycles does my practice go through each year?

_____

_____

_____

_____

_____

If I wanted to increase my profit by 15%, how could I make more income or cut expenses?

_____

_____

_____

_____

_____

What is the basis for my current fee structure?

_____

_____

_____

_____

_____

When was the last time I raised my fees?

_____

_____

_____

_____

_____

EXERCISE: DETERMINE YOUR PROFIT DRAINS, PROFIT GAINS

You probably lose profit in ways you are not noticing, and you could be more profitable in many ways you don't consider. Here is a checklist of ways that profit can seep out of a practice and a checklist of ways to make your practice more profitable. Check those that apply to you.

Profit Drains

- ❑ I have either no business plan or a weak business plan.
- ❑ I don't have enough liquidity or cash on hand, so I am always borrowing money.

- ❑ I offer the wrong services to the right people.
- ❑ I offer the right services to the wrong people.
- ❑ I am in a location that is not conducive to getting or retaining clients.
- ❑ I don't have a good accounting system for accurate tracking of finances.
- ❑ I have too much credit card debt.
- ❑ My income can't support my lifestyle.
- ❑ I communicate poorly with my clients regarding fees.
- ❑ I spend too much time doing menial work and too little time earning money.
- ❑ I have poor self-care, resulting in feeling burnt out.

Profit Gains

- ❑ Every dollar I spend on my business contributes to furthering my profitability.
- ❑ I have less paperwork since I automated my systems.
- ❑ I work only with serious clients.
- ❑ I reduced my debt and high interest payments.
- ❑ I pay attention to financial details.
- ❑ I collect fees as soon as possible to eliminate accounts receivable.
- ❑ I put profitability ahead of comfort or appearance.
- ❑ I have a good accounting system in place to be able to see my current finances and budget at a glance.
- ❑ I am a skilled manager of my practice.
- ❑ I made a list of my expenses and cut them by 50%.
- ❑ I leverage my time and efforts to get the most money in the least amount of time.
- ❑ I surround myself with bright people who are dedicated to my success.
- ❑ I have multiple profit centers.
- ❑ I think expansively and am building a practice to last well into the future.
- ❑ I spend 90% of my time delivering services and generating referrals, 10% of my time doing all else.

→ FIELDWORK

Look at ways you can plug some of the most obvious profit drains. Circle the items that you can take action on this month to increase your profitability.

JUSTIFYING EXPENSES

When your practice is not profitable, you may wonder how to justify your expenses. You will need to trim your existing expenses in order to operate on a leaner budget, while taking the steps to increase your income by using the marketing strategies from Months 5 and 6. At some point in time, as you begin to earn more income, you may wonder how to justify which expenses to re-incur. I challenge my clients in this situation to bring back an expense only if it produces several times its cost in immediate revenue.

Bryson is struggling to sustain a very small psychotherapy practice while he continues to work at an agency job. Last year's taxes showed that he barely broke even in his private practice. I asked him to find a way to cut his expenses for the current year, to increase his profit line. He made a list of all his expenses and highlighted the most essential direct expenses that he would continue to pay for, and eliminated the rest. The direct expenses he kept included: rent, phone, licensure fees, association dues, supervision, business coaching classes, and postage for small mailings. The direct and indirect expenses he eliminated included: week-long trainings that involved travel, advertising in an association magazine, plans to purchase a new computer, staffing (the bookkeeper who did his billing), a referral network he belonged to that provided him with occasional clients, publications, and books. He also scrapped his plans to replace a worn sofa in his office and paint the office or buy new artwork to spruce it up.

After a year of focused marketing and cost cutting, Bryson built his practice to the point where it now yields him the same amount of income as his agency job, an increase of 25% in his profit. He wanted to bring back some expenses that he had cut, but at the same time he liked the increased profitability, so he wanted to do this with caution. I asked him to make a list of all the expenses he wanted to reinstate and then evaluate each one to see if it would produce several times its cost in revenue.

Bryson completed this exercise and came to the next business coaching class with three items he thought fit that criteria: buying a new computer, advertising in the magazine, or painting the office. He thought the computer would increase his profitability by allowing him to compose and print flyers and mailers more effectively to promote his practice, and by giving him better control over his accounting so that he could continue to do his own book-keeping, even as his practice grew. He thought that advertising in the magazine might provide him with more clients, although the results had been spotty in the past; he liked advertising as a way to have more of a presence in the local community. Painting the office could increase revenue by making a nicer office, he said, and that would entice clients to stay longer because his space was more conducive to therapy. One of his clients had recently mentioned how dingy the office looked.

Bryson asked the business coaching class for their feedback. The class decided that the only two items that met the revenue criteria were purchasing the computer and advertising. The painting was too iffy for the class to consider it a revenue increaser. Bryson decided that the computer was a better bet, and if he continued to stay profitable, the advertising would be the next item he would add back.

If profitability is your primary goal, take a hard look at your list of expenses and prioritize them. Get feedback from others about which expenses to cut, which to keep, and which to add back in time to keep adding to your profit.

THE RIGHT FEE

Your profitability depends in large part on how much you charge for your services. Your fee for services should:

- reflect your vision of the practice;
- adhere to your business goals and business plan;
- reflect current market forces;
- uphold the value or perceived value of your services.

Your fee should *not* be based on:

- *Anxiety.* Emotion doesn't have a place in deciding how much to charge. Decide on a fee that is fair, meets the right criteria, and reflects your business objectives. Don't raise or lower it based on your worries or fears of keeping or losing a client.

- *Guilt.* Some therapists feel guilty about charging what they are worth. Feelings of fear regarding success or confusion about reconciling profit and service are often the sources of guilt.
- *Zero-sum game mentality.* This mind-set says that there is only a fixed amount of money in the world. If I take more, you get less. If I win, you lose. This is both illogical and demeaning to your clients.
- *Love.* Some clients confuse the caring or affection with which therapy is often delivered with love, and feel offended at having to pay for love. You are not selling love. A senior therapist in New York told me that he explains it to his clients this way, "You pay me for my skill. The love I choose to give is free."

EXERCISE: YOUR CURRENT FEE

Start to examine your fee by completing the following statement.

My current fee for services is: ______________________________

My fee is based on: ______________________________

____

Changes I need to make regarding my fee: ______________________________

____

→ FIELDWORK

Evaluate your fee this month. Are you happy with your fee? If not, can you charge a fee you love? Do you need to raise your fee? Lower it? Make it clearer for clients to understand? Make a plan for how to correct it and take action.

EXERCISE: RAISE YOUR FEE

If you need to raise your fee, do it in the least disruptive manner, using the following checklist as a guide.

❑ I give my clients clear notice of fee changes, verbally and in writing (because money is so emotional, its best to make all communication regarding money very clear).

❑ I give my clients ample notice of fee changes (30 to 60 days) since any change in the frame of therapy may trigger decisions to leave. This way my clients have time to leave well.

❑ I anticipate a reaction. Most of us don't like change of any kind, especially about increasing prices.

❑ I am available to process any reaction with my clients. For that reason, I inform them in the beginning of the session, not on their way out the door at the end.

❑ I help them to use their reactions as part of the therapeutic process, a chance for deepening their work. I calm my anxiety and present the change cleanly.

❑ I don't offer an overly-long explanation. A long explanation may soothe my anxiety when I tell my clients that I am raising my fee, but it doesn't necessarily help them.

BUILDING A BUSINESS TO SELL

Your long-term financial health is important, so think about building a business that you can eventually sell. Is it possible to sell a therapy business? Yes, but you will need to start positioning it today. In order for your therapy business to be attractive to buyers, it needs to have multiple transferable assets.

Too often, a therapy business has only one asset, and it's a nontransferable one—the therapist's relationship to his or her clients. Even though you are the star attraction of your business, your cachet can't be easily transferred to a potential buyer. Can your clients be transferred to a buyer? That depends on whether your clients perceive that their main attachment is to you, to the practice, or both. Review Month 7 to see how to increase your client's attachment to both you and your practice, and consider how you might transfer the attachment to a therapist who bought your practice by asking these questions: What creates the main rapport that I have with my clients? Could I quantify this for a potential buyer? Could I teach a buyer to do what I do and work in the way I work? If so, what would be the best way to do this?

One therapist who was selling her practice had a very distinctive way of working with addictions, and the bulk of her clientele came from the 12-step community. When she decided to sell her practice, she carefully screened buyers so that she found a therapist she liked and respected. She defined the methods she used and prepared a manual for the potential buyer, developed a procedure for training the potential buyer, set aside 5 months to make a good transfer (for example, she had the buyer sit in on a month's worth of sessions with every client), and in the end the majority of her clients (65%) stayed with the new owner.

What price can you expect to get for your business? While a manufacturing company might be sold for five times its annual earnings because it has a product, plant, staff, and system in place, a therapy business without these elements in place might sell at one to two times its annual earnings. You can add to this ratio by having as many tangible assets as possible.

Create tangible value that is transferable. Turn your ideas into programs, document those programs, and establish your methods of therapy in writing and on video. Create as much product as possible. Write, research, and publish to validate your methods. Begin to train others in your methods, so that you have a pool of potential buyers when you are ready to retire. Here's a list of six tangible assets that can add to the selling price of your practice and how to accomplish each one:

1. *Brand name.* If you can name your type of services in a recognizable way as separate from your identity, you have a salable asset. You can more easily sell your methods than sell yourself. *How to do it:* Look at your professional field for examples of this. You will find programs and methods that are trademarked. Read Tom Peters's classic article, "The Brand Called You" (Fast Company Magazine, August 1997, available at www.fastcompany.com). Go to the United States Post Office Trademark Office Web site (www.uspto.gov) for complete information how to trademark a brand name. Brand names carry value, since they have an identity that is separate from their developers.

2. *Direct-mail list.* Build a large direct-mail list for your practice of clients and referral sources. A practice with a direct-mail list of 5,000 current names can add significantly to the value of a business. *How to do it:* Use your advertising and speaking engagements to build your mailing list, not only to generate referrals. Keep a good database. Ask to buy direct-mail lists from colleagues or other organizations who support your work. Get permission

from those on your list to transfer their names to the new owner; be ethically correct by only transferring the names of those who have given their permission.

3. *Promotional materials.* Develop brand-name recognition via your promotional materials now, with brochures that highlight the method or the program name more than your name. *How to do it:* Take the time and effort to create a good package of materials. Keep a portfolio of your winning advertisements, brochures, or flyers that have generated good results for your practice, along with the details of those results. This is part of the package you can offer someone who wants to reproduce your results.

4. *Measures.* Have a system to track your effectiveness over time. *How to do it.* If you develop a great survey for clients that measures their satisfaction and you have used this not only to boost client satisfaction, but also as part of your promotion, this transferable measure is a definite asset for a potential buyer. Keep good files recording all the diagnostic tests and surveys you use.

5. *Ancillary products.* If your state sanctions selling products to clients under your licensure (some do and some don't; ask your licensing board), you can develop a product line of materials to sell—pamphlets, audio- or videotapes, training tapes, books (your own or others), nutritional supplements. Even if you have not promoted your product line sufficiently during your owning of the business, it doesn't lessen its potential value to another buyer. *How to do it:* Get legal advice regarding licensing agreements for all written and recorded products. Keep thorough records and originals of all scripts, tapes, videos, and manuscripts. Make the packaging reflect the quality and match your brand.

6. *Practice management.* If you have created a thriving practice with easy-to-understand administrative systems in place, you have an additional asset. See Month 10 for strategies to optimize your systems. *How to do it:* Find a billing system that is user friendly. Document your office resources in a manual—include staffing procedures, outside contractors, maintenance services, written agreements you use. Present a potential buyer with a clear, complete management program for the practice.

➜ FIELDWORK

Create a plan for the long-term financial health of your practice by positioning it as a business that can be sold when you are ready to retire. Consider which of the above transferable assets already exist in your practice and which you need to develop.

MONTHLY SKILL SET: RAISE YOUR MONEY IQ

As an entrepreneur, you need to be smart about money. Raise your Money IQ by reading, thinking, observing, and becoming curious about how money operates in your practice, in your profession, and in the world. Here's a quick checklist of ten statements to help measure your money IQ. Check those that apply to you now.

❏ *I know what services people happily pay for, regardless of income level.* Your clients will gladly pay for what they want, versus what you think they need. Articulate your services to speak to what your clients want—get coached to do this if you don't know how.

❏ *I know the value of my unique skills.* The essence of your business is your unique value as a therapist. If you define this well, for yourself and your clients, you can charge what you are worth.

❏ *I know my market.* Know what others who are doing similar work are charging and why.

❏ *I educate my clients.* Find ways to educate your clients about the efforts you make to be a great therapist, so that they can understand the investment you make in terms of time, money, and training.

❏ *I encourage my clients to focus on their goals and results.* When clients ask about your fees, understand the real question: they want to know if they will be getting their money's worth. This is a fair question, because it's what we all want. Help your clients become a partner in their own results.

❏ *I add value.* What are you doing each day for your clients and your practice? Continually offer more for existing and new clients.

❏ *I am a good boss to myself.* If you are working very hard and not making much money, you may be paying yourself too little. Raise your prices, raise your self-esteem, and lower your resentment.

❑ *I model a winner.* Pick a model of practice that you think is excellent and follow it as closely as you can. You don't need to reinvent the wheel. If you know a therapist who is doing good work and has the business part of his or her practice handled, borrow his or her way of working until you get the same results.

❑ *I work to be the best in my field.* In today's competitive marketplace, you need to stand out based on some aspect of your business. Invest in yourself and master some area of your field. Orient your practice around that strength.

❑ *I set boundaries that protect my income.* Develop policies that will support you and insure a fair income for you. Just because you are a sole proprietor doesn't mean that everything has to be negotiable. (For example: I have a set fee and will not compromise to go below this fee; Or, I collect my fees at the time of the session and stay current with my accounts receivable.)

Monthly Review

This month we looked at the essential elements for enhancing profitability, including how to set your fee, raise your fee, increase your profit, and build a business to sell. The fieldwork for Month 8 includes:

■ Resolve negative beliefs about money by using the affirmation process from Month 2. Use your support system, as well as the reading list in Appendix B, to shift limiting beliefs.

■ Analyze your financial data.

■ Plug some of the most obvious profit drains and put in place some profit gains.

■ Evaluate your fee and raise it if necessary.

■ Create a plan for the long-term financial health of your practice by building a business that can be sold when you are ready to retire.

Part III
Charting an Evolutionary Path to Success

MONTH 9
Stamina: Creating Business Strength and Endurance

True to our business model, the first four months of this workbook focused on all aspects of your preparation—physical, mental, emotional, and spiritual. The next four months focused on the building blocks—articulation, marketing, security, and profit. Now, we are at the final four months of this program and it's time to add some finishing touches—stamina, optimization, expansion, and flow—to your practice.

In a house, the finishing touches include the craftsmanship and detailing that make a house feel like a home. In business, adding finish means looking at *positioning*. Positioning, a buzzword in business, means the relationship between your business and your community, your clients, and the marketplace. This position is not fixed; it evolves over time, as you change and grow.

Since the position of your business evolves, you need to understand its evolutionary spiral. We know that we continually evolve as human beings, both internally, in our consciousness, and externally, in the things we create. But we don't always recognize that our businesses go through evolutionary stages. We busily focus on the daily tasks that are necessary to help our practices succeed, while failing to see the evolutionary spiral of our businesses over time. As a result, we miss the larger framework, a pattern of undercurrents and emerging phases that develops in similar ways for all businesses.

Certain themes consistently emerge at different stages of small-business development—concerns about survival and competition, a move toward stability, a drive

Position yourself and your practice for long-term success by learning how to anticipate future challenges. This month, explore the early stages of business evolution to see how to develop greater stamina and endurance, deal with competition as it occurs, transform envy into excellence, and stay true to your business vision.

My Monthly Prep Form

Answering these questions each month will help you to chart your progress and define your next goals.

1. What have I accomplished since last month that I feel positive about? What are my wins?

2. What challenges am I facing this month?

3. What opportunities are available to me right now?

4. What blocks me from taking advantage of these opportunities?

5. How could I make life or work easier or better for myself right now?

6. My goals for this month are:

to expand, a push to affiliate, and so on. These themes tend to occur across the board in all businesses and follow a similar progression. As such, they are the evolutionary markers of a business. Although the markers are not strictly linear and don't arise in identical ways, if you are familiar with them and know where to look, it's possible to see the developmental path of any business. You can spot which stage is currently occurring, and if you understand the ramifications of the particular stage, you will know what tasks the business owner needs to attend to in order to master the challenges of that stage. You can predict what will happen next as the business continues to evolve. You have a perspective from which to lubricate instead of obstruct inevitable business changes. You can begin to enjoy the bumpy ride of business a lot more by highlighting the most positive aspects inherent in each stage. Business success becomes easier.

In my work as a business coach, I listen beyond my clients' presenting complaints and concerns to hear the subtle, underlying expressions that signal these developmental markers. Phrases that clients use when describing the state of their business, or issues that they mention let me know where they are in their evolutionary path, and whether a shift is about to transpire or is getting blocked. When I am able to explain these signals to a client, he or she can gain a new perspective on the situation. I can alert a client to the stage he is approaching, help him identify the challenges of that stage, and emphasize the tasks and objectives he will need to accomplish to do well at that stage.

I find that many clients welcome having an evolutionary perspective on business, because the actual experience of transitioning through a developmental phase is often not a conscious or especially desired event. Like most change, it just happens. Since business evolution is not linear, you need a model that can help you see the distinct stages that you may move into, move out of, and revisit from time to time.

BUSINESS EVOLUTION

Nature works on change; the world around us is in a state of constant flux. Change in one's business often occurs as a response to a changing environment and small business as are especially reactive to external forces. But even though business evolution is constant and can be reactive, it is not necessarily random. It can be charted.

The idea of charting business evolution is new for most therapists in private practice. For clinicians in private practice who are more often than not unschooled in the process or theory of business, one's business success or failure can feel not only random, but intensely personal as well. We naively think that our business success or failure is based primarily on factors that involve our psychology, or our skill level, or other personal issues; while this may be true, rarely do we factor the developmental arc of business into the success or failure equation. Sometimes, business situations that we experience are simply indicators of a stage that any business invariably passes through. Business evolves by moving through spirals of lower-order action to newer, higher-order ways of being, just as we human beings tend to do.

We accept that human beings go through developmental stages with some predictability. Parents of children anticipate the tantrums that occur during the "terrible twos" and the sullen behavior of a preteen child. Cultures go through predictable developmental stages as well: Almost all cultures pass through phases of clan to tribalism to feudalism to authoritarian systems of government.

Business, which is just another invention of human beings, goes through its own evolutionary patterns that can be identified and predicted. Businesses go through early phases of survival, mid-life stages where matters of organization, achievement, and affiliation dominate, and mature phases where matters of integrating core values, defining legacy, and reinvention take over. But while understanding the phases and having some ability to predict or anticipate what is next can be helpful and calming to the business owner, prediction is only part of the toolkit a business owner needs to succeed.

Knowing that a child is in the terrible-twos phase can help anxious parents put tantrums in perspective; but just knowing what is going on doesn't solve all the problems of living with a rambunctious toddler and may not make the daily task of trying to get a squirming bundle of energy to lie down for a nap any easier. Similarly, knowing the stage one's business is currently in helps a therapist in private practice gain perspective and perhaps feel less alone, but doesn't tell the business owner how to turn around an ailing practice, keep it filled with clients, or make it more profitable.

Business consultants who rely on an evolutionary approach usually refer to the work of Don Beck and Chris Cowan, whose book *Spiral Dynamics* defines the current thinking about the hidden codes that shape human nature and drive organizational change. Their work is an extension of the biopsychosocial systems concept of Clare Graves, an early student of Maslow. Graves, Professor Emeritus at Union College, proposed an eight-stage, value-based system of evolution that he applied to human beings, societies, business, and government. Beck and Cowan refined his work, giving each stage a color, clarifying the principles of the model, and then testing it worldwide—most notably to help Nelson Mandela take South Africa out of apartheid.

I use the spiral dynamics model as my primary tool in understanding business evolution, finding it to be a flexible and fascinating indicator of business development. To make it more applicable to the small-business owners I coach, I have narrowed the model that Beck and Cowan presented in a macro format. My adapted model focuses less on the far-reaching aspects of each stage and more on the specific objectives and tasks that small-business owners need to accomplish to transition successfully from stage to stage, using with the many strategies and exercises that I have developed over time.

During the next 4 months we will examine all eight stages of the spiral dynamics model, in my adapted form. You will find that the adapted form provides you with fascinating concepts to think about to help keep your practice on the cutting edge. Each month I will give you exercises, fieldwork, and skill sets to help you apply concepts of business evolution.

SPIRAL DYNAMICS

Beck and Cowan assigned eight colors to represent the eight progressive stages of human development: beige, purple, red, blue, orange, green, yellow, and turquoise.

Every stage is important to examine, because you need to master the values of each stage in order to evolve to the next. Ken Wilber, who further defines spiral dynamics in his book *A Theory of Everything,* calls this progression the need to "transcend and include." You don't want to skip stages, because then you may not have incorporated the values and objectives inherent in that particular stage of development; it's hard to learn to run fast if you never really mastered the mechanics of walking. Each value-based stage will strengthen and polish your business abilities, and your practice will reflect your new abilities.

I want you to understand the basics of this model: The easiest way to think about spiral dynamics is to see how it applies to a large movement of evolution, such as human society. Human societies all emerged from primitive, survival-based beginnings. This first level of spiral dynamics, called beige, represents the stone-age human society, when our ancestors relied on base instincts to exist. In beige, a sense of self, as we would think of it today, is barely awakened or sustained, since so much energy is focused on surviving. We see beige in very primitive societies, or those that are shell-shocked, war-torn, or facing starvation. Beige also occurs in businesses facing bankruptcy or circumstances that elicit survival behavior.

As beige human societies band together, they grow and evolve to the animistic purple stage, which is marked by ethnic bonding, a reliance on ritual, magical thinking, and adherence to myths to counter the realities of a harsh environment. Kinship and lineage establish political links. We see purple in isolated or third-world societies, gangs, athletic teams, and in some clannish corporate cultures or family businesses.

Red, the stage of power, tribalism, and emergence of a separate sense of self, evolves next. Society feels like a jungle, full of threats and predators; territorialism becomes primary. Red is seen in feudal empires, frontier approaches, epic legends, feudal kingdoms, and gangs of rebellious youth. Businesses operate in red when they feel threatened by downsizing or competition. The maxim "business is war" speaks to a red mentality.

The rigors of beige, purple, and red lead a society to gravitate toward blue, the stage that places a high value on order, control, protection, and stability. At this stage, societies esteem laws, convention, and conformity. Blue can be seen in governments of authoritarianism, totalitarianism, and dictatorship, and in religious fundamentalism. In business, blue is seen in bureaucracy of all kinds. In health care, the managed care movement is a representation of blue.

The lack of personal freedom inherent in blue leads a society to shift to orange, a stage of independence, free-market capitalism, and entrepreneurial energy. The orange stage values rational thought, science, achievement, and materialistic gains. Orange thinking is prevalent in Western first-world countries and some formerly blue ones, such as China and Russia. In business, orange takes the form of expansion, marketplace alliances, and all types of entrepreneurial endeavors.

The intense materialism of orange creates the evolutionary shift to green, where sharing, mutuality, and environmental sensitivity are valued. A spiritual focus pervades; attention to feelings and caring supercede the concerns of achievement; the culture remembers to cherish the earth, humanism is valued.

People at this stage shift toward diversity and multiculturalism, striving to be egalitarian and pluralistic. Currently, green is seen in certain pockets of societies among ecological, humanistic psychology, and human rights movements. In business, green can be seen in a trend toward employee-ownership, diversity, sensitivity training, political correctness, and global networks that link both like and diverse concerns.

Next comes yellow, a stage that intentionally provokes chaos, invites newness, and values flexibility and synchronicity. Knowledge and competency are valued; integration is key. Yellow is a futuristic stage, and no society currently exhibits yellow, but some "spiral wizards" see yellow thinking emerging in Stephen Hawking's *A Brief History of Time*, chaos theory, ecoindustrial parks, and in business, forward-thinking start-up companies and magazines such as *Wired*.

Ken Wilber says that a shift to yellow represents "second tier" thinking, whereby one can grasp the entire spectrum of development and see that each level is crucially important for the health of the overall spiral. From the heights of yellow, he imagines, a society or business could integrate each stage, rather than feeling that its worldview is the only correct one.

Turquoise, the final conceptual stage, values harmony and holistic principles. In turquoise, a business could see all of the many levels of interaction that are possible and utilize the state of "flow" for the best, easiest performance from individuals. One's work would be filled with vision and one's feelings and practical information would enhance each other. Turquoise societies would be attuned to the delicate balance of interlocking life forces and aspire to spiritual connectivity. Beck and Cowan see glimpses of turquoise in universal systems thinking, integral-holistic theories, Gandhi's and Mandela's pluralistic integration, and the growth of transpersonal psychology.

Beck and Cowan present their model as a formulation of spiral intelligence: They conceive of the spiral as an organizing principle with eight stages, which contains many disparate elements, can double back upon itself as spirals do, and is open to many different metaphors or perceptions, based on who is using or viewing the model. The following chart is a very brief representation of Beck and Cowan's color-coded spiral dynamics model. While this chart does not capture the complexity of their model as presented in their book, *Spiral Dynamics*, seeing each stage listed by its color, thought structure, and value-based bottom line makes it easier to apply the model pragmatically for our purposes.

Color	Thinking	Value Systems—Bottom Lines
Beige	Automatic	Basic survival
Purple	Animistic	Myths, traditions, and rituals
Red	Egocentric	Power, glory, and exploitation
Blue	Absolutist	Authority and stability
Orange	Materialistic	Success and material gain
Green	Humanistic	Equality and humanism
Yellow	Systemic	Choice and change
Turquoise	Holistic	Harmony and holism

ADAPTING THE MODEL FOR PRIVATE PRACTICE

As fascinating as this evolutionary model is, I found it needed some adaptation for use in small businesses. First, I saw that small businesses eventually go through all the stages of the model. And because business evolution is rarely linear, your practice may go through stages more than once. For example, if you build a practice and then move to a new city and have to start over, you will repeat the early stages of survival. But if you mastered the values and objectives of survival the first time, rebuilding is not nearly so difficult.

If you try to skip any stages, you may find yourself without the full range of skills and abilities that going through the stage would have offered you. I want you to be well-prepared for all situations, so I have adapted the model to do four things:

1. Explain the signals that alert you to the stage you are in or approaching.
2. Address the challenges of each stage.
3. Identify the tasks and objectives you need to learn.
4. Highlight the values and most positive aspects inherent in each stage.

Each month we will explore a few stages to help you understand your evolutionary path, position yourself securely for the future, and refine your practice in a value-oriented approach.

Here is a chart of the spiral dynamic color-coded stages as I have adapted them for your use. It emphasizes the tasks and objectives for you, the business owner, at each stage.

Color	Thinking	Spiral Dynamics Objectives Adapted for Therapists in Private Practice
Beige	Automatic	Counter instinct to go beyond survival.
Purple	Animistic	Remove the mystery from business.
Red	Egocentric	Claim power and deal with competition.
Blue	Absolutist	Optimize systems to promote stability.
Orange	Materialistic	Pursue opportunity and achievement.
Green	Humanistic	Temper entrepreneurial zeal with humanism.
Yellow	Systemic	Increase choices and invite newness.
Turquoise	Holistic	Build an ideal practice that flows.

BEIGE: COUNTER INSTINCT TO GO BEYOND SURVIVAL

This month we will look at the first three stages, all of which point you in the direction of developing more business stamina and endurance. By achieving the objectives of beige, the first stage, you learn how to go beyond survival. And since a small business can be counted on to go through ups and downs, knowing how to get beyond survival is a strategy that you will need to remember from time to time.

As mentioned earlier, the first step is to recognize the surface issues, feelings, and behaviors that signal that you and your practice are in beige; then we will look at what you need to do to meet the inherent challenges of that stage; lastly we will examine the strategies for meeting the objectives of beige, how to counter the "fight or flight" base instincts that survival elicits, and how to address your survival problems with a plan, instead of a panic, so that you learn to go beyond simply surviving and move forward.

At different points in their careers, any therapist in private practice can find herself or himself dealing with issues of survival. You might be brand new in private practice, in the "bootcamp" phase, and wondering how you will survive the year. You might be an experienced clinician who has suffered a drop in clients, due to an unexpected personal or professional crisis. Any number of circumstances can cause a therapist to find his or her entire practice, or one particular aspect of it, in beige.

No matter how you got there, the signals that you are in the beige survival stage are that you feel fearful and anxious. And given those feelings, it is not surprising that you may revert to reacting from instinct. While reacting from instinct is understandable in the face of fear, it rarely makes for good business. Let me give you an example:

Fred, 66, had been in private practice for a dozen years. Therapy is his second career and he is thinking about retiring. His wife unexpectedly developed a serious illness and needed a lot of care. He cut back his practice to almost nothing to take care of her and they moved out of state to be closer to their children. Fortunately his wife began to recover. However, her illness and his lack of productivity had taken a toll on their finances and Fred needed to get back into private practice and make some money soon. But he was exhausted, was living in a new city, and hated having to start over at this late point in life.

At a professional meeting in the new city he meets another therapist who asked him to form a partnership. Fred thought logically that they were strangers and that he should take his time to think this through, but his fear and his instincts to fear (fight or flight) pushed him to say yes, fast, as a way of making something happen. They signed a lease on a building, occurred debt to outfit the office, purchased expensive advertising, and signed a partnership agreement.

Clients came, his schedule filled, and Fred was finally working again. Then problems began to surface in the partnership. Over the next year the relationship between Fred and his partner became rancorous. Their personality differences now seem insolvable. Fred is making some money and working again, but in this specific aspect of his practice, his partnership, he finds himself in beige.

How does he know he is in survival? this constant feelings of fear and anxiety signal that he is in beige. "I can't sleep at night, thinking about how upset I am with my partner and my situation. When I do sleep, I have nightmares about this. I know I should ask for legal help, but I am paralyzed when it comes to spending any more money. I have no one to talk to, especially not my wife because she is recovering and I don't want to upset her; I don't have any colleagues here I really know or trust. I am trying to figure it out myself, going around and around the same issues. I just hate going into that office every day and my partner and I are no longer speaking. We have to memo each other any necessary communication. When anyone asks me how I am doing, I just say fine, but I'm not. I feel like this is a personal failure. I am ashamed. I reacted too quickly to being out of work and got myself into a mess."

Because being in beige feels like a personal failure, therapists feel embarrassed and cover up the problem; a sense of denial is all too common. Even though all our prior months' work together has tackled many of the things you need to know and do to build a strong practice, some aspect of your practice may still be in beige. We may not have adequately addressed this aspect to get it past survival, or you may not have clearly recognized or admitted that it exists. Now, in Month 9, this is your chance to enhance the work you have done so far and really strengthen your practice. Create more stamina and endurance as a way of adding some finishing touches by taking another clear look at your practice for any aspects that are survival-based and have not been dealt with adequately. Use the following checklist to identify if you are struggling with survival issues in any way, and then see the next strategy, *taking control*, that helps you to meet the challenges and go beyond them.

EXERCISE: KNOW THE SIGNALS OF BEIGE

Check those items that are true for you. Checking two or more items means that some aspect of your practice is in beige.

- ❑ I am secretly worried about all or some important aspect(s) of my practice.
- ❑ I feel blank or numb when I try to come up with solutions.
- ❑ I get good advice, but can't seem to follow through on any of it.
- ❑ I am in a reactive mode, feeling a lot of fear and anxiety, not a proactive mode.
- ❑ I am losing money, losing clients, losing sleep, and/or losing confidence.
- ❑ I don't want to ask for help (from supervisors, coaches, peers, other experts or consultants.)

- ❑ I don't have a plan, I don't like to think about the future of this problem, I just hope for the best.
- ❑ I won't invest any money to deal with this issue, even though it makes sense to get some help.
- ❑ This business problem is making me feel quite depressed.
- ❑ I am isolated and don't have anyone I can talk to.
- ❑ I feel embarrassed or ashamed that I have this problem.
- ❑ My practice (or some aspect of it) is worsening and making me feel like a failure.

Taking Control

Going through and then beyond survival, even the survival of one aspect of your practice, means that you will have to defy your fear-based instincts, which are counterproductive and push you in the unhelpful direction of fight or flight and impulsive action. You need a clear-thinking business-survival strategy to help you regain a sense of control, move you through your fear, and meet the challenges of beige. The survival strategy I want you to use, although simple, may not seem easy, because it asks a lot of you, just when you are feeling at your least resourceful. It requires that you have three elements:

1. a plan;
2. an intention;
3. a commitment.

Becoming planful is the first step to feeling more in control of your situation. Make a written daily, weekly, and monthly plan, and then follow them. Look at it every day. Modify it. The more structure you put in place when you are in beige, the better. This is the time to write a list of good habits and productive actions that you will take each day, each week, and each month, and then follow them, no matter what.

Along with the plan, you will need willpower, and you get that by connecting to a higher purpose, via your broadest intention. In beige, you will normally feel discouraged; your confidence is shaken. Fear makes us see in tunnel vision, with a narrow, tight focus. Take time each week to broaden your perspective and see the big picture, by remembering your intention. Lean back on your inner entrepreneur (Month 2) for constructive energy. Use affirmations, meditation, professional support, and anything else that helps you to feel connected. Remember your business vision. Go for daily walks in nature, pray, sing, chant, draw, be with others. Be as creative as you can for an hour each day. Use this energy to remotivate yourself on behalf of your business.

In addition to having a plan and intention, you also need to make a big commitment to your practice right now, even though you feel like pulling in and pulling back. You are building a business that you want to last: Invest in it now. If you don't make a large commitment, in terms of energy and resources, if you don't seriously invest in your practice even as it is failing, you may not have a practice left to discuss. The investment can be in the form of time, energy, money, training, supervision, coaching, support, or any other resource that will help you to build or rebuild your practice. Think big and take a major step in the direction of your future.

Reach out to those who have been through business ups and downs and who can help you put your business back on track. Join a professional group and go to the meetings. Let others who are wiser in business help you think through a plan and set goals, and then ask if you can be accountable to them in order to get yourself and your business back on track. And know that I am supporting you in your efforts to endure and succeed, no matter how long it takes.

EXERCISE: TAKE CONTROL IN BEIGE

Identify any aspect of your practice that is in beige and complete the following statements to help you become a businessperson that plans, instead of panics.

My Plan

My daily action plan consists of:_____

_____

_____

_____

_____

My weekly and monthly actions include: _____

_____

_____

_____

_____

My Intention

I am staying in a positive mind-set by:_____

_____

_____

_____

_____

My understanding of the big picture of my situation is: _____

_____

_____

_____

_____

My Commitment

The resources I am giving to my practice: _____

_____

_____

_____

_____

The support system helping me consists of:_____

_____

_____

_____

_____

→ FIELDWORK

Use the beige corrective strategy this month to fix any aspect of your practice currently in beige. Make sure you refer it each week and ask for help from others.

PURPLE: REMOVE THE MYSTERY FROM BUSINESS

To be successful in private practice, one needs more than stamina or endurance; one also needs fortitude. Fortitude develops as you become more comfortable being in command of your business operation. If you are surviving, but unsure about how your business works, either in totality or in some specific aspect, your feelings of confusion or bewilderment may signal that you are in the purple stage.

In purple, you are making a go of your practice, but business, either all of it or parts of it, including your successes or your failures, is still a mystery to you. You engage in magical thinking about your practice. Since you don't understand what accounts for your good or bad business results, you rely, consciously or unconsciously, on myth, tradition, superstition, or rituals. You deny your role and don't claim responsibility for what happens in your practice, because it really seems as though the reasons for what happens in your business have little to do with you.

I see the purple stage play out with therapists most often in three areas: money, clients, and organization.

One therapist says, "I never know how much money I have or am making until the end of the year when my accountant does my taxes. She figures it out. I just go through the year hoping for the best. Sometimes I get down pretty low in my bank account, other times it looks like I have plenty of money. I don't know how my finances work. Money somehow shows up when I need it."

Another says, "I am unlucky. I work hard, but maybe I work in the wrong area, or maybe I just have the wrong skills. I seem to end up with clients who are not serious about therapy. I miss out on opportunities all the time. I have bad luck with referrals."

Another says, "I do a lot of things with my paperwork and my billing that make no logical sense to me, but I feel afraid to change them. I don't want to rock the boat."

It's not unusual for very experienced, savvy therapists to have some aspect of their practice in the purple stage. A chiropractor who has been in business for 20 years and does well for herself has a very convoluted way of handling her billing. She has six different bank accounts she deposits checks into and out of. When I asked her about this, she immediately grew defensive. "I know it's odd, but this is the way I have been doing it for my entire time in practice. My accountant laughs at me and I feel somewhat ashamed of this and I agree it's cumbersome, but I don't think I should change it." Purple thinking when it comes to billing and an unconscious purple ritual to match.

Of course the primary solution for purple is to get more informed and knowledgeable about business. By this time in your practice-building program, if you have been following the exercises and suggestions in the workbook, you are well on your way in that direction. The following exercises are designed to supplement your ongoing action plan and give you a way to add some additional polish to your practice in this area.

Develop Conscious Rituals

Rituals in business are neither good nor bad; rather, they are useful or nonuseful, conscious or unconscious. If you develop useful rituals for your business, you can use them to reduce anxiety and increase business creativity.

The most anxiety-filled part of my work as a therapist/business coach has always been my role as a presenter. My personal struggle with performance anxiety has made this part of my work difficult for me. Over the past few years I have tried many things to overcome my anxiety: much coaching by experts, stress-reduction tools, energetic techniques, but remnants of the anxiety remain.

One of the most disconcerting parts of presenting is tied to my self-image, and I used to have a hard time deciding what to wear. Before a speaking engagement, it wasn't unusual for me to spend a miserable hour trying on and flinging off clothes that looked fine when I was packing my suitcase but, in the hour before the presentation starts, with my anxiety at fever pitch, all seem to look wrong.

One morning, watching me go through my last-minute clothing debacle prior to being part of a conference panel in front of several thousand people, my husband, an Italian and an admitted clotheshorse, said, "Honey, I think your problem is that you don't have any *good* clothes."

By *good*, he meant: You should have several presentation outfits that you never touch or wear except for speaking engagements. They should be the most expensive, best items of clothing in your closet. They should be the clothes that you absolutely love to own and to wear. Then you could look forward to getting dressed, knowing that speaking means you get wear your very favorite, most expensive, best-looking outfits.

I loved this idea: ritualized, very special clothing, worn to soothe the most difficult, anxious part of my work. Now I shop for special outfits that are only worn when I present and are awarded a special place of their own in my closet. These items represent luxury to me, but they are worth the expense. I feel calmer the moment I put these outfits on, no matter what city or country I am in. This is a useful and conscious purple ritual that I call *Having Good Clothes*.

EXERCISE: DESIGN A USEFUL PURPLE RITUAL

A useful, conscious ritual can help you achieve a sense of calm when your practice makes you feel anxious. Use the following format:

1. The anxiety-filled part of my practice I want to address is:_____

_____

_____

_____

2. My useful ritual will accomplish: _____

_____

_____

_____

3. The steps or aspects that create my useful ritual are:_____

_____

_____

_____

4. My name for this ritual is: _____

_____

_____

_____

➥ FIELDWORK

Now test this conscious ritual in the real world. Does it help reduce your anxiety? Make you feel more in control of a situation? Make life or work easier or more fun? If not, tinker with it so that it achieves these goals.

Increase Attentiveness

To evolve beyond purple, you need to become more actively curious and conscious about how things work in your business. Track the progress of your practice over time. Get better organized, watch your finances, upgrade your systems, and above all, recognize that intimately understanding all aspects of your business is not harmful, it is helpful.

You can bring your creativity and playfulness into this task by creating a metaphor to help you stay continually informed. The metaphor must have pleasurable associations for you, as it helps you to organize the daily work of maintaining your business and and keeps you interested in your business's needs and workings over time.

I use the metaphor of gardening. I learned to garden 10 years ago, when I moved to a house with a sunny side yard. I created a small kitchen garden planted with herbs, perennial flowers, and seasonal vegetables.

The needs of the garden are predictable and unrelenting. In the early spring I clean up the planting beds that are filled with debris, leaves, sticks, and old plants. I prune the roses and replace plants that did not survive the winter. I fertilize beds. I spend hours planting, weeding, and irrigating. As summer approaches I harvest my vegetables and weed or water daily. By late fall I hurriedly clean and prune, fertilize beds, and prepare for a dormant season. Then I rest during the winter and read gardening books, dreaming of new perennials to plant or finding a space for one more climbing rose bush.

My practice has similar needs. At times I am seeding the practice by thinking of new groups to run, making notes for the next book I want to write, or taking steps to establish new referral sources. I spend time eliminating or pruning the practice by cutting expenses that no longer serve me well. For example, after three years of paying for advertising with no results in a directory of mental health therapists, I ended my contract and "transplanted" those funds to other sources of advertising. With a business, as with a garden, something is always needed.

EXERCISE: THINK ABOUT YOUR PRACTICE AS A GARDEN

Think about your practice as a garden. What do you need to do this week, month, or season? Think about each took listed, make some notes next to each one, and list the actions you will take to maintain your practice.

fertilize_____

_____

weed_____

_____

organize _____

_____

prune _____

_____

seed _____

_____

plant_____

_____

transplant_____

_____

harvest _____

_____

irrigate _____

_____

prepare _____

_____

inventory _____

_____

rest _____

_____

dream _____

_____

RED: CLAIM POWER AND DEAL WITH COMPETITION

The red stage signifies the emergence of claiming business power. Having overcome the immediate crises of survival in beige, having removed the mystery from business in purple, you start to feel resilient. In red, you feel proud to have built a functioning private practice, you like manifesting your ideas and your vision, you like feeling capable in business. You can make things happen for yourself and your practice. You have staying power!

That's the good news.

Here's the bad: As your sense of a business self emerges, unwelcome feelings surface too. You feel protective of your ideas and your referral sources. You become territorial, vigilant, and watchful. Competition looms. Envy makes her grand entrance.

- How is it that Mary, right down the street, is doing better than I am and has more clients? She started her practice after I did and we have the same degree!
- What gives Joe the nerve to charge $120 for individual therapy sessions? I have as much experience as he does and I only charge $85!

- Why does Pat have so much of an easier time filling her workshops than I do?
- Why does Ed pay for such a large ad in the local magazine? What does he know that I don't?

Welcome to Red, the stage where you learn to claim power, expand your business awareness, and deal with competition. If you want to keep growing, you can't avoid red. The old maxim, "What doesn't kill us makes us stronger" applies especially to the red stage. Two strategies for having an easier time with the challenges inherent in the red stage are:

1. Define yourself versus defend yourself.
2. Transform envy into excellence.

Define Yourself Versus Defend Yourself

When anyone feels threatened and protective, he or she naturally becomes defensive. But if, in the red stage, you position your practice defensively, you will find yourself taking action and making decisions based not on who you are and what is right for you, but as a reaction to what your competitors are or are not doing. Defensive positioning distracts you from your business vision and makes owning a business much less satisfying.

Carol has had an occupational therapy practice for 3 years. She has 15 hours filled each week, not quite a full practice, but getting there. Beth is another occupational therapist in the same city, whom Carol knows and respects. The two therapists have similar ways of working and similar specialty areas; Carol feels they are often competing for referrals and opportunities. Carol complains, "Every time I go visit a doctor or a potential referral source, he or she says to me, "Do you know Beth? You two do such similar work."

Carol keeps an eye on what Beth does. When Beth takes an ad in a newspaper advertising her services, Carol thinks she should so that too, to keep up. When Beth gives a talk to the local hospital, Carol feels pressured to find a similar venue for herself, to keep up. She runs her practice defensively, trying to keep up with Beth.

The problem is that Carol has her own goals, her own vision, and when she stays so focused on Beth, she forgets herself. One day she called me excitedly to say she had just agreed to give a series of weekly classes on coping after a major illness at the local recreation center. "Last time Beth did these classes, but they agreed to use me this time, " she crowed. I asked her to tell me about the classes. "Well, actually they take a lot of time. I will be spending about two hours on each class each week, preparing for it and then giving it. It's on a Tuesday night, which is my bowling league night, so I will miss my bowling for 2 months, I guess." She began to sound less sure of herself.

"What do you get paid?" I asked.

"I get $25 for each one-hour class."

"Hmm. That is much lower than your hourly session rate. Do you see this as a marketing experience? Will you get clients from doing this?"

"You know, I don't think so. Most of the people who attend really don't go further with therapy than the class."

"What do you get from this, then? It doesn't pay well, you can't use it for marketing, it takes time out from one of your most favorite activities." I asked.

"I don't know. I didn't think through it that far. I just know Beth wanted it and I got it instead."

In the face of competition, how do you hold onto yourself and stay the course? Do you get caught up with what others are doing? The best way I know to define yourself is to keep reviewing your vision and your goals, to remember your direction, to stay true to what is important for you.

EXERCISE: REVIEW YOUR BUSINESS VISION

In Month 4, you wrote your vision, purpose, and mission statement. Review it now and then answer the following questions.

How does my business vision, purpose, and mission statement look to me today?

_____

_____

_____

_____

_____

Do I need to make any changes to it or update it to have it reflect who I am and what I now know?

_____

_____

_____

_____

_____

What progress have I achieved?

_____

_____

_____

_____

What steps am I taking this month to move forward?

_____

_____

_____

_____

How can I stay true to myself and my direction, even when others are taking a different route that also looks good to me?

_____

_____

_____

_____

MONTHLY SKILL SET: TRANSFORM ENVY INTO EXCELLENCE

During the red stage, envy visits us. Since I go in and out of the red stage in my business evolution, I, too, feel envious of others from time to time. I used to feel embarrassed about my envy; after all it isn't a "nice" emotion. At the root of my envy, and perhaps yours as well, is longing and desire for more: more power, more money, more success, more ease, more fun, more fame—you name it. I long for things that feel beyond my reach, and when I see that they exist in others, I am jealous.

But, I am also curious. Asking questions has been a great antidote for my envy. I approach therapists and coaches whose success I envy and ask to interview them. "How did you do it?" I ask. I really want to know, and before too long my envy has shifted into admiration or fascination as I discern someone else's take on life or work. I love learning, and envy has been a springboard for learning. The objects of my envy have become my teachers, generously showing me how to achieve results more easily, more elegantly, or with a lot more intelligence than I could have ever imagined.

When I hear about a strategy for success, I play with it. I try it out, adapt it, use it, ask others to use it, and then finally devise a version I can teach. When you learn how to model and adapt strategies of success, you never need to feel envious for very long.

You have probably already had some business experience with modeling. When I first wanted to know how to be a therapist, I looked to my own therapist/supervisor, Marilyn Ellis, LCSW. Marilyn is a very successful psychotherapist who developed a unique style of practice, and she was a generous model for me and for several dozen other therapists in my local area that she supervised. Some of her supervisees built practices that followed her model very closely, and others borrowed her model and modified it to fit their style of working. She is always open to helping others develop their own successful practices and she taught me a lot about being an excellent therapist and operating a diverse private practice.

Many therapists have a similar experience of trying to model an admired therapist or supervisor, trying to emulate his or her practice and hoping for similar results. But the skill of modeling can be complicated, and the results are often uneven.

Model Success

When trying to model someone else's strategies, paint with a broad brush at first: Try to identify and replicate everything. Once you begin to get results, then you can refine and eliminate unnecessary elements. At this point you will be able to adapt the strategy to fit your style.

One of my close friends lost 10 pounds and got very buff and strong. I liked how she looked with her weight loss and her toned muscles. I was jealous first and curious second, so I decided to model her success and asked her to tell me exactly how she accomplished her weight loss. She explained her regimen in detail. It started with getting up early each morning to exercise, a part of the regimen she felt was very important for several reasons. Now, I hate to get up early, so I listened but secretly decided not to model that part. She eliminated all sugar in her diet. I love dessert and decided I would also not follow that part. She hired a trainer for weight definition. I am too busy for another appointment in my calendar and decided not to model that part. Did I succeed at her plan? Of course not. Here's a better way to model success:

EXERCISE: REPLICATE RESULTS

Use this process to identify and model strategies for success:

1. Think about something you desire for your business and identify someone who gets the results you would like to achieve. He or she is your model.
2. Observe or interview that person to try to understand all the elements of his or her strategy. If you can't interview this person, observe all you can and deduce the rest.
3. Give the strategy you are modeling a name (*e.g., Getting Buff and Strong*).
4. State the goal and objectives of the model.
5. List the elements (based on observation and/or interview with the therapist).
6. Include a time line of how long you will work at this to achieve it, and add markers along the way.
7. Include a specific budget of money, energy, and other resources.
8. Develop a way to track your results.

➔ FIELDWORK

Use this exercise to transform something you have envied about another person into a model or a strategy you can follow, and begin this month. Get support for this by telling someone in your professional support system what you are up to. Devote sufficient resources to your modeling attempt. Don't scrimp.

Monthly Review

This month you explored the first 3 stages of a color-coded evolutionary model that focuses on how to make your practice stronger with more staying power. The fieldwork for Month 9 includes:

■ Design a beige corrective strategy to correct any aspect of your practice that is barely surviving. Make sure you refer to it each week and ask for help from others.

■ Use your conscious ritual in the real world. Note whether is helps reduce your anxiety, and/or makes life or work easier or more fun. If not, tinker with it so that it achieves these goals.

■ Add a new model or strategy into your practice or your life that has previously been a source of envy. Get support for this, by telling someone in your professional support system what you are up to.

■ *In addition,* stay in close contact with your professional support system (review Month 3). Continue to use a business affirmation each month to sustain your intentions (review Month 2). Pursue your goals and objectives on your monthly prep form, prioritizing for ease and then completing the easiest ones first (review Month 1).

MONTH 10
Optimization: Upgrading Your Practice

The early stages of business evolution that we explored last month—beige, purple and red—can make an entrepreneur feel on edge and hypervigilant. Business seems like a rough ocean, with lots of ups and downs. You may long for calmer waters and where "no problem" becomes your motto. If so, you are ready to explore the blue stage of spiral dynamics, where the business owner's objective is to create a well-systemized, smooth-functioning, upgraded private practice. Sound good? Read on.

Even if you are still in the midst of the earlier stages, you can help your practice make this shift to blue by first evaluating the current status of your operations and then moving them in the direction of optimization. Here is a quick way to see if you have downgraded your practice in any of four distinct areas—management, organization, connection, or entrepreneurial drive. Review the Downgrade Checklist to see how you measure up: Checking even one item can mean that you need to put the next strategy, the Practice Upgrade Plan, into effect.

Optimize and upgrade your practice. This month, focus on strategies that enhance your practice management, broaden your network, and diversify your services so that you can run a problem-free operation that can handle continued growth. Also, get comfortable with a normal and important entrepreneurial emotion: ambition.

My Monthly Prep Form

Answering these questions each month will help you to chart your progress and define your next goals.

1. What have I accomplished since last month that I feel positive about? What are my wins?

2. What challenges am I facing this month?

3. What opportunities are available to me right now?

4. What blocks me from taking advantage of these opportunities?

5. How could I make life or work easier or better for myself right now?

6. My goals for this month are:

EXERCISE: DOWNGRADE CHECKLIST

Check what is true for you at this time. Checking a minimum of 5 out of the 20 items signals a practice that is not optimal and needs upgrading.

- ❏ I have too many tasks to do each day and never get a sense of completion.
- ❏ I don't put aside a regular time during my week for my administrative or financial responsibilities.
- ❏ My papers are sitting in piles on the floor or desk, anywhere but in a filing cabinet.
- ❏ I would feel better and perhaps work better if I were more organized.
- ❏ Other people (my clients, family members, friends) have been known to complain or tease me about my lack of organization or my messy office.
- ❏ I make mistakes with clients (errors, double-booking, etc.) due to my level of inefficiency or distraction.
- ❏ When my office is cluttered, I feel cluttered and less peaceful inside my mind.
- ❏ I put off doing all paperwork until the end of the day, when I am most tired.
- ❏ I need staff for my scheduling, filing, billing, or other administrative tasks that I can't fully handle, but I am reluctant to pay for or ask for help.
- ❏ I work alone all day and feel isolated.
- ❏ I miss collegiality and wish I were part of a bigger system or that I worked with others.
- ❏ I have a very insular life, socially and professionally.
- ❏ I have a limited number of professional contacts.
- ❏ I feel like a very small practice and wish I were larger or more solid.
- ❏ I have weak community ties.
- ❏ I haven't built a reputation in my field even though I have been in my profession for a long time.
- ❏ I think small and miss out on seeing the opportunities or growth that others spot more easily.
- ❏ My practice doesn't feel like a real business; it's more of a hobby.

❏ I don't know what growth or expansion would mean for my practice or how to get there.

❏ I don't have feelings of drive or ambition, which I see and admire in others.

BLUE: OPTIMIZE SYSTEMS TO PROMOTE STABILITY

If you checked any signals of downgrading as being true for you, you need a plan to help you upgrade your practice: to improve your practice management, increase your stability, expand your offerings, enhance your connections with others, build a stronger reputation, and get more comfortable with normal entrepreneurial feelings, such as ambition. The blue stage promotes all of these objectives for a business owner, and gives you ways to let your small practice feel larger and more stable.

This month you will be using a five-point plan that does all that. At each step of the plan you will find exercises and fieldwork to consider, as well as skills to learn and practice.

The Practice Upgrade Plan
1. Run a business, not a hobby.
2. Diversify your services.
3. Connect to a broader network.
4. Go beyond competency.
5. Embrace your ambition.

Run a Business, not a Hobby

Some therapists approach their private practice as a hobby, not a serious business. Turning a therapy practice that is essentially a hobby into a business feels like growing up. It's time to take your practice by the hand and, like a responsible parent, give it some tough love to help it mature.

In earlier months, you inventoried your current practice policies. Now it's time to review your policies and remove all the hobby elements or inconsistent aspects of your practice management. Use the Practice Management Checklist in the next exercise. Feel free to adapt this checklist so that it resonates with your particular practice, adding or subtracting items as needed to make it relevant for your business. There are 20 items on the checklist that signify good practice management. If you can check off every item as true, you are firmly in the blue stage and have a professionally managed practice. If you leave many items unchecked, you are in the beginning stages of Blue, and can use the checklist items as goals to add to your monthly prep form to help you evolve.

EXERCISE: PRACTICE MANAGEMENT CHECKLIST

Check each item that is true for you. This checklist functions as a guide for optimal management. Complete the fieldwork that follows this checklist, and return to this list during the next several months until you can check off all the items and have an efficiently managed practice.

- ❑ I use a written business plan, which lists my objectives and goals, to guide my practice.
- ❑ I know my top five business goals for this year and the action steps to take in order to accomplish each one.
- ❑ I continually look and ask for ways to upgrade my administration systems, including billing, record keeping, and filing.
- ❑ I have an accountant, lawyer, and business coach to whom I can turn for advice.
- ❑ I am in control of my day-to-day operations.
- ❑ Each working day I take one action designed to strengthen my business.
- ❑ I return calls promptly and follow up on information in a timely manner.
- ❑ I devote one specific time each week to handling all my business paperwork.
- ❑ My office is well organized and set up to let me do my best work.
- ❑ If I employ staff, we have first-rate communication. They know how to please me and perform their job with minimum input from me.
- ❑ My office is a pleasant environment for both me and my staff.
- ❑ I have a client policy sheet that states all my policies in writing. It is openly displayed in my waiting room and given to each new and prospective client.
- ❑ My clients know that I will hold firmly to the boundaries of my policies.

❏ I educate my clients about how they can get the most out of our working relationship in therapy and become my ideal clients.

❏ My time at work is a valuable commodity and I manage it carefully.

❏ At least 75% of my total time at work is spent doing what I do best—seeing clients and delivering service.

❏ No more than 10% of my time at work is spent handling paperwork or on unbilled calls or meetings.

❏ I reserve 10% of my working time for training, reading, writing, contemplating, networking, or learning so that I stay energetic, interested, and on top of my field.

❏ The remaining 5% of my working time each week is spent working on the business—improving the overall health of my practice.

❏ I discuss my practice management policies with a coach or colleagues whom I trust, so that I can get feedback and advice to continually improve my business.

➜ FIELDWORK

Pick three items this month to complete on the Practice Management Checklist. Adopt higher professional standards. Take a long, hard look at all of your policies. Let a trusted colleague or a business coach review your practice operations and help you correct the areas that are weak and inconsistent, so that you can have the professional feel of a larger company, even though you may be a small business.

Diversify Your Services

There are many strategies of diversification that a sole practitioner can use, to feel like he or she is in a bigger practice. Diversifying does three things for a small business:

- It allows you to have more than one source of income and energy fueling your practice. A highly diversified practice can eliminate the feelings of boredom some practitioners face from doing the same thing every day.
- A diversified practice eliminates a sense of boredom within your clients by giving them more than one choice. Each of us likes to have choices. When you go to a restaurant, you expect to be able to choose from a

menu of items. Your clients may appreciate some choices within your business, too.

- Diversification lets you develop additional "practice muscles." Years ago, health-fitness experts realized the value in cross-training—incorporating more than one form of exercise into a workout to keep an athlete in peak condition. Just like an athlete, it's good for therapists to become cross-trainers, to diversify, to become more flexible, versatile, and well-balanced.

EXERCISE: DEVELOP MULTIPLE PROFIT CENTERS

Circle the items you want to include in your services. The goal of each service is to generate income for your practice.

- workshops
- classes or groups
- weekend retreats
- telephone or e-mail consultations
- on-site consulting for corporations and organizations
- organizational development (team building, mediation, leadership training, etc.)
- conducting assessments or supplying testing materials
- expert witness testimony
- self-publishing and distributing books, workbooks, or pamphlets
- audiotapes
- videotapes
- additional product sales
- writing articles, books, or other materials for outside publication
- radio or television appearances
- public speaking engagements
- other training or teaching endeavors
- program development for yourself or others
- licensing your programs to others
- Web site with membership fee

→ FIELDWORK

Add an additional profit center to your practice within the next six months; make it a permanent feature of your business. Set aside the resources, space, and a budget to finance the profit center and treat it like a separate, yet valuable part of your existing practice. Track the income and time involved separately. Note the cross-referrals it gives you. When it is well established, consider adding another one. If you add one additional profit center each year, you will have a full, diversified practice within five years.

Connect to a Broader Network

When I coach individual clients, I often recommend that they double the amount of people they know. I do this because the current thinking about networking is changing. The old business maxim *It's not what you know, it's who you know* has changed to *It's not who you know, it's* how many *you know*.

One of my favorite writers, Malcom Gladwell, wrote a book about small things that have a huge impact. *The Tipping Point* looked at the business and social power that is inherent in the quantity, not quality, of relationships you can develop. The power comes not from the depth of your relationships, but from their sheer number. Using a series of studies he showed that those who know the most people, especially superficially, have a much greater chance to gain business success. Superficial acquaintances will actually provide you with more reach and success than friends and family, because the acquaintances who operate outside of your natural social or business world are more likely to broaden your reach. Gladwell concluded that the new definition of poverty is not deprivation—it's isolation.

Therapists in a sole proprietorship are often the most isolated (and at times impoverished) businesspeople I know. Therapists tend to be isolated by the type of work they do, which is private and confidential; by the nature of their introverted personalities; and isolated by the lack of networking within and between various therapy professions. Overcoming the poverty of isolation will be one of the most important strategies of expansion you can acquire, and it must become a lifelong pursuit. Here are five possible steps to take that can broaden your network and how to achieve each one.

1. *Form alliances.* You can become part of an alliance or group practice. *How to do it:* Forming alliances with others is a creative endeavor that can function in many ways. Form a group practice that bands together in one office, sharing rent and expenses, generating referrals for each other, and enjoying the energy and collegiality that is created by a larger practice. Or join with others to operate as an association without walls: Each therapist maintains a separate office, but participates together in a range of events or to share costs. Jointly sponsor workshops, share print or direct-mail advertising costs that promote the entire group, form a regular supervision or professional support group, or even share administrative help that rotates from office to office.

2. *Cultivate diversity in your professional network.* It's easy to isolate yourself professionally and socially. It takes intention to have a life outside of your work. *How to do it:* Cultivate more diversity within your professional network by connecting with those who are in other professions. Start with small steps. Seek out difference. Gravitate to any committee or activity that is new to you. Your networking efforts might include connecting with groups of businesspeople, teachers, community activists, and a variety of therapy professionals to give you access and reach within some other pockets of your local community. Take a day a week to have lunch with business owners who are clearly outside your field. After one year, you will have 50 new sources for ideas, expanded thinking, and referrals. You can also network professionally online, using the Internet to join the e-mail lists of professional groups.

3. *Develop more hobbies.* You can let your network expand naturally by developing hobbies and pursuing them with the same energy you give to your work. *How to do it:* If you tend to be consumed with work, add a hobby and get to know others engaged in the same pursuit. Your hobby will do many things for you professionally; it will give you rich metaphors to use with clients, challenge you in ways that your profession does not, and hopefully get you out of your office and out of your house, enabling you to develop more connections with others.

4. *Read outside your field.* Purposefully try to open your mind to all points of view and new topics. *How to do it:* Look at what you read and make sure it's broadly based. Read magazines that stretch you to understand a new point of view. This strategy offers several benefits: Reading outside your field is a great way to develop a broader understanding of topics to use as metaphors with your clients, so that you can illustrate therapeutic ideas using nontherapeutic

words. It will also give you some topics to talk about when you are making small talk, an essential skill for effective networking.

5. *Expand your "weak ties."* Pursue acquaintances, not just old friends. *How to do it:* The key to Gladwell's strategy is to appreciate and pursue those less-than-profound relationships. Cultivate acquaintances, not just friends. More is more. Take a break from deep relationships and let yourself get to know a lot more people.

EXERCISE: BROADEN YOUR NETWORK

Answer the following questions to identify your current networks and how to expand them.

What networks am I connected to right now?

_____

_____

_____

_____

_____

How I can build on my current efforts or create a new strategy to broaden my network?

_____

_____

_____

_____

_____

What resources do I need to put my plan in action?

_____

_____

_____

_____

_____

What specific steps will I take this month?

____

____

____

____

____

→ FIELDWORK

Pick one network-broadening strategy (form alliances, cultivate diversity, develop hobbies, read outside your field, or expand weak ties). Use your answers to the above exercise to create a plan. Take steps this month to broaden your network.

Go Beyond Competency

There are approximately 500,000 clinically trained psychotherapists (social workers, psychologists, licensed counselors, and psychiatrists) in the United States; each year, thousands more graduate from school. The number of massage therapists is skyrocketing, too. Ten years ago 90 schools taught massage therapy; today you can find close to 900. The field of personal coaching has exploded, with an estimated 10,000 people calling themselves coaches; training centers and associations are forming to train and accredit thousands more. The marketplace is filled with experienced therapists who are trying to stay in business, as well as newer therapists who are just getting started and are willing to charge low prices. To succeed in this market, you need to build a reputation by honing your skills and highlighting your experience.

EXERCISE: HIGHLIGHT YOUR EXPERIENCE

Answers the following questions.

How could I become truly excellent in my practice? (*Hint:* Find one specific aspect of your practice to master, not everything.)

_____

_____

My plan:

_____

_____

_____

_____

What is my an annual investment in training to maintain excellence? (*Hint:* In this market, you need to stay on top. Try to invest 5% of your gross income in training.)

_____

_____

My plan:

_____

_____

_____

_____

Have I oriented my practice around my area of greatest expertise? (*Hint:* When you are putting a lot of time and money into a specific area of your training, make sure you put this area of expertise at the center of your services. This is what you want to become known for.)

_____

_____

My plan:

_____

_____

_____

_____

_____

Does my professional image match my level of mastery? (*Hint:* Make sure you are charging a high enough fee. Packaging conveys meaning, like it or not.)

_____

_____

My plan:

_____

_____

_____

_____

_____

_____

➵ FIELDWORK

Pick one of these four action steps to help you to go beyond competency and decide on a long-term plan, one that you can accomplish during the remainder of the year that will increase your reputation and mastery of your craft. Write down your plan and take the first step now.

MONTHLY SKILL SET: EMBRACE YOUR AMBITION

In 1996 I attended the International Coaching Federation annual conference. The ICF has grown to become the largest professional association of coaches, with 5,000 members in 30 countries, but in 1996 it was a newly formed organization and just a few hundred members came to the conference. Our keynote speaker was Cheryl Richardson who was the ICF President at the time, and her topic was building a coaching practice. (Cheryl is now a *New York Times* best-selling author and a frequent guest on Oprah and other television shows, but at that time she was less well-known and the coaching profession was still quite new.) She told the audience that her coach, Thomas Leonard, had advised her that one of the easiest ways to build a successful coaching practice was for her to decide to become the very best in her field. He encouraged her to set no limits on her abilities, her role, or her drive. As she spoke, she expressed some surprise to find herself having risen to the top of her profession in such a short time, with an even bigger vision ahead of her.

I thought about her talk in the following months. As the daughter of an entrepreneur, I understood the desire for business success, but as a social worker and a new coach, ambition did not sit well. I wondered how to reconcile the desire to be of service with the desire to be at the top of one's profession. How would aiming high make practice building easier? I questioned my preconceptions about ambition. What if ambition, instead of signifying something negative to me, such as self-absorption and narcissism, was really a type of fuel that fed big visions?

Without giving free reign to my ambition, I tended to keep a lid on my goals and vision. I didn't allow myself to imagine great things for myself, only good things. I avoided opportunities, and potential connections that seemed too large for me, and didn't allow myself to get too enthusiastic or excited, for fear I would just get disappointed. With my great discomfort about ambition, I kept any visionary thoughts about my practice to myself.

But as I began to play with the notion of ambition as fuel, I could see that it was a natural entrepreneurial emotion and an important energy source that helped to invigorate big dreams. Ambition acts like a stimulant and helps me aim higher, do more, and spread my wings. I don't always act on my feelings of ambition, as I don't act on every feeling that goes through me, but I learned to embrace, accept, and enjoy the feelings as they emerge. Recognize and embrace your feelings of ambition, too, which are a natural consequence of your becoming more entrepreneurial.

EXERCISE: RECOGNIZE YOUR AMBITION AS FUEL

Answering the following questions can help you normalize this entrepreneurial emotion, and allow your feelings of ambition to fuel your goals.

1. What did I learn about ambition from my family or from my history?

    _____

    _____

    _____

2. How might letting my feelings of ambition surface help me in manifesting my vision?

    _____

    _____

    _____

3. What do I fear about letting my natural ambition surface?

    _____

    _____

    _____

4. What needs to shift inside me to understand ambition as a fuel?

    _____

    _____

    _____

5. What steps can I take to get more comfortable with this feeling in daily life? In professional life?

    _____

    _____

    _____

6. What specific time will I put aside each week for daydreaming, meditating and being open to thoughts of my business vision, letting all my feelings (including those of ambition) emerge?

_____

_____

_____

Monthly Review

This month we looked at a five-point upgrade plan to help your business become more polished and systemized. Your fieldwork for Month 10 includes:

■ Check more items on the Practice Management Checklist. Adopt higher professional standards and ask more of yourself as a therapist, and of your clients. Run a tight business, not a loose hobby.

■ Add an additional profit center to your practice within the next six months as a permanent feature of your business. Set aside the resources, space, and a budget to finance the profit center and treat it like a separate, yet valuable part of your existing practice.

■ Plan to take steps to broaden your existing network.

■ Decide on a long-term plan to enhance your reputation. Take the first step this month, but make the plan one to accomplish over time.

■ *In addition*, continue to use a marketing plan, one that helps you to structure your efforts and measures your progress (review Month 6).

MONTH 11
Expansion: Increasing Your Capacity for Growth

To stay on the cutting edge of your profession, you need to welcome opportunity and growth. You need to shape your practice to reflect your personal development and to respond to the changing marketplace. This month, we examine the stage of evolution that values entrepreneurial energy, expansion, and possibility thinking, and that encourages you, as the business owner, to pursue opportunity and achievement: the orange stage. We also address how to add humanistic values to your entrepreneurial zeal: the green stage.

"I am chomping at the bit, ready to leave managed care (the blue stage) after eight years," a psychologist says. "I have a full practice in managed care and I have mastered the bureaucracy and the procedures it requires. But I want to earn better money and I want to feel autonomous. I want to treat patients my own way, without having to get an insurer to approve my methods each step of the way. I've been a company man, now I want to be my own man."

Another therapist says, "I want to shift into a career in consulting. I've been a family therapist forever. I would be reaching out to a new market and having more impact, in a bigger pond, with a bigger payoff."

Another therapist says, "I feel ready to take on more in my life. I want to explore. I want to double and then triple the size of my practice, add staff, employ other therapists, buy a large building, create a holistic health center."

Feeling entrepreneurial, wanting to achieve more, seeking new directions, or making a break for independ-

Expansion and growth are important goals for many small-business owners. This month, expand your practice by learning how to select the best opportunities for growth and prioritize your use of time. Then add balance to your expansion plan to become a model of the services you offer, as you create strong community connections.

My Monthly Prep Form

Answering these questions each month will help you to chart your progress and define your next goals.

1. What have I accomplished since last month that I feel positive about? What are my wins?

2. What challenges am I facing this month?

3. What opportunities are available to me right now?

4. What blocks me from taking advantage of these opportunities?

5. How could I make life or work easier or better for myself right now?

6. My goals for this month are:

ence all signal that a natural, inevitable, evolutionary shift is about to occur, taking you, the business owner, from the safety and security of blue into the dynamic, entrepreneurial zeal of orange.

ORANGE: PURSUE OPPORTUNITY AND ACHIEVEMENT

In orange, the self seeks meaning in individualistic terms. The business owner seeks accomplishment in entrepreneurial terms. As a result, orange can feel quite energizing and exciting. Business becomes a way of learning more about who you are and how the world works—you test out your abilities, form strategic alliances, and manifest your goals and vision.

You may already be in orange, in which case this month will help you polish and direct your entrepreneurial energy. Or you may be in an earlier stage but wanting to add some of this zeal into your current life. To approach the orange stage, you need to adopt the abundance attitude that we explored in Month 2, whereby you believe that expansion is possible for you. It's very difficult to grow your business if you don't believe that there is enough out there—enough ideal clients, enough money to be made, enough prospects and opportunity, or enough resources for you to have the practice you desire.

Having an abundance attitude doesn't mean that you live in a fantasy. A successful entrepreneur holds dual realities: You see life as it is, with its pragmatic limitations, and at the same time you see that opportunity is ever present.

A *Washington Post* article "No Fat Cats Allowed" (August 17, 2002) described a Young Entrepreneurs' Organization (YEO) seminar in Washington, DC, attended by hundreds of CEOs who create businesses of all kinds that average $5 million in gross revenue. The reporter noted that the YEO attendees shared one common notion—their unshakeable optimism about the vast opportunity they saw for themselves and others, even in the face of an unstable, unpredictable marketplace.

If having an abundance attitude is the first step for moving into orange, an eagerness to take action is the second. While it's nice to sit back and meditate on abundance, taking action makes things happen. But with so much opportunity, what actions are best to take? Imagine you are standing on the bank of a swiftly flowing river. Business opportunities, potential clients, and collaborative possibilities are rushing by. If you stand on the bank, the river seems to move fast and you only get a fleeting glance at the opportunities before they are gone. You are safe and dry, and wondering: How do I get into that flow without getting my feet too wet? Answer: You can't.

You will need to wade out, making some missteps along the way as you navigate the rocks and hidden pockets of silt and dirt, maybe falling down a time or two, holding a strong intention about the your ability to withstand the flow. As you finally learn to stand in the flow of the river comfortably, swaying gently with the currents, you can see close at hand all that goes by you, and decide when to make your move.

Spotting Opportunities

When a therapist complains that there is *too* much opportunity at his or her doorstep and it all looks enticing, I know I am coaching someone in the orange stage. "There is so much I would like to do. It all has potential. What do I tackle first?" I am asked.

Each month in your prep form you have a space to note the opportunities that are available to you. I put this in the prep form hoping that it would help to open your eyes to the opportunities that surround all of us. But you may still be missing some important opportunities because you don't recognize what is flowing by, or don't know how to sort through the multitude of possibilities in order to select the ones that are right for you (by right for you, I mean those that will help you achieve your stated business vision). Opportunity comes in so many different forms. Use this checklist to note those that exist or you could create.

EXERCISE: EXISTING OPPORTUNITIES CHECKLIST

Check the existing opportunities you see for yourself, and circle those that you are not ready to move toward now, but will consider in the future.

- ❑ partnering with others in new ways;
- ❑ brainstorming with colleagues about growing my practice;
- ❑ networking with new people just for fun;
- ❑ thinking bigger and bolder;
- ❑ reorganizing what I already have or do;
- ❑ finding more than enough needed resources;

- ❏ making additional phone calls or recontacting potential referral sources;
- ❏ modeling a successful strategy of someone else and following through to make it my own;
- ❏ spending money to make more money;
- ❏ trying something brand new in my business, just because I want to;
- ❏ taking a bold risk that resonates with my vision;
- ❏ doing something that no one else I know has tried;
- ❏ doing something that everyone else I know has tried;
- ❏ taking a class or a workshop that stretches my skills;
- ❏ completing everything on my to-do list within one week;
- ❏ saying yes to things I would normally reject;
- ❏ doubling my goals in my prep form for the month and accomplishing them all;
- ❏ going into unfamiliar situations just to experience novelty;
- ❏ creating a project, budgeting for the project, and carrying it out to completion.

Answer these questions to further identify opportunities. Based on your answers, decide which opportunities you might pursue this month.

1. What is missing in my business or life right now?

   _____

   _____

2. What do I wish I could create?

   _____

   _____

3. What feels beyond my reach and why?

   _____

   _____

4. What aspect of my business vision is still not manifesting for me?

   _____

   _____

5. What opportunities are available to me that I currently don't take advantage of?

_____

_____

6. What will it take for me to act on these opportunities?

_____

_____

7. What opportunities are available to me if I extend my reach and really stretch?

_____

_____

8. What is it worth to me to make this happen?

_____

_____

9. What is my first step?

_____

_____

10. When will I take it?

_____

_____

11. Who will I ask to support my endeavors?

_____

_____

Sorting Opportunities

As you begin to tap into the abundant flow of opportunities, you may feel overwhelmed and in need of direction. Entrepreneurial types are known for having too many irons in the fire, saying yes more than they say no, needing to sort and prioritize on a regular basis. Even if you are not yet highly entrepreneurial, you still need a way to evaluate opportunities you spot. To select the best opportunities for yourself, develop a filter. A filter is a screen of questions you look through, similar to a photographer's lens, to bring certain objects into sharp focus and blur the rest.

Simone is an executive coach with a lot of marketing ideas, projects, and plans. She is very good at designing a plan and getting it off the ground, and as a result she has a strong business going with many new projects in the works. She spends 80 hours a week in her office, and her husband and children complain that she is the "invisible woman."

My work as her coach is to help her concentrate on her priorities and take things off her plate. I coach her to ask herself two filtering questions when evaluating whether a "great, brilliant" new opportunity is right for her.

1. What am I willing to delegate or let go of in order to take on this new project?
2. Will it cut into my existing family time?

Unless she can eliminate something or delegate it, and unless she can answer no to the second question, she does not get my okay, as her coach, to take on a new project. We laugh together as she tries to creatively negotiate or bargain with me about adding more into her schedule, because the new opportunities seem very compelling, but we both know that for her, this is serious business. The path to a well-lived life is not always defined by what we add into our already busy lives; sometimes a great life is achieved by what we let go of.

EXERCISE: FILTERING OPPORTUNITIES

Pick one opportunity from the previous exercise that interests you and use the following set of questions to evaluate it.

1. Is it profitable? If so, what is the timeline for profitability?
2. Will this take me closer or further from my business vision?
3. Will this make me a better therapist, coach, or healer?
4. Will this be fun, an adventure, uplifting, good for my soul?
5. Will this help me create more community in my life or isolate me?
6. What other paths could this lead to?
7. What does my head say about this? What is my gut feeling?
8. What will I lose if I say no?

9. What will this cost me if I say yes?
10. What will this give me?
11. What do I need to let go of or delegate in order to take this on?

→ FIELDWORK

Pick several or all the filtering questions from the above list to evaluate the opportunities that you spot this month. Based on the answers to your questions, decide if an opportunity or project is one you want to act on or pass on. If you decide to act on an opportunity, make a plan, get support, and go for it!

Prioritize Your Time

For most entrepreneurs, time is a prized asset. Time is often more valuable than money. To protect and best use your time, devote concentrated blocks of time to each activity, instead of doing things piecemeal. Rely on your calendar to guide your use of time. For example, schedule a minimum of two hours in your calendar each week (a block of two hours on one day, or one hour on two days of the week) for administrative time (such as posting checks, creating invoices, filing, returning calls, scheduling clients, writing treatment reports, reviewing client notes, preparing written materials, responding to e-mails, etc.), instead of just trying to fit it in five minutes here or there.

I like to divide my weeks into work, spirit, and buffer, time, a system taught to me years ago by coach and entrepreneur Jeff Raim:

Work means activity that brings you *both* joy and money.
Spirit means time that replenishes your soul and increases your energy.
Buffer is a catch-all phrase meaning everything else.

I asked Simone, who was so immensely busy with her work, to rearrange her calendar into work, spirit, and buffer days. She found she had six working days a week, Monday through Saturday, and one buffer day each week on Sunday when she rested and did things around the house. There were no spirit days in her calendar that she could see, except now and then when her husband put his foot down and insisted that they go out.

Simone was in danger of burning out because she had no refueling time. Spirit days were the first thing we prioritized, in order to replenish her energy.

I requested that she block out one spirit day each week, minimum. A Sunday spent cleaning the garage and running errands didn't count—it was just more buffer time. I also checked Simone's definition of work days, asking if they brought her money *and* joy. She said, "sometimes." I told her that until she could say yes, those days counted as buffer days. "That means I have only buffer days," she said sadly.

With only buffer days in her calendar, it was no surprise Simone felt exhausted most of the time. As she began to reorganize her work and life into spirit, work, and buffer days, she reported feeling more energized and happier and said that her husband and children were appreciative as well.

↪ FIELDWORK

Categorize the days of your calendar into spirit, work, and buffer time. Notice how your days look now, and begin to change your calendar so that you have primarily work and spirit days in your week, with a marked reduction of buffer time.

GREEN: TEMPER ENTREPRENEURIAL ZEAL WITH HUMANISM

Although the spiral dynamics evolutionary model is value-based, sometimes the values of a particular stage don't sit well with a therapist. The orange stage values achievement and expansion. Some therapists resonate with these values, but others don't. Fortunately, evolution has a pendulumlike way of correcting one-sidedness, so if the orange stage was too materialistic for your tastes, the next evolutionary stage, green, which promotes fairness and sensitivity, may offer some welcome balance.

Rick, an acupuncturist who owns a wellness center, faced this value clash. For several years his wellness center was struggling with not enough revenue. He created an aggressive marketing plan, spent his time on community outreach, and doubled the staff of practitioners and revenue. Rick gave frequent talks to organizations in the community, linked his wellness center with other businesses, and sought opportunities to increase growth and expansion of his center.

But, along with this entrepreneurial activity, Rick complained that his business activities had disconnected him from his core values. He complained that he had developed a hard business edge.

"I have gotten to the place where I see every get-together, every party or casual meeting as a marketing opportunity. I literally can't stop marketing. It takes the fun out of social events, because I am always thinking about who I should be talking to, how I should be talking up the wellness center. That's not how I want to relate to people.

"Also, I don't want to be just a boss, I want to create something more meaningful with my staff. I want them to feel a sense of ownership and interest in the viability of the center. As the owner, I need to think about how to stop being autocratic and get them to be more equal with me. The center espouses a holistic approach to wellness in the treatment services we offer, and I want my business structure to reflect that as well."

Once a business is sufficiently entrepreneurial, the natural evolutionary pull is to begin to incorporate humanistic values. Green incorporates the ideals of community building, sharing, benevolence, and the ecological well-being of everyone in the business and in society at large. In green, the old hierarchies of boss and employee tend to fall away and become imprecise, so that power can be shared. Remember, spiral dynamics is based on the process of *transcend and include*, so nothing you know or learn gets lost or forgotten. In green, you keep hold of the gains you have made up until now; you just open your heart further and, as a good business owner, add in a healthy dose of compassion.

EXERCISE: GREEN VALUES CHECKLIST

Check business values that articulate who you are or want to become, in regard to your practice. Checking a majority of the items signals a readiness to shift into the green stage by incorporating humanistic principles into your business.

- ❏ I am effortlessly passionate about my work.
- ❏ I am an articulate educator.
- ❏ I am highly collaborative.
- ❏ I am interested in building a larger vision.
- ❏ I am grounded in my desire to serve others.

- ❑ I am confident about what I have to offer to the world.
- ❑ I am self-aware, continuing to grow personally.
- ❑ I am a model of the services I offer to others.

→ FIELDWORK

Allow yourself to adopt and express these values in your actions and your work this month. Become a model of your services to others. How will you do this? What kind of plan and resources do you need to further this goal?

EXERCISE: CONGRUENCE CHECKLIST

Become congruent as a business owner and model the services you offer. Check the items that apply and create a plan to accomplish each one.

- ❑ *I am on a strong financial track.* It's hard to be an effective therapist when you are overly concerned about money. Get business coaching and financial advice so that your business prospers and you achieve financial independence.

  My plan:

  ____

  ____

  ____

  ____

- ❑ *I decorate my office so that I love spending time there.* If you love to spend time in your office, you will be happier when you are at work. Bring in fresh flowers, a favorite painting, comfortable furniture, and surround yourself with colors that make you feel good.

  My plan:

  ____

  ____

  ____

  ____

❑ *I find solutions for all the complaints I have regarding my work.* By now, you understand the value of correcting all of the problem areas in your practice so that you have no energy drains. Make your practice a problem free zone.

My plan:

_____

_____

_____

_____

❑ *I get all my personal needs met outside of my practice.* Too often over-worked therapists have a practice but no life. I want you to have both. Devote time to hobbies and satisfying relationships outside of your work.

My plan:

_____

_____

_____

_____

❑ *I get my own therapy, ongoing clinical supervision, and business coaching.* Remember to set aside resources for therapist self-care. Get the support you need first, so that you have a full well from which to give to others, not an empty tank. Have a strong professional network that encourages your success.

My plan:

_____

_____

_____

_____

Loving Your Practice

In green, your compassion needs to extend to others as well as to your own practice. There are so many areas of our business we don't love. These are usually the ways we feel bound, pushed, or burdened by our practices. This is normal, because a business has many needs and demands, and we must respond to those needs to keep our business viable. But just like any other entity, it does better if we respond to it with love, sensitivity, and compassion. This next exercise will help you to become more benevolent toward your practice by thinking of it with love each day.

EXERCISE: SEND LOVE TO YOUR PRACTICE

Step 1: Think about your practice, exactly as it exists today. See it or sense it, in your mind's eye, as a separate entity from you. Do this with eyes open or closed. Take your time. Then fill in the following statements.

I picture my practice in my mind as _____

_____

My feelings about my practice are _____

_____

Critical thoughts or judgments I have about my practice are _____

_____

Body sensations, including tension, I feel when I think about my practice are

_____

_____

Step 2: Now contrast these answers with the way you think about a person, place, or thing that you love unconditionally, with your whole heart and mind. It might be a place in nature, a pet, a person, or even some activity. See or sense this beloved person, place, or thing in your mind's eye, with eyes open or closed. Take your time and then complete the following statements.

I picture this beloved person, place or thing in my mind as_____

_____

My feelings about this beloved person, place or thing are ________________

____

Thoughts or judgments I have about this beloved person, place or thing are

____

____

Body sensations I feel when I think about this beloved person, place or thing are ____

____

Step 3: Make a note of all the differences and similarities between your list. You will probably notice that you have pictured your practice differently than you pictured the beloved person, place, or thing. One picture might be in dark colors, or blurred, the other in light shades with clearly defined objects. Take notice of the submodalities for each list. You may also notice that you are holding more critical thoughts and judgments about your practice than you are about your beloved person, place, or thing and that you have different body sensations when you think about the two. Think about your practice with love by transferring the submodalities of the beloved object to your thinking about your practice. See your practice in your mind the same way you see your beloved object. Use the same internal tone of voice when you talk to yourself about it. Try and have the same body posture and sensations when you think about your practice. Notice what happens when you consciously try to be more loving in the way you think and talk about your practice.

→ FIELDWORK

Each day, imagine that you are sending love to your practice, by thinking in a loving way, the way a good parent would think loving thoughts about a child. Imagine that you can send love unconditionally to every neglected, unappreciated, misunderstood, irritating aspect of your business. Think of an affirmation or an image that will help you to hold onto this experience, so you can think of your practice with a loving heart. What specific actions will you take to hold this love in place?

MONTHLY SKILL SET: CREATE COMMUNITY

Do you know what position your practice holds in the community? How your business is linked with the community around you defines your positioning. Linking can be more than networking; linking can mean actually building community, and you do this by recognizing the ways your practice is already connected to existing communities and then strengthening those existing bonds.

Even if you don't feel connected to any sense of community, your practice is, by the fact of its existence, linked to others. For starters, you have a position within your neighborhood (your local community), within your professional community, and within the society at large. These links may be dormant, because you do little to set them in motion or strengthen the bonds, but they do exist. If this is the case, your task as a green business owner will be to become more aware of your existing connections and activate or nurture them by circular positioning.

Marlene, a social worker, was a single parent of a college-age child. Faced with an empty nest syndrome for the first time in her life, she felt disconnected and at a loss for how to be part of a community. Her small psychotherapy practice functioned smoothly. In her words, it "could be fuller, but I am satisfied. I just feel empty in my life with my child gone. He was the focus of my daily existence."

Marlene had time and energy to spare, and I suggested that she enlarge her circles of community. Marlene said she had ties to her local community and to several professional organizations, but few ties to the community at large. She began to look around to see what linkages she could create. "I'm not going to volunteer in the sense most people think about it," she decided. "I am intent on connecting. To me, connecting means I will make relationships with others who share my passions, as opposed to licking stamps or collecting canned goods. I want to feel a part of something bigger than myself."

Marlene made a list of ten personal, unfulfilled passions, that included singing, astronomy, and hypnotherapy. She also made a list of existing organizations that sponsored the activities she was interested pursuing. After taking a few months to explore some different organizations, she decided to join a statewide volunteer choir that specialized in giving free performances throughout the state to hospitals, nursing homes, and events.

"I have a loud voice, I love to sing, and this is the most positive, fun way I could imagine to connect to an existing, larger community," she exulted. "But I am warning you, Lynn, it won't do a thing for me professionally." I didn't disagree, but we decided that at the end of the year, we would chat and she could evaluate whether this circle of community had any impact on her practice.

At the end of December we met for a follow-up session. Marlene came in shaking her head and grinning. "You must know something I don't. I just did my taxes. Do you know I actually increased my revenue a bit this year, by about $10,000 from last year? I added six new clients during the past 5 months. I can't imagine how this happened, but 4 of them came from singing in the choir!" She laughed and said to me, "Did you know this would happen?"

I solemnly pronounced one of my favorite mottos: "I take credit for all local miracles."

She laughed and said, "You know, I joined the choir just to feel connected after my son left for college. I had a ball, met some great gals from all over the state, and we sure sang up a storm in a lot of different places. I had such fun, I just can't tell you. As a child, I was never allowed to sing in the house, because my father worked the night shift and we had to be very quiet during the day, so being able to sing loudly with others was just a kick.

"I even agreed to do some administrative work for the choir because they needed some help and I had a little time. I guess the choir appreciated me because I began to notice that when we would perform at hospitals or any health-related event, some of the members would promote me! Maybe they felt proud of me, maybe they just thought it was a way to give back, I really don't know. I certainly never expected to have a cheerleading team, but after certain performances, someone related to the hospital or the nursing home where we were singing would come directly over to me and say, 'I hear you are a social worker who works with families. I'd love to have your card.' I ended up with a few new referral sources, and, as I said, several new clients. But best of all, I got to sing."

EXERCISE: IDENTIFY YOUR CIRCLES OF COMMUNITY

Identify the circles of community that exist around your practice.

1. Draw a series of concentric circles, or use the drawing provided, and imagine that your practice is a dot in the middle. Each circle repre-

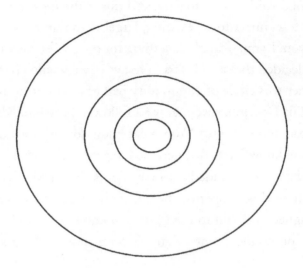

sents an existing community that surrounds your practice, such as your local community, professional communities and organizations, and then the larger societal or national community we all belong to.

2. Name the existing circles of community that surround your practice. Don't be concerned about whether the connections between the communities and your practice are active or dormant.

3. Pick one circle. Think how you could add value to that circle. Don't contribute money—for this exercise you must get personally involved and give something of yourself to this community. Feeding the circle will enrich your immediate environment, one form of reciprocation.

4. The reciprocal nature of circular positioning works only if you contribute from a desire to really enrich a particular community. As you build stronger relationships based on adding value to a community, the community naturally reciprocates. I call this "karmic marketing," because with this strategy, what goes around, comes around.

5. Create a plan of action to make the time and have the energy to add value in this way.

6. Focus on the pleasure of making connections with others. Be giving and try to improve your environment and your world. Follow your passion. Notice what comes back to you and your practice over time.

➔ FIELDWORK

From your diagram, pick one circle (one existing community) to start with this month. Give back to this community and add value to your professional and personal life. Sometimes this approach has a direct impact on practice building. Sometimes the impact is less direct. Your practice may or may not be enhanced based on this strategy, but your life will definitely be.

Monthly Review

This month you explored how to expand your practice with new opportunities and then add humanistic values to keep it well-balanced. The fieldwork for Month 11 includes:

- Develop a filter to help you evaluate and select the right opportunities to pursue.

- Use the categories of spirit, work, and buffer time to prioritize your calendar, increase your work and spirit days and reduce buffer time.

- Express green values in your actions this month. Aspire to congruence, so that you become a model of your services to others.

- Think about your practice with loving energy each day.

- Enhance your links to a community of your choice.

- *In addition,* continue to operate a profitable practice by tracking your finances each month, looking for ways to contain costs and enhance revenue (review Month 8).

MONTH 12

Flow: Integrating Multiple Perspectives

As a small business owner, do you know the inherent value in a *small* business? It's flexibility; being small allows you to have more agility. John Grinder, developer of neurolinguistic programming used to say, "The person with the most flexibility wins." He meant that in a negotiation, the person who was mentally flexible and could see multiple points of view would also see the widest array of possible solutions at any given moment, and if that person were also behaviorally flexible, he or she could more easily adopt any one of those solutions—hence having a better chance to achieve a successful outcome. A small business offers you flexibility—the freedom to change, shift, reshape, and improve your business easily in response to a frequently changing marketplace, profession, and society.

This month, I want to help you look ahead to the future of your practice, and see the many alternatives and options available, so you can increase your flexibility. Seeing multiple choices and options and then knowing how and when to take action can make you a highly strategic business owner, and you will have an edge over others who are unable to adopt to the changing world around them.

The last two color-coded stages of spiral dynamics, yellow and turquoise, are often the most exciting for therapists to consider because they introduce the concept of flow into business—a time where your business operates easily, in a conscious, yet effortless way. As the business owner, you are able to integrate all the hard work you

Go with the flow—position your practice so that it invites synchronicity and ease. This month, go beyond a traditional medical model, by adding choices and options with personal growth and coaching services and by increasing your level of self-motivation. Then celebrate the completion of your year-long coaching program.

My Monthly Prep Form

Answering these questions each month will help you to chart your progress and define your next goals.

1. What have I accomplished since last month that I feel positive about? What are my wins?

2. What challenges am I facing this month?

3. What opportunities are available to me right now?

4. What blocks me from taking advantage of these opportunities?

5. How could I make life or work easier or better for myself right now?

6. My goals for this month are:

have done to build your ideal private practice with the many options and new opportunities that interest you, and as a result, synchronicity happens. No matter where you are in your practice development, by using this month's exercises and concepts you can explore alternative ways of doing business, and as a result, welcome some flow.

YELLOW: INCREASE CHOICES AND INVITE NEWNESS

In 2002, I gave a series of two-day workshops in Australia. I spent the last day of each workshop introducing the adapted spiral dynamics model of evolution, asking a few therapists in the audience to come to the front of the room and talk about their practices, to see where they fit on the evolutionary model. One therapist asked to come up in front of the group so she could get some clarification. "I am not sure where I fit on the chart of evolution. Let me tell you my situation and perhaps you can help me figure it out."

This therapist had been in a very prosperous practice for almost 20 years, and had strong links and alliances to her community of professionals. She looked at the audience and said, "I know I am where many of you say you wish to be, with lots of clients, a well-functioning practice, a good life, no problems on the horizon. But I am not satisfied. I want to go in a new direction."

Here she paused and her voice turned brittle. "I know that doing this may challenge my retirement plans, and my husband has voiced his concerns, since he is retiring soon and thought we would retire together. But I'm not ready to stop working. I feel like I am turning my world upside down and inviting chaos. I want to practice my profession in a very different way from what I am doing now, with new methods I am currently learning, and maybe starting over, finding clients that want to work with these methods. I'm not sure why I am doing this, but by this time next year, I know that my practice will have changed dramatically."

I projected a slide of all of the adapted color-coded stages of spiral dynamics on a screen above her head and I asked the audience to tell me where this therapist was heading. "Yellow!" they called out, and they were right.

If a business owner in a functioning, profitable practice speaks to a longing to break out, do something new, take a risk, invite chaos—he or she is voicing the yellow stage. When a prosperous therapist chooses to change direction radically, not based on financial necessity but for the purpose of change itself, driven by deeper, core feelings of innovation, again think yellow.

Yellow means thinking out of the box, which, for a therapist, can translate into going beyond a traditional medical model. Two ways to do this are to:

1. Adopt a personal growth model of business.
2. Diversify into areas such as coaching.

Adapt a Personal Growth Model

Gerald Celente, author of *Trends 2000*, says that a major trend surfacing in our aging, relatively affluent population is the desire for high-quality longevity. We want to live well as we live longer. We yearn for long-term physical and mental health—to stay interested in life until the day we die. According to Paul Zane Pilzer, author of *The Wellness Revolution*, a longing to solve the issues of aging and vitality will fuel a trillion-dollar industry over the next decade. This trend points the way for an expanded role for the therapy profession, *if* therapy can move from a traditional medical model, which emphasizes treatment of pathology, toward a personal-growth or coaching model, which emphasizes personal development and healing over one's life span.

The difference between healing and cure is a primary distinction for the personal growth model versus the medical model. Abraham Verghese, writing in the *New York Times* ("The Healing Paradox," December 8, 2002) explained it this way:

> *Therein lies the rub: we are perhaps in search of something more than a cure—call it healing. If you were robbed one day, and if by the next day the robber was caught and all your goods returned to you, you would only feel partly restored; you would be "cured" but not "healed"; your sense of psychic violation would remain. Similarly with illness, a cure is good, but we want the healing as well, we want the magic that good physicians provide with their personality, their empathy and their reassurance.*

With an alternative model, such as a personal growth model of business, your role is less that of an expert and more that of a collaborative partner in change. While you may still diagnose and offer treatment, you see a client's problems in a larger context. You offer services designed to help people resolve immediate issues, but also to help them further a process of personal development. Treatment becomes part of a long-term strategy of wellness.

The goal in personal-growth is to improve, transform, or enrich a person's quality of life. A personal-growth model may embrace a wide range of Eastern and Western methods designed to extend and enhance the way we grow, live, and eventually die. Instead of clients feeling forced to come for services because they are ill (the medical model), clients voluntarily and proactively seek services, to stay as fit and well as possible. Use the following checklist to see if gravitating toward alternative models, as opposed to traditional medical models, makes sense for you and your practice.

EXERCISE: ALTERNATIVE MODELS CHECKLIST

Check those items that fit for you. Three or more checks signal a readiness to adopt an alternative model, such as the personal growth model.

- ❑ I want to help clients not just heal, but also have an optimum life.

- ❑ I like learning and using methods that don't fall within the current medical model.

- ❑ I want acknowledgment and compensation when I use innovative or alternative methods of therapy.

- ❑ I consider that an eclectic approach is my best way of working.

- ❑ I want to assume total financial control of my practice and not rely on any third-party payers.

- ❑ I am comfortable having the responsibility for profitability rest entirely on me, as the business owner.

- ❑ I tend to get bored doing the same type of treatment each year.

- ❑ I like to keep learning and want to stay on the cutting edge of healing technology.

- ❑ I have an articulated basic message, links, and connections with my community, curiosity about what the public wants, a desire to produce tangible results, and interest in methods that will keep my clients engaged.

- I am willing to work in a long-term mode with "lifetime clients" who I will see at different stages of their lives.
- I believe in the importance of a value-added practice for new, existing, and returning clients.

Stages of Personal Growth

What would a personal-growth model look like as applied to your practice? In conceptualizing your own model of personal growth, consider your philosophy of service, your training, and your professional style. To create the five-stage, personal-growth model for a therapy business that I use, I considered three factors: the stages of personal growth, the goal of services for each stage, and the specific range of services that could be offered.

The first three stages, which I call *survival, recovery,* and *progress,* are most familiar to therapists and reflect standard therapy services. The last two, *pleasure* and *awareness,* are often not considered as part of a therapist's repertoire. Developing a personal growth model for your business requires that you offer a full range of services for a person at all stages of life.

Although I organized this model to reflect five distinct stages, I recognize that personal development is rarely linear. In times of stress or loss we all regress to the "lower" stages of survival, and in times of calm, approach the "higher" stages of awareness. There is a normal back-and-forth movement to each person's development. You may find that your clients move between stages, at times needing services from one, at other times from another.

It's also not unusual to work with a client who needs services from two extremes of the model at the same time. For example, I have worked with clients who are at a survival level in terms of their relationships, but at a pleasure level in terms of their careers. Look at the following model, adapt it to fit your style and method of working, and allow the broad concepts of personal development to guide you. The following chart defines the five stages of personal growth, the markers that signal what stage is currently activated for a person, and the focus of services that can be offered for that stage.

Stage of Personal Growth	Presenting Markers of Person	Focus of Your Services
1. survival	in crisis; at a low point of existence; in extreme emotional, psychological, or physical pain with concerns about stability, self-protection, or personal preservation	reduce effects of crisis; change self-destructive behaviors; calm or shift affect (emotion); find solutions; treat trauma; keep person safe; help establish or protect a fragile sense of self
2. recovery	out of crisis; has occasional upsets at work and/or home; feels less desperate; is ready to explore a deeper connection to self and others	support staying out of crisis; change self-destructive behaviors; learn to appropriately express and feel emotions; generate own solutions to problems; set and maintain boundaries; improve relational skills and connections; consolidate gains; explore and examine deeper causal issues below the surface
3. progress (in a medical model reaching this stage signals the end of therapy, but in a personal-growth model it is a halfway point)	functioning; able to set and achieve primary goals; stable; has relationships; can cope better with life's problems	develop a life vision; define large goals; build stronger ties to family, friendships, and community; find spiritual direction; enhance self-care; develop creativity; sustain previous gains; enhance quality of life

Stage of Personal Growth	Presenting Markers of Person	Focus of Your Services
4. pleasure	functioning well; finds satisfaction and pleasure in life; has a peaceful and enthusiastic outlook; has relationships with an extended, loving community; sees opportunities for pleasure and profit	deepen practices of spirituality; sustain pleasure and a playful outlook; appreciate nature; heighten relaxation; recharge energy; get continually nurtured; open one's heart; take in more love and passion; enhance compassion
5. awareness	peak time of life; has accomplished personal and professional goals; supports sense of happiness with relationships; has met vision and mission; is still learning and growing	feel supported, inspired, and reinforced; live a life based on integrity; resolve old business and practice forgiveness; have peace of mind; open doors on life's further possibilities; give back to others; explore legacy; reflect on life experiences; create a wonderful life

When adopting any new healing model, it works best to first try it on oneself. Think about your life in general and specific aspects of your life: How would you match my stages of personal growth to your life? My experience of this exercise is that it is both sobering and enlightening. Complete the following exercise and then consider how you can shift your attitude, behaviors, and feelings to increase the level of personal growth in any or all areas of your life.

EXERCISE: IDENTITY YOUR STAGES OF PERSONAL GROWTH

On the left is a category of your life, and on the right, space to identify the stage of personal growth you experience in each category.

Stage of personal growth (survival, recovery, progress, pleasure, awareness)

My life in general _____

My life aspects:

My career_____

My relationships to friends _____

My finances _____

My health _____

My self-care_____

My ability to have fun_____

My relationships to family _____

My spirituality_____

1. How will I shift an area to the next stage of development?

_____

_____

_____

_____

_____

2. What internal changes do I need to make? What external changes do I need to make?

_____

_____

_____

_____

_____

3. What specific actions will I take this month to further my development?

_____

_____

_____

_____

_____

➡ FIELDWORK

Using the preceding exercise as a guide this month, target the areas of your life and work that you want to advance to the next stage of personal growth. Take steps each week to improve any or all categories of your life, so that you become a model of the stages of personal growth to which your clients aspire.

Range of Services

Now that you have some familiarity with this model and can understand how it applies to your own life, think about your clients and where they are in regard to the five stages of personal growth. What specific services do you have to offer for each stage?

Many therapists working in the medical model of treatment have a host of services for clients in the first two stages, survival and recovery, but little to attract and retain clients in the later stages of progress, pleasure and awareness. If you want to have a practice that meets clients at all the stages of development, you must make sure that you have services that will appeal at each level.

You may have a client who has developed to a later stage, or one who comes in at a later stage. You want to offer services that promote higher levels of self-value and a deeper connection with others. Keep the following points in mind when in thinking about the services you offer, especially for the later stages:

- _Focus attention on the_ depth _of services._ Pick no more than one or two services per stage. More important than breadth of services is how deeply you are able to work with others. This model pushes you to become expert in a few services and then orient your practice around your strengths.

■ *Let your practice be unique.* This is a practice where your creativity, your ability to be different and spot trends will be a major asset. Instead of having to do things the traditional way, you can be inventive. Your practice may not look the same as anyone else's; this can be a strength. To be distinctive, play to your strengths and your passions.

■ *Have an overarching vision.* Get ready to work with clients over the long term. In a personal-growth practice you may see clients for many years, perhaps in a revolving door method where they come in and out of your office at different stages of their personal development. See the big picture of health and wellness, so that your practice is part of a large vision. Keep your emphasis on excellent services of a high nature.

■ *Your services can include ones you already offer or ones you add.* Make a list of possible services, including individual or group sessions, workshops, classes, retreats, audiotapes, books, newsletters, trips, and other services you can offer. Include a full range of your talents and skills, including the practice of art, music, healing, and spirituality. Offer services alone, or in collaboration with others. Offer services for an individual client, or include members of his or her family or extended community. Be sure you have a clear and concise way to articulate these services to clients.

EXERCISE: LIST YOUR PERSONAL GROWTH SERVICES

Make a list of the services you have for each stage. Use the following format:

Stage	Goal of Services	Specific Services I Offer
survival		
recovery		
progress		
pleasure		
awareness		

→ FIELDWORK

If you decide to adopt this alternative business model, decide how you will let new and existing clients know about your expanded range of services. What marketing materials need to be adjusted to reflect your additional information? How will you verbally talk about your expanded services in your basic message? What, if anything, do you need to alter on your list of policies or procedures?

Diversity into Coaching

Therapists in the yellow stage often want to diversify, and one popular way to do that is by adding coaching services. I have mentored many new coaches for years, but two years ago I reached out to the coaching community and asked selected senior coaches who were therapists as well to share their experience transitioning from therapy to coaching. The result was a ground-breaking book of first-person essays that I enjoyed editing, *The New Private Practice: Therapist-Coaches Share Stories, Strategies, and Advice.* The contributors offered inside advice on all areas of coaching—how to get started in coaching, what fees to charge, how to get new clients, and other trade secrets. They wrote openly about their experience coaching CEOs, executive teams, lawyers, people in transition, and professional and amateur athletes. The book is a balanced, highly entertaining read that answers a lot of questions for therapists about what coaching is and isn't, how to get trained, and how to break into new markets.

As a result of being a therapist-coach for several years, a teacher-trainer for a large coach-training organization (CoachU), a mentor of new coaches, and my involvement with this book project, I understand a lot about how and why therapists turn to coaching. Similar to a personal-growth model, a coaching model attracts clients who are searching for untraditional ways to grow and allows therapists to work outside of the conventional limitations of psychotherapy.

Coaching changes the settings in which therapists usually work, and the nature and intention of the work allows therapists and clients a lot of flexibility in achieving goals. Therapists are often natural coaches already, so the transition from a therapy practice to one that includes coaching can be satisfying, easy, and profitable.

Before coaching was defined as a separate profession, it was understood as a style of relating, one that has been used in a variety of settings (sports, business, and, of course, therapy) for decades. But since the 1980s, coaching has been promoted primarily by the coaching industry as a separate profession. Some therapists find that they naturally use a coaching style and becoming a coach is an easy transition: others find it quite outside their style of working. Take the next assessment to see if diversifying with coaching is in your future.

EXERCISE: DEVELOP A COACHING STYLE

Check those items that reflect your current style. Four or more checks means that you are already using a coaching style in your work. Then answer the additional questions.

My current style focuses on:

- ❑ genuineness (versus detachment)
- ❑ guidance (versus a nondirective approach)
- ❑ cognition (versus eliciting emotion)
- ❑ mutuality and appropriate self-disclosure (versus specifically eliciting transference)
- ❑ empathy (versus neutrality)
- ❑ support and counsel (versus analysis or interpretation)
- ❑ here and now (versus focus on past)
- ❑ interpersonal focus (versus intrapsychic focus)
- ❑ ego strengthening (versus ego regression)
- ❑ transparency of therapist and practice (versus not revealing)

1. What coaching skills do I already use in my current practice or in my work as a trainer, teacher, or workshop leader?

   _____

   _____

   _____

   _____

   _____

2. How can I transfer these skills to other settings or populations outside my office walls?

_____

_____

_____

_____

_____

3. What opportunities to diversify my practice exist that I am not taking advantage of?

_____

_____

_____

_____

_____

4. How could I articulate these services (in my brochures, business card, flyers, etc.) so that my referral sources understand that I have diversified?

_____

_____

_____

_____

_____

5. What additional information, training, research, or mentoring could I get to make this diversification more valid and successful?

_____

_____

_____

_____

_____

TURQUOISE: BUILD AN IDEAL PRACTICE THAT FLOWS

The yellow stage encourages a business owner to consider options and newness, and the last color-coded stage of evolution in spiral dynamics, turquoise, invites a business owner to integrate all that has come before into a holistic, harmonic connection, which I think of as *flow*. The flow stage, turquoise, while primarily conceptual and idealistic, undeniably permeates well-functioning businesses from time to time. Turquoise marks those wonderful moments when synchronicity and optimal performance come together, making your private practice a joy to own and operate.

In turquoise, your business operates without effort. Your practice is on an even keel, you attract the clients and opportunities you desire, money accumulates, you love using your craft, work is a pleasure. This doesn't happen by magic, but as a result of the preparation, building blocks, and finishing touches you have put in place. But it no longer feels like work. You are in the zone, where everything is integrated. I like to think about turquoise as a state, rather than a stage. This state shows up in our practices at different moments, but I find that there are ways to invite these moments and increase their frequency, to get your a practice humming, and to remove all complaints and problems.

We have looked at many strategies to help you do this: Here is one more that can help keep your practice balanced between ebb and flow, operating on an even keel. The purpose of this strategy is to modify the uneven flow of business by having a series of steps to even out times of either too little or too much business.

EXERCISE: DEVISE YOUR EBB AND FLOW STRATEGY

Fill in the following sections to have a plan for balancing the uneven nature of business.

Too Much Ebb?

Diversify. Have at least three different profit centers, so that the ups and down get spread out and you can move between one thing and another when business is slow.

My plan: _____

_____

_____

Develop a referral engine. Build a self-generating engine that keeps going easily and yields a steady, slow stream of referrals.

My plan: _____

_____

_____

Build a strong cash reserve. Save money to build up a financial reserve to tide you over in lean times. Pay yourself first—before you pay bills, put 10 percent of your earnings each week into a savings vehicle.

My plan: _____

_____

_____

Add value. Keep doing more for existing clients to improve retention and referrals. Think about ways you can benefit and educate your clients.

My plan: _____

_____

_____

Too Much "Flow"?

Resist the pressure to do more. Maintain your boundaries and your spirit time in the face of too much business. Start by developing a waiting list and a good Rolodex of referrals you can make.

My plan: _____

_____

_____

Hire staff. This is the time to let others help you organize and manage the influx of new business. Have someone else book your appointments. Delegate all administrative activities. Get a reliable office manager.

My plan: _____

_____

_____

Leverage your time. See the maximum amount of people you can in the least amount of time.

My plan: _____

_____

_____

_____

➙ FIELDWORK

Choose one or more of the preceding strategies to balance your ebb and flow and put it into effect this month. Get support for your efforts, by structuring your plan, deciding on a budget or resource allocation, and then alerting your professional support system or your advisory circle to help you achieve your goals.

Personal Flow

It's hard to help your business reach a flow state, unless you are actively attempting to keep your personal life flowing as well. According to Mihaly Csikszentmihalyi, author of *Flow,* the two main strategies that add flow to life are: (1) focus on shaping and improving our external environment, and (2) focus on how we experience our external environment. I have found that the second strategy, my internal experience of my environment, can increase my sense of flow if I keep my focus on certain life-giving concepts. The next exercise is a set of these concepts that you can learn to embody, to enhance your well-being and internal experience of flow.

EXERCISE: ENHANCE YOUR INTERNAL FLOW STATE

Consider how you might embody the following life-giving concepts. Make some notes in the spaces given of your thoughts and plans.

Candor, rather than deception:

_____

_____

_____

Integrity, rather than incompleteness:

_____

_____

_____

Aliveness, rather than withdrawal:

_____

_____

_____

Appreciation, rather than disappointment:

_____

_____

_____

Simplicity, rather than entanglement:

_____

_____

_____

Ease, rather than difficulty:

_____

_____

_____

Meaningfulness, rather than futility:

_____

_____

_____

MONTHLY SKILL SET: STAY MOTIVATED

Inviting a flow state into your business means that you stay proactive, not passive. Unfortunately, it's hard to stay proactive in your practice building, month after month, year after year. All of us are vulnerable to backsliding. You are at the end of this year's program. As future months go by, you may notice that you procrastinate and miss deadlines. Action slows down. Phone calls don't get made. Plans for expansion take a back seat. You have a list, but hate to look at it. Whereas once you felt inspired and motivated to build your practice, now you feel frustrated or, once again, anxious.

I understand how difficult it is to hold onto business gains and keep moving forward over time. In a sole proprietorship you wear a lot of hats. You will default to the roles you most like to do and ignore the others. If you like to deliver service the most, that's what you will tend to do, overlooking the other roles you need to attend to in order to keep your business going well. The key skill to performing well in *all* your roles will be your degree of self-motivation.

Motivation is the fuel that inspires us to action. Self-motivation is your way of claiming that fuel, and the final business skill set that I want you to develop this year. Based on John Keller's research about motivation, I have broken the concept of self-motivation into four distinct aspects and adapted each for your use. To self-motivate, you need to:

1. Consistently arouse your own interest.
2. Create relevance in your daily actions.
3. Develop an expectancy of success.
4. Produce satisfaction through a combination of intrinsic and extrinsic rewards.

1. *Consistently arouse your own interest.* Keeping your interest at a high level is an important element to staying invested in any career. Sustaining interest doesn't just happen; you must plan for it and dedicate a percentage of your budget to it. The longer you stay in practice, the more you must challenge yourself in this area. *How to do it:* Arouse your interest in your work by continually learning. Expose yourself to new ideas and experiences, for the purpose of staying fresh. Go beyond courses in continuing education training, and pursue more far-flung experiences. Dedicate 5% of your budget each year to new experiences and/or training that will keep your interest aroused.

Actions I will take: _____

_____

_____

2. *Create relevance in your daily actions.* You can create relevance by continually integrating your practice into a larger worldview. When the purpose of your practice means more to you than just providing a source of personal income or a service for a small pool of clients, you will be inspired to take larger steps. *How to do it:* Create relevance by identifying a theme for your practice that expresses your overarching purpose as a therapist. Recognize that your business goals and tasks are the way you manifest this larger vision and how you connect your small practice to a larger worldview. Define the larger purpose of your work. Articulate a theme that helps you feel that your work fits into a bigger picture of life. Write the theme on a card and post it in places where you will see it often.

Actions I will take: _____

_____

_____

3. *Develop an expectancy of success.* Develop relationships with others who succeed in business. Inspire yourself by reading biographies of others who have succeeded, despite difficult odds. You can always find accounts of people who faced more problems than you do, yet accomplished awe-inspiring goals. *How to do it:* Read business magazines, like *Fast Company*, that offer first-person accounts of the successes of contemporary entrepreneurs. If you give yourself enough case examples, you will see that succeeding in business is not unusual. Surround yourself with inspiring stories and examples of others who express optimism and a belief in possibility. Join a group of active businesspeople (such as the chamber of commerce) who can help normalize your experience of business success.

Actions I will take: _____

_____

_____

4. *Produce satisfaction through a combination of intrinsic and extrinsic rewards.* Utilize a reward system. Two types of rewards increase motivation: intrinsic (self-focused rewards) and extrinsic (externally focused rewards). To stay motivated, you need a combination of both. Intrinsic rewards include feelings of satisfaction, joy, and pride. Extrinsic rewards may come in the form of money or other tangible markers of success. *How to do it:* Structure rewards at set intervals. Schedule difficult tasks early in the day, so that by noon you can reward yourself by reading your novel, going for a walk, or playing with your children. Have a circle of friends and peers who you can call for a quick verbal pat on the back when needed—another reward. Keep two lists each week— one for wins and a second one for current goals. Break down the goals into small action steps. The smaller the steps, the more chance for frequent rewards—you will accomplish many small steps versus one large step. Have someone you account to each week who can hold you to your tasks and celebrate your progress.

Actions I will take: _____

_____

_____

Monthly Review

This month we looked at strategies to help you become more flexible, expand your existing services and welcome more flow into your practice. Your fieldwork for Month 12 includes:

■　Target the areas of your life and work that you want to advance to the next stage of personal growth. Take steps each week to improve any or all categories of your life, so that you become a model of the stages of personal growth to which your clients aspire.

■　Decide how you will let new and existing clients know about your expanded range of services. What marketing materials need to be adjusted to reflect your additional information? How will you verbally talk about your expanded services in your basic message? What, if anything, do you need to alter on your list of policies or procedures?

■　Balance your ebb and flow. This month get support for your efforts, by structuring your plan, deciding on a budget or resource allocation, and then alerting your professional support system or your advisory circle to help you achieve your goals.

■　*In addition*, continue to review the workbook during the course of the next 12 months, to stay motivated, focused, and engaged in continuing to build your ideal private practice.

AFTERWORD
Celebrating Success

If you have gone through the 12 months of this workbook, completing each exercise and tackling the fieldwork, keeping up with your monthly prep form, and using the support of others to guide and advise you, then I have no doubt that you have had many successes. You will have expanded your business awareness and savvy, defined your long- and short-term goals, carried out many of those goals and become more confident in your abilities as a business owner.

I hope you have seen your vision start to take shape, attracted more ideal clients, made more money, gotten your life and your work better organized, and noticed the many opportunities that exist for you. If you go back to retake the Private Practice Success Program Assessment from Month 2, you will probably score much higher. As a result of your efforts, actions, and intention, you may notice flow and synchronicity occurring, those days and weeks when everything seems to click.

You deserve many hugs and much praise for your willingness to learn and change and grow. You deserve all the real, tangible extrinsic rewards that a business can offer as well as the intangible rewards of satisfaction and pride. Congratulations on building your ideal private practice.

If you have not reached your level of expectation from this workbook program, it doesn't mean that anything is wrong with you or with the program. You may simply need more time and more support to achieve the results you desire. Take another year and go back through the program a second time. One therapist recently told me she had to reread my first book four times over three years, before she could really utilize the ideas, but that by the forth time it all made sense and her progress was speedy and successful. Don't underestimate the value of repetition.

Timing is everything. I have talked to many therapists who attended a weekend workshop, enjoyed it, but weren't ready or able to make any changes in the way they worked. But they listened and absorbed what was said and later, maybe a month or maybe several years, when the time was right, instituted key strategies and were on their way! I hope you will give yourself internal permission and external support to achieve your business goals in your own way, at your own pace, with your own sense of timing.

Support is everything, too. Let others help you build your business. Become part of a peer coaching group, or hire an individual coach. See "How to Use This Workbook" at the beginning of this book (p. 11) for information about how to join a facilitated telephone coaching group that will give you expert guidance and support specifically for this workbook. If you are feeling stuck, get more energy by bringing more people onto your team.

I also hope you have had fun in the process of reading this workbook, and that the progression of going through it month by month made your business (and your life) easier and richer for you. Please know that it has been my great pleasure and delight to be with you on your practice-building journey. I wish you continued success, all the ease possible, and all my best.

I always offer my e-mail, because I love to hear how you are doing and how the program is working for you. Over the years I have been blessed to hear from people all over the globe. If you want to contact me at any point, just to say hello and let me know how you are progressing, please do so by e-mailing me at: lynn@privatepracticesuccess.com. Although I am somewhat limited in my ability to respond, I read and appreciate every e-mail I receive.

You are also welcome to stay in touch with me throughout the year by subscribing to my free email monthly newsletter, which contains my most current thoughts and ideas about practice building. Subscribing connects you to the global community of thousands of other therapists around the world who share your challenges and your dreams. To subscribe, go to: www.privatepracticesuccess.com.

APPENDICES

APPENDIX A
Monthly Prep Forms

MONTH 1: MY MONTHLY PREP FORM

Answering these questions each month will help you to chart your progress and define your next goals.

1. What have I accomplished since last month that I feel positive about? What are my wins?

   _____

   _____

   _____

   _____

   _____

2. What challenges am I facing this month?

   _____

   _____

   _____

   _____

   _____

3. What opportunities are available to me right now?

   _____

   _____

   _____

   _____

   _____

4. What blocks me from taking advantage of these opportunities?

_____

_____

_____

_____

5. How could I make life or work easier or better for myself right now?

_____

_____

_____

_____

6. My goals for this month are:

_____

_____

_____

_____

_____

MONTH 2: MY MONTHLY PREP FORM

Answering these questions each month will help you to chart your progress and define your next goals.

1. What have I accomplished since last month that I feel positive about? What are my wins?

   _____

   _____

   _____

   _____

   _____

2. What challenges am I facing this month?

   _____

   _____

   _____

   _____

   _____

3. What opportunities are available to me right now?

   _____

   _____

   _____

   _____

   _____

4. What blocks me from taking advantage of these opportunities?

_____

_____

_____

_____

_____

5. How could I make life or work easier or better for myself right now?

_____

_____

_____

_____

_____

6. My goals for this month are:

_____

_____

_____

_____

_____

MONTH 3: MY MONTHLY PREP FORM

Answering these questions each month will help you to chart your progress and define your next goals.

1. What have I accomplished since last month that I feel positive about? What are my wins?

    _____

    _____

    _____

    _____

    _____

2. What challenges am I facing this month?

    _____

    _____

    _____

    _____

    _____

3. What opportunities are available to me right now?

    _____

    _____

    _____

    _____

    _____

4. What blocks me from taking advantage of these opportunities?

_____

_____

_____

_____

_____

5. How could I make life or work easier or better for myself right now?

_____

_____

_____

_____

_____

6. My goals for this month are:

_____

_____

_____

_____

_____

MONTH 4: MY MONTHLY PREP FORM

Answering these questions each month will help you to chart your progress and define your next goals.

1. What have I accomplished since last month that I feel positive about? What are my wins?

Completed all activities to set up my Private practice. Agreed new hours at work so I know have a day off. Had a lovely holiday and battery recharged.

2. What challenges am I facing this month?

Laying foundations to ensure I keep on top of my admin. Getting my first client. Ensuring I focus the correct amout of time on work and others.

3. What opportunities are available to me right now?

My details are now on the centre website. I have set up my own website. Registered on the counselling Directory.

4. What blocks me from taking advantage of these opportunities?

_____

_____

_____

_____

_____

5. How could I make life or work easier or better for myself right now?

_____

_____

_____

_____

_____

6. My goals for this month are:

_____

_____

_____

_____

_____

MONTH 5: MY MONTHLY PREP FORM

Answering these questions each month will help you to chart your progress and define your next goals.

1. What have I accomplished since last month that I feel positive about? What are my wins?

   reading completing chapter 4 & 5 of the workbook and feeling quite inspired.

2. What challenges am I facing this month?

   Not currently had any enquiries - being patient as it is early days (3 weeks)

3. What opportunities are available to me right now?

   - Need to set up a facebook page and think how I can use this quite effectively
   - update suggestions from counsellor directory view

4. What blocks me from taking advantage of these opportunities?

_____

_____

_____

_____

_____

5. How could I make life or work easier or better for myself right now?

_____

_____

_____

_____

_____

6. My goals for this month are:

_____

_____

_____

_____

_____

MONTH 6: MY MONTHLY PREP FORM

Answering these questions each month will help you to chart your progress and define your next goals.

1. What have I accomplished since last month that I feel positive about? What are my wins?

   _____

   _____

   _____

   _____

   _____

2. What challenges am I facing this month?

   _____

   _____

   _____

   _____

   _____

3. What opportunities are available to me right now?

   _____

   _____

   _____

   _____

   _____

4. What blocks me from taking advantage of these opportunities?

_____

_____

_____

_____

_____

5. How could I make life or work easier or better for myself right now?

_____

_____

_____

_____

_____

6. My goals for this month are:

_____

_____

_____

_____

_____

MONTH 7: MY MONTHLY PREP FORM

Answering these questions each month will help you to chart your progress and define your next goals.

1. What have I accomplished since last month that I feel positive about? What are my wins?

   _____

   _____

   _____

   _____

   _____

2. What challenges am I facing this month?

   _____

   _____

   _____

   _____

   _____

3. What opportunities are available to me right now?

   _____

   _____

   _____

   _____

   _____

4. What blocks me from taking advantage of these opportunities?

_____

_____

_____

_____

_____

5. How could I make life or work easier or better for myself right now?

_____

_____

_____

_____

_____

6. My goals for this month are:

_____

_____

_____

_____

_____

MONTH 8: MY MONTHLY PREP FORM

Answering these questions each month will help you to chart your progress and define your next goals.

1. What have I accomplished since last month that I feel positive about? What are my wins?

    _____

    _____

    _____

    _____

    _____

2. What challenges am I facing this month?

    _____

    _____

    _____

    _____

3. What opportunities are available to me right now?

    _____

    _____

    _____

    _____

    _____

4. What blocks me from taking advantage of these opportunities?

_____

_____

_____

_____

_____

5. How could I make life or work easier or better for myself right now?

_____

_____

_____

_____

_____

6. My goals for this month are:

_____

_____

_____

_____

_____

MONTH 9: MY MONTHLY PREP FORM

Answering these questions each month will help you to chart your progress and define your next goals.

1. What have I accomplished since last month that I feel positive about? What are my wins?

    _____

    _____

    _____

    _____

    _____

2. What challenges am I facing this month?

    _____

    _____

    _____

    _____

    _____

3. What opportunities are available to me right now?

    _____

    _____

    _____

    _____

    _____

4. What blocks me from taking advantage of these opportunities?

_____

_____

_____

_____

_____

5. How could I make life or work easier or better for myself right now?

_____

_____

_____

_____

_____

6. My goals for this month are:

_____

_____

_____

_____

_____

MONTH 10: MY MONTHLY PREP FORM

Answering these questions each month will help you to chart your progress and define your next goals.

1. What have I accomplished since last month that I feel positive about? What are my wins?

   _____

   _____

   _____

   _____

   _____

2. What challenges am I facing this month?

   _____

   _____

   _____

   _____

   _____

3. What opportunities are available to me right now?

   _____

   _____

   _____

   _____

   _____

4. What blocks me from taking advantage of these opportunities?

_____

_____

_____

_____

_____

5. How could I make life or work easier or better for myself right now?

_____

_____

_____

_____

_____

6. My goals for this month are:

_____

_____

_____

_____

_____

MONTH 11: MY MONTHLY PREP FORM

Answering these questions each month will help you to chart your progress and define your next goals.

1. What have I accomplished since last month that I feel positive about? What are my wins?

   _____

   _____

   _____

   _____

   _____

2. What challenges am I facing this month?

   _____

   _____

   _____

   _____

   _____

3. What opportunities are available to me right now?

   _____

   _____

   _____

   _____

   _____

4. What blocks me from taking advantage of these opportunities?

_____

_____

_____

_____

_____

5. How could I make life or work easier or better for myself right now?

_____

_____

_____

_____

_____

6. My goals for this month are:

_____

_____

_____

_____

_____

MONTH 12: MY MONTHLY PREP FORM

Answering these questions each month will help you to chart your progress and define your next goals.

1. What have I accomplished since last month that I feel positive about? What are my wins?

_____

_____

_____

_____

_____

2. What challenges am I facing this month?

_____

_____

_____

_____

_____

3. What opportunities are available to me right now?

_____

_____

_____

_____

_____

4. What blocks me from taking advantage of these opportunities?

_____

_____

_____

_____

_____

5. How could I make life or work easier or better for myself right now?

_____

_____

_____

_____

_____

6. My goals for this month are:

_____

_____

_____

_____

_____

APPENDIX B
Short List of Recommended Reading for Marketing and Profit

Note: Further reading lists are available in the book Building Your Ideal Private Practice *and on my Web site: www.privatepracticesuccess.com. This targeted reading list is offered to specifically support your work in Month 6 and Month 8.*

ADDITIONAL MARKETING IDEAS

1. Grodzki, L. (2000). *Building your ideal private practice: A guide for therapists and healing professionals.* New York: Norton.

2. Grodzki, L. (Ed.). (2002). *The new private practice: Therapist-coaches share stories, strategies, and advice.* New York: Norton.

I am recommending my books to you first. If you haven't read them, they will help. *Building Your Ideal Private Practice* contains many marketing ideas and actions, more than can fit in this workbook, all adapted for a therapist's sensibilities and ethics. If you are trying to market a coaching practice, *The New Private Practice* is a collection of 16 behind-the-scenes essays by successful therapists-turned-coaches: how they got started, what it took to market their practices, how they broke into the field, what they charge, who they coach, and why.

3. Edwards, P., Edwards, S., & Douglas, L. (1998). *Getting business to come to you* (2nd ed.). New York: Tarcher/Putman.

This book of more than 600 pages dovetails closely with my thinking about abundance and marketing. I have never met the authors and didn't read their book until well after I had written mine, but we are first cousins in our approach. Because this book is for small-business owners in general, not everything that they recommend is exactly right for a therapy practice. But they offer so much to choose from you can still use many, many ideas. The book has a nice, easy-to-read layout and is full of good advice, reading lists, resources, and products.

4. Baber, A., & Waymon, L. (2002). *Making your contacts count* Woodbridge, CT: Amacon.

Lynne Waymon is a colleague of mine and a true networking maven. This is just the latest of her many good books on networking. Her Web site, www.contactscount.com, lists all her books and the tapes that she has produced with her sister, Anne, that help even very introverted people approach networking with confidence. If you feel shy or unsure about networking, her books and tapes will help.

5. Godin, S. (1999). *Permission marketing.* New York: Simon & Schuster.

Seth Godin is the bad boy of business, but I like his irreverent take on marketing. In this book, he helps to clarify the distinction between marketing by promotion or by permission. He can helps you formulate a Web site and marketing materials to enable you to build a big list of potential clients or referrals sources who really want to hear from you and receive your information.

6. Beckwith, H. (1997). *Selling the invisible: A field guide to modern marketing.* New York: Warner Books.

Some of my clients really like this book because Beckwith is entertaining and entrepreneurial, but also cognizant of how hard it is to sell intangible services. He focuses on how to build relationships with your customers, rather than sell them services, and normalizes the process of marketing as "everybody's first task in business."

7. Harrow, S. (2002). *Sell yourself without selling your soul.* New York: HarperCollins.

A clear, practical book on how to create publicity and build credibility for yourself when you want to reach out far beyond a small, local practice; it helps you to know how to develop a press kit, master media interactions, prepare for interviews, etc.

8. Larkin, G. (1999). *Building a business the Buddhist way.* Berkeley, CA: Celestial Arts.

If all marketing is still feeling too hard-sell for you to warm up to, read Larkin's gentle, yet savvy book about business from a spiritual point of view. She has a good section on marketing basics that will help you target your specific market quickly and easily, while still maintaining all the concepts of right livelihood.

SHIFTING NEGATIVE MONEY BELIEFS

1. Mellan, O. (1994). *Money harmony*. New York: Walker.

A gentle, straightforward book that can help you to identify your money profile—hoarder, spender, money monk, avoider, or amasser—and has lots of useful exercises to help you transform your inner conflict to harmony.

2. Nemeth, M. (1999). *The energy of money*. New York: Ballantine Wellspring.

Nemeth offers a spiritual approach to working through beliefs and old patterns, using a positive and abundant frame of reference.

3. Kinder, G. (1999). *The seven stages of money maturity*. New York: Delacorte Press.

A Buddhist teacher who is also a Harvard-trained financial planner, advocates a kinder, value-based approach to developing adult attitudes about money.

APPENDIX C

Sample Business Budget for a Sole Propietorship

Income	$ Amount	Profitability Formula
Client Sessions		
In person sessions	_____	
Phone sessions	_____	
Consulting	_____	
Speaking engagements	_____	
Reports	_____	
Classes	_____	
Workshops	_____	
Products	_____	
Other: _____	_____	
Total Income	_____	= 100% Revenue

Expenses	$ Amount	Percentage of Revenue
Direct expenses		
Phone	_____	.5% _____
Postage	_____	.5% _____
Rent	_____	10% _____
Supplies	_____	.5% _____
Utilities	_____	.5% _____
Printing	_____	1% _____
Repairs	_____	.5% _____
Accounting/Administration/	_____	2% _____
Bookkeeping	_____	1% _____
Advertising	_____	1% _____
Licenses	_____	.5% _____
Insurance total:	_____	2% _____
Malpractice	_____	_____
Disability	_____	_____
Self-Employment taxes	_____	15% _____
Total Direct Expenses	_____	**35%** _____
Indirect expenses		
Books/Publications	_____	.5% _____
Office Cleaning	_____	.5% _____
Dues	_____	1% _____
Education/Training	_____	2.5% _____
Therapy/Supervision	_____	2.5% _____
Equipment/Maintenance	_____	.5% _____
Furnishings	_____	.5% _____
Meals	_____	.5% _____
Parking/Transportation	_____	.5% _____
Travel	_____	1% _____
Other: _____	_____	_% _____
Cash reserve	_____	5% _____
Total Indirect Expenses	_____	**15%** _____
Total Income	_____	**100%** _____
Total Expenses	_____	**−50%** _____
Net Profit	_____	**= 50%** _____

APPENDIX D
12-Month Master Plan

A plan of the entire year, with monthly objectives, fieldwork assignments, and additional words of advice.

MONTH 1

Physical Preparation: Taking an Honest Inventory

Your Objectives this Month

Gain clarity about your current challenges, assets, and liabilities. Use the assessments and charts offered (The Strong Start Survey, list of assets and liabilities, gains and drains, and the Self-Care Checklist) in order to develop a better understanding of your existing situation. Strengthen your capacity for positive expression regarding your practice. Learn to speak about what is going well in your work, with enthusiasm, by sharing success stories.

Your Fieldwork

- Take the Strong Start Survey and evaluate your answers using the categories of energy level, motivation, direction, and action.
- Prioritize your list of 90-day goals from easy to hard, and complete the three easiest ones.
- Enhance your self-care by taking two action steps.
- Speak positively with others about your strengths.
- Share your success story with others.

Words of Advice

Beginnings are important to me. Before beginning a practice-building program, I want you to know where you are starting from. Use the assessments, charts, and checklists to evaluate your situation, then let them spark your interest about the next steps that you can take. Want to move ahead faster this month? Focus on your self-care. Recharge and rebuild yourself, so that you have the energy and resilience to carry out the 12-month program. How many items can you complete this month on the Self-Care Checklist? Each month, as you acquire new business skills, remember to continue to enhance your well-being and self-care.

MONTH 2

Mental Preparation: Honing Your Entrepreneurial Mind-Set

Your Objectives this Month

Become mentally resilient as you learn to think the way a successful entrepreneur thinks. First, use the Private Practice Success Program Assessment to identify your business acumen and point you in the direction of further business understanding. Then start to think through the common challenges and obstacles that surround the business of therapy. Develop solutions to the obstacles so that you anticipate what to do to overcome normal problems that occur. Build on last month's inventory by developing your ideal client profile, to identify those clients you most want to attract. Create a business affirmation that will strengthen you mentally and eliminate negative, self-sabotaging beliefs.

Your Fieldwork

- Shift your challenges about the business of therapy to opportunities. Choose several opportunities you listed and add them to your goals on your prep form.
- Establish your ideal client profile and communicate it to your new and existing clients.
- Use a business affirmation each day this month and clear away any negative thoughts.
- Revisit your inner entrepreneur once a week for new understandings.

Words of Advice

The business affirmation is a very powerful antidote for a normal business owner's anxiety. Plan to use a series of business affirmations during the year to stay calm and motivated. An affirmation is a positive, bold statement about what you want to achieve in your business; holding the same, self-assured, goal-oriented thought every day trains your mind to focus on your future direction. You can select different affirmations to use each month as you progress in your business development, creating affirmations that reflect the topic of each month.

MONTH 3

Emotional Preparation: Building a Reserve of Support

Your Objectives this Month

You need strong, consistent professional support as you deal with the normal ups and downs of owning a business. Create a three-tiered professional support system, and use that system to help you think through your business challenges. Learn how to recenter yourself when business gets rough, so that your know how to soothe your own anxiety and stay calm and focused. Refine your skill of goal setting, so that your goals feel energizing, instead of draining. Explore and correct the source issues behind the symptomatic business problems that may occur. Bring together advisors to support you in achieving your goals, using a formal advisory board or an informal advisory circle.

Your Fieldwork

- Increase your collaborative efforts at hiring, attracting, or being attracted to people who support you.
- Ask three people to help you brainstorm solutions for your top business problems.
- Pick two business symptoms and possible source issues to address on your own.
- Make sure that you have a positive way to relate to the goals you focus on each month.
- Create your advisory board or advisory circle.

Words of Advice

Many therapists pay too little attention to their need for strong, consistent professional support; they don't appreciate how much easier business becomes with the right support in place. You will need to be proactive in this regard. Seek out and create the support you need. Do yourself a favor and put a professional support system in place now, using the exercises and suggestions to guide you; later, when the tasks of building your practice become even more challenging, the support you need to succeed will be ready for you to utilize.

MONTH 4

Spiritual Preparation: Orienting Your Practice Around Values and Vision

Your Objectives this Month

Does your business have a soul? A business flourishes when the owner invests the business with integrity, core values, and vision. Examine your current practice for integrity breaks—signs that problems at the foundation of your business need your immediate attention and then repair any integrity breaks you identify immediately. Develop an aligned business vision based on your core values, strengths, and talents, and imagine it existing within a predictable future; identify trends and learn to "trend up." Clarify your strengths and talents; prioritize your core values. Write a vision, purpose, and mission statement that elicits your passion. Become more purposeful, so that you make your vision a reality.

Your Fieldwork

- Evaluate your integrity breaks and correct them so that your practice operates with high level of integrity.
- Let others help you to spot trends in your profession, your regional area of practice, society at large, and use those trends to position your practice for the future.
- Work with and refine your vision, purpose, and mission statement.
- Become purposeful by stretching into new behaviors to become the person who will manifest your business vision.

Words of Advice

Your business can embrace a spiritual component when you build a practice based on vision. Align your business vision with your heart, so that you feel the vision at the center of your being. Make sure that your vision speaks to the best of who you are and what you want to do, now and in the future. Too many therapists don't think they need a business vision, because they don't think they have a real business. They operate in a reactive mode, reacting to circumstances instead of setting intentions. Your business deserves better than that. By recognizing that your practice should be based on an aligned business vision, you can build an ideal private practice, one that allows you to do your very best work.

MONTH 5

Articulation: Communicating Your Value as a Professional

Your Objectives this Month

How you talk about your business speaks volumes. Learn to communicate who you are and what you do with genuine enthusiasm, so that you are an effective spokesperson for your practice. Articulate your basic message—a verbal introduction that highlights the best of what you have to offer. By finding the right words to say, you can begin to attract the right clients into your practice. Expand the reach of your message by learning some key strategies of public speaking, step by step: Learn how to verbally ask for referrals when you talk with others; strategize how to give talks successfully for the public, from your own office; introduce yourself to organizations as a speaker, making sure that you have professional promotional materials. Finally, learn what it takes to interest speaker's bureaus and meeting planners in hiring you as a speaker. Through all of this, integrate the skill of enrolling—learn how to persuade potential clients or audience members to become paying clients, so that when you speak, your caseload can expand.

Your Fieldwork

- Practice your basic message in front of a mirror or with friends, family, colleagues, and new acquaintances. Get feedback from at least five other people you trust about how you come across.
- Add a referral request to your basic message when you use it as an introduction. Try out this longer introduction on at least 10 people this month.
- Decide on a plan either to sponsor yourself for a high-touch talk or to find a sponsor to help you extend the reach of your message.
- Apply the concept of enrolling to your practice and speaking engagements.

Words of Advice

Articulating your basic message is a cornerstone strategy of practice building; when effective, a basic message makes it possible for you to continually attract referrals just by talking with others. Creating a basic message is a process. Don't rush. Take your time, go over the exercises, write and rewrite, practice on a number of people. Use the professional support system that you began to create last month to give you feedback and encouragement. Refine your basic message during the month and experiment by using it out in the real world.

MONTH 6

Marketing: Generating a Flow of Quality Clients

Your Objectives this Month

Remove all elements of promotional marketing in your practice-building efforts, and instead use strategies of attraction marketing. Attract your ideal clients by extending the reach of your basic message beyond public speaking, to the areas of writing and networking. Learn how to write effective, personalized referral letters; enhance your newsletter using the concept of enrolling. Improve your marketing materials, so that they focus on the benefits and results of your practice. Identify the networking strategies that would be easiest to use and follow through on increasing your networking efforts. Develop a marketing plan so that you structure and optimize your marketing actions.

Your Fieldwork

- Write or improve your newsletter this month and remember to use the principles of enrolling.
- Send out two of your five personalized referral letters this month, and set up a system to keep track of when you sent the letters, and how and when you will follow up.
- Select one of the three strategies that increase your leverage when networking, meet practice angels, develop your rolodex, or host a gathering of colleagues, and begin to contact people this month.
- Create a written marketing plan and find someone to be accountable to, and follow through on your plan week by week.

Words of Advice

Marketing becomes less difficult when you use strategies that emphasize your existing style. Note the abundance of marketing ideas I suggest, or read further in the Appendix B to find additional ideas; then decide to only use those strategies that are most comfortable and easy for you. Use only those marketing ideas that already fit with your personality. The recommended reading list in the Appendix B includes a wealth of marketing ideas, and tips, so that you don't ever need to be at a loss wondering what to do next.

MONTH 7

Security: Establishing a Solid Client Base

Your Objectives this Month

An ideal practice is one that has a solid client base—clients who stay with you, return to you, and/or refer to you. As a business owner, you can build a client base by understanding the stages of attachment, and their counterpart in the business world. Learn how to encourage client loyalty, advocacy, and enthusiasm. Listen effectively to what clients say they want, not just what you think they need, and then include client language in your materials. Check your business boundaries to make sure that you create sufficient psychological security for your clients. Continually educate clients about the value and the meaning of their ongoing therapy. Track results, so that clients can measure the gains they make. Support all termination, so your clients have an experience of ending well.

Your Fieldwork

- Notice and correct any dissonance in your language with new clients. Improve your ability to resonate with everyday language.
- Correct any boundaries, policies, or procedures that don't strengthen your first stage of client connection, and don't promote client loyalty, respect, and retention.
- Continually educate your clients so that they understand both the process they are in, and the value of the work they do with you.
- Support all termination. Let new and existing clients know that you want to support their ending therapy, as well as you did their beginning.
- Pick one or more of the added-value ideas or create one of your own to put in place each year.

Words of Advice

Building a solid client base isn't just a factor of luck or personality; it's not entirely based on your clinical skill, either. A solid client base is based on many elements, including some business approaches. Understanding how to encourage feelings of trust, respect, and endorsement in clients says a lot about how you have set up your practice. Take your practice to a new level of sophistication by learning how to appreciate the natural stages of attachment that clients and customers enter into. Develop a secure and steady relationship with your clientele, by creating a practice that has strong boundaries, added value, an ongoing educational component, and provides measurable results.

MONTH 8

Profit: Making Peace with Making Money

Your Objectives this Month

A business, by definition, is an entity that makes a profit. To become more profitable, identify and address any negative beliefs you may have about money that are clouding your ability to be a good money manager. Reconcile the concepts of profit and service for yourself, and then check the profitability of your practice against a profitability formula. Analyze your business budget and track your profit picture. Examine the elements of a profitable or unprofitable practice, by using the profit gains and drains checklist. See how to set and raise fees the right way. Begin to install the elements that will help you to sell your business for a final profit when you are ready to retire.

Your Fieldwork

- Resolve negative beliefs about money by using the affirmation process from Month 2. Use your support system, in the Appendix, to shift limiting beliefs as well as the reading list.
- Analyze your financial data.
- Plug some of the most obvious profit drains and put in place some profit gains.
- Evaluate your fee and raise it if necessary.
- Create a plan for the long-term financial health of your practice by building a business that can be sold when you are ready to retire.

Words of Advice

Too often, very expert, skilled therapists in private practice find themselves going broke. Staying profitable in a small business requires that you are comfortable managing money. Become savvy about money and profit. Use the Appendix B to review a list of books that can help you change any of your negative ideas about money and business. If you want to build a business not just to own, but one you can also sell, you need to start long before you are ready to retire. Start now, by making a plan. Design your business so that is an remains an asset both now and in the future.

MONTH 9

Stamina: Creating Business Strength and Endurance

Your Objectives this Month

When you understand the evolutionary spiral of a small business, you can position your practice so that it grows in the direction you desire. Examine an innovative, adapted model of business evolution, and focus on the first three stages that enhance business stamina. Eliminate any survival-based aspects of your practice and learn to become more planful in your response to obstacles and problems. Remove all of the mystery from business by giving more attention and awareness to how, exactly, your business works. As your practice strengthens, get comfortable with feelings of power—business power! Learn two strategies for dealing with competition, including how to transform your envy into a pursuit of excellence.

Your Fieldwork

- Design a beige corrective strategy to correct any aspect of your practice that is barely surviving. Make sure you refer to it each week and ask for help from others.
- Use your conscious ritual in the real world. Note whether is helps reduce your anxiety, and/or makes life or work easier or more fun. If not, tinker with it so that it achieves these goals.
- Add a new model or strategy into your practice or your life that has previously been a source of envy. Get support for this, by telling someone in your professional support system what you are up to.
- Stay in close contact with your professional support system (review Month 3). Continue to use a business affirmation each month to sustain your intentions (review Month 2). Pursue your goals and objectives on your monthly prep form, prioritizing for ease and then completing the easiest ones first (review Month1).

Words of Advice

After looking for a better way to help clients anticipate their future business challenges, I am now a big fan of the evolutionary model of spiral dynamics, especially in the adapted form that you are offered this month where you can see not only what the challenges of each stage entail, but also what your objectives are as a small business owner. Use the exercises to help your practice endure and stay viable, while still finding strategies that help you to take an easier path to private practice success. Pay close attention to the strategies that help you to overcome the normal concerns about competition, and that can allow you to stay focused and less anxious, even when you are in a crowded marketplace.

MONTH 10

Optimization: Upgrading Your Practice

Your Objectives this Month

Want more ease? Make your practice a problem-free zone, by upgrading your systems and management position. The five-step upgrade plan addresses the essential elements of a well-run business. Use the Practice Management Checklist to evaluate your organizational skills, and as a guide to better business management; the more items you check off this month, the smoother your practice becomes to operate. Diversify your services so that your practice can ride out marketplace changes. Broaden your existing network so that your practice has a depth of connection, and so that you have profitable links to organizations, associations, and larger communities. Go beyond competency, toward mastery as a professional; enhance your technical and clinical skills and services. Find new ways to embrace the natural, entrepreneurial feelings of ambition, so that you can continue to grow and evolve in business.

Your Fieldwork

- Check more items on the Practice Management Checklist. Adopt higher professional standards and ask more of yourself as a therapist, and of your clients. Run a tight business, not a loose hobby.
- Add an additional profit center to your practice within the next six months as a permanent feature of your business. Set aside the resources, space, and a budget to finance the profit center and treat it like a separate, yet valuable part of your existing practice.

- Plan to take steps to broaden your existing network using one of the specific strategies offered.
- Decide on a long-term plan to enhance your reputation. Take the first step this month, but make the plan one to accomplish over time.
- Continue to use a marketing plan, one that helps you to structure your efforts and measures your progress (review Month 6).

Words of Advice

Taking the care and time, on the front end of a business, to optimize your systems makes life and work easier in the long run. Upgrade your administrative and management approach. Pay attention to detail. Treat your practice as though it is a serious business, instead of a hobby, by giving it the time, energy, and resources it deserves, so that it can become robust and productive.

MONTH 11

Expansion: Increasing Your Capacity for Growth

Your Objectives this Month

A hallmark of a mature and successful practice is that the business owner welcomes changes in the marketplace as an opportunity for newness and growth. Grow your practice by learning to spot and then select opportunities, and then prioritize your time by restructuring your calendar. As you build a practice that is highly entrepreneurial, integrate the values of fairness and mutuality. While you extend compassion to others, extend some compassion to your practice, too; send love to your business daily. Focus attention on your community ties to strengthen the position of your practice in relationship to the various communities that surround it.

Your Fieldwork

- Develop a filter to help you evaluate and select the right opportunities to pursue.
- Use the categories of spirit, work, and buffer time to prioritize your calendar, increase your work and spirit days and reduce buffer time.

- Express green values in your actions this month. Aspire to congruence, so that you become a model of your services to others.
- Think about your practice with loving energy each day.
- Enhancing your links to a community of your choice.
- Continue to operate a profitable practice by tracking your finances each month, looking for ways to contain costs and enhance revenue (review Month 8).

Words of Advice

Building an *ideal* private practice means integrating entrepreneurial zeal with humanistic values. Business can be a highly creative endeavor; experiment with ideas, expand your horizons, and reach for more. At the same time, allow your business to reflect the caring and compassionate values that matter to you most, so that you create a business environment that brings out the best in you and everyone you work with.

MONTH 12

Flow: Integrating Multiple Perspectives

Your Objectives this Month

Position your practice to take advantage of the benefits of being a small business: your ability to be innovative, flexible, and stay on the cutting edge of your profession. Go beyond a traditional medical model of private practice by incorporating alternative models of business. Invite some newness into your practice by adopting a personal-growth model and expanding your services. Explore the model by using it with your own life, then think how it can benefit your clients. Consider the elements of a coaching model and see if that style fits well within your practice. Bring the concept of flow into your practice: balance the ebb and flow of your business and heighten your internal sense of flow. Use the self-motivation strategies to keep your business successful over time.

Your Fieldwork

- Target the areas of your life and work that you want to advance to the next stage of personal growth. Take steps each week to improve any or all categories of your life, so that you become a model of the stages of personal growth to which your clients aspire.

- Decide how you will let new and existing clients know about your expanded range of services. What marketing materials need to be adjusted to reflect your additional information? How will you verbally talk about your expanded services in your basic message? What, if anything, do you need to alter on your list of policies or procedures?

- Balance your ebb and flow. This month get support for your efforts, by structuring your plan, deciding on a budget or resource allocation, and then alerting your professional support system or your advisory circle to help you achieve your goals.

- Continue to review the workbook during the course of the next 12 months, to stay motivated, focused, and engaged in continuing to build your ideal private practice.

Words of Advice

Enjoy the gains you have made this year. Celebrate your success. Use the self-motivation ideas to stay focused and proactive over time. Continue to invest in yourself and in your practice. If you didn't meet your expectations this year, go back through the workbook, review each month, and increase your professional support system. Review "How to Use This Workbook" (page 11) and "Celebrating Your Success" (page 271) for more ideas about additional support that can help you move forward more easily with this program. If you give yourself enough time, support, and resources, this program will work for you and you, too, can achieve your business vision.

index

Lynn Grodzki, LCSW, PCC, is the author of *Building Your Ideal Private Practice: A Guide for Therapists and Other Healing Professionals* and editor of *The New Private Practice: Therapist-Coaches Share Stories, Strategies, and Advice.* She divides her time between her psychotherapy private practice and her work as a business coach. She offers workshops and lectures internationally on the topic of practice-building and is a teacher/trainer for CoachU, a large coach training program. Grodzki lives in Silver Spring, MD, with her husband and two middle-aged dogs.